Debates in Modern History

BRITISH CULTURE
AND ECONOMIC
DECLINE

Debates in Modern History

BRITISH CULTURE AND ECONOMIC DECLINE

Edited by
Bruce Collins
and
Keith Robbins

Weidenfeld and Nicolson
LONDON

George Weidenfeld and Nicolson Ltd
91 Clapham High Street, London sw4 7TA

ISBN 0 297 82038 9

Typeset by BP Integraphics Ltd, Bath, Avon
Printed in Great Britain at The Bath Press, Avon

Contents

Contributors

Among Keith Robbins' many books are biographies of *Sir Edward Grey* (1971) and *John Bright* (1979), as well as *The Eclipse of a Great Power: Modern Britain 1870–1975* (1983) and his Ford's Lectures *Nineteenth-Century Britain: Integration and Diversity* (1988). He was Professor of History at University College, Bangor 1971–80 and has been Professor of Modern History at the University of Glasgow since 1980.

Peter Payne is a distinguished historian of British business and entrepreneurship whose publications include *British Entrepreneurship in the Nineteenth Century* (1974), the chapter on British entrepreneurship in *The Cambridge Economic History of Europe* vol VII Part I, and *Colvilles and the Scottish Steel Industry* (1979). He has been Professor of Economic History at the University of Aberdeen since 1969.

W.D. Rubinstein is an authority on wealth-holding and British elites. He has written *Men of Property: The Very Wealthy in Britain since the Industrial Revolution* (1981), and his essays on this subject have been published as *Elites and the Wealthy in Modern British History* (1987). He is Professor of Social and Economic History, Deakin University, Australia.

Harold James is a British historian of Germany whose books are: *The Reichsbank and Public Finance in Germany, 1924–1933* (1985), *The German Slump: Politics and Economics 1924–1936* (1986) and *A German Identity, 1770–1990* (1989). He is a Professor of History at Princeton University.

Bruce Collins is a British historian of the USA. His research has been on the mid-nineteenth century with books on *The Ori-*

gins of *America's Civil War* (1981) and *White Society in the Antebellum South* (1985). He is currently working on a book *America: Present and Past* which explores contemporary dilemmas from an historical perspective. He has been Professor of International History at the University of Buckingham since 1988.

Preface

Politicians and journalists have been debating since the 1960s whether or not Britain was a nation in decline. So, too, economic historians have long been engaged in assessing Britain's long-term economic performance. But the deep economic recession of the late 1970s and early 1980s, and the political assertion by the government headed by Mrs Thatcher since 1979 that Britain needed a new ideological commitment to reverse decades of real decline, gave greater edge, urgency and importance to the debate. Historians other than economic specialists began to consider in detail whether one of the more intriguing phenomenon of the twentieth century was the decline of Britain broadly defined. This was not simply a British intellectual reaction. American writers in the 1980s wondered whether their country would follow Britain on a long downward path.

Contemporary interest in a complex historical process does not usually make for the most dispassionate history. But this particular debate is both fascinating and wide-ranging. The precise issues are likely to be imprecisely defined. Political feelings can sometimes mould historical judgement, but that fact should quicken our interest in debate rather than send us scurrying to avoid matters of larger public interest that might threaten the purity of our historical assessments.

This volume describes the complexities of a major debate and provides authoritative analyses of its British dimensions. It then takes the debate further by offering two major international comparisons.

The origin of this volume was a symposium organized at the

University of Glasgow in May 1986. Professors Payne and Rubinstein (among others) presented papers at that symposium, which drew together over forty participants. The editors would like to thank the following whose financial support made it possible to bring an extremely distinguished group of speakers and discussants together: the Economic and Social Research Council; General Occidentale; the Alexander Stone Lectureship in Bibliophily (University of Glasgow). One of us owes a debt of gratitude to Dr Jane Ridley (University of Buckingham) for offering very helpful comments as a British historian on the work of an Americanist.

Bruce Collins
Keith Robbins
October, 1989

Keith Robbins

British Culture versus British Industry

Experience shows that the relationship between 'culture' and 'industry' is enigmatic. It is possible to plan a particular pattern of industrial development, using the most sophisticated techniques to identify the optimum location, and to employ the latest methods of organization, only to find that this development fails to 'take off'. Managers and planners have naïvely believed that they can shift systems around the globe and have the same industrial outcomes wherever a factory is located. However, we now know that very different levels of productivity are often obtained from region to region and country to country, despite the fact that the objective conditions of manufacturing appear very comparable. For want of a better term, we often speak of 'cultural factors' which either inhibit or stimulate change and enterprise. Even so, some historians in the past have been very unwilling to place much reliance upon the explanatory value of such factors. It is not so much that when they hear the word culture they reach for their word-processors as that they have often preferred to look for more readily quantifiable explanations of industrial change. 'Cultural factors' have seemed nebulous, to be brought into the discussions only when all other explanations have failed, or been found only to tell a part of the story. Most writers will accept that there is some relationship between the culture of a society and its ability to participate in industrialization: the difficulty is to say in precise terms what it is and how important it is. There is at present a lively and inconclusive debate on this central issue; it is the purpose of this introduction to set it in context and indicate the areas of continuing contention.

The Wiener/Barnett Thesis

Enterprising historians know that there are books for all seasons. When it was first published in 1981, Martin J. Wiener's *English Culture and the Decline of the Industrial Spirit 1850–1980* seemed to match theme and moment to perfection.[1] Mrs Thatcher had just begun her first administration. There was an atmosphere of doom and despondency about Britain's immediate past record and future prospects. It was time to consider afresh the problem of Britain's 'retardation' and offer some fundamental explanation for the 'decline' which was frequently perceived. Professor Wiener was well aware of the atmosphere of that decade and saw the possibility of an extended meditation on Britain's plight. He could produce a work of scholarship which would also have an immediate public resonance. To write such a book would have the incidental benefit of demonstrating the importance of history. It would also be an advantage that he would be writing about the British predicament from an American perspective. He would not be hindered in his judgment by the loyalties of a native.

This was not a peculiar transatlantic hobby. British commentators had also been busy identifying the 'decline' and putting it into what they believed to be the appropriate context. Wiener himself quotes the view expressed by Correlli Barnett in a newspaper article in 1975 that the 'English disease' was 'not the novelty of the past 10 or even 20 years ... but a phenomenon dating back more than a century'. Barnett was gearing himself up for a more extended assault on targets he had already clearly identified. His *The Audit of War* appeared in 1986. Its main focus was upon Britain's industrial performance during the Second World War. Its verdict was comprehensively damning. Britain had neither the skills nor the resources to meet her own needs and was critically dependent upon the United States for vital components and sophisticated techniques. However, the analysis of Britain's wartime performance was prefaced by a chapter which set the scene for this abysmal débâcle. Barnett established the existence of something he called 'New Jerusalemism'. In 1940, as he supposed, while 'Winston Churchill and the nation at large' were fighting for sheer survival in the face of German might, members of 'the British cultural elite' were busy with design studies which would transform Britain into a green and pleasant land after the war was won. It is implied that this elite had little to do with the actual business of winning. The blueprint that emerged after 1945 prevented Britain from remedying the industrial defects which were only too apparent to those who really understood the world. In his final chapters Barnett sets out to show just why this was so.[2]

The reception accorded these two books went beyond normal reviews and debate in academic journals. They touched a chord in many quarters and, in a general sense, have contributed to certain shifts in public policy. Industrialists, politicians, bishops and vice-chancellors all felt obliged, to greater or lesser degree, to betray a certain acquaintance with what we may call the Wiener/Barnett thesis concerning the 'decline of Britain'. It was not necessary to have read the detailed expression of this view since its broad outlines were frequently referred to in the press and on radio and television. In his Green Paper of May 1985, the then Secretary of State for Education and Science, Sir Keith Joseph, warned universities that they needed 'to be concerned with attitudes to the world outside higher education, and in particular to industry and commerce, and to beware of "anti-business" snobbery. The entrepreneurial spirit is essential for the maintenance and improvement of employment.' Higher education as a whole should be alert both to the hazard of blunting it and positively seek to encourage it. Here are more than echoes of the thesis that there have been and are certain elements in British culture which have stifled enterprise to the ultimate detriment of the country's prosperity.

It is no cause for concern that two history books should have had a wider resonance. There is no virtue in believing that historians should only devote themselves to topics which have no bearing upon public issues. By the same token, however, it is proper to address the questions that have been raised in a continuing debate and to put them before the public at large in a fashion that is at once scholarly and accessible. That is what this collection seeks to do.

Decline Without a Fall

The fundamental problem confronting anyone interested in this central problem is to determine the appropriate framework of reference. Professor Wiener approached his task from a background which had included work on early twentieth-century English intellectual and cultural history. He wrote a study of the political thought of Graham Wallas. Barnett, on the contrary, had written extensively on military history ranging from *The Desert Generals* to *Britain and Her Army*. He had already had one shot at a broader theme in his *The Collapse of British Power*. Naturally, Barnett and Wiener have both read more widely but nevertheless their original historical formation still shows through clearly. It is apparent not only in their treatment of particular topics but also in the aspects of their theme which they do not consider at all. To write persuasively about as complex a problem as 'decline' requires an ability to synthesize and structure relevant material drawn from very diverse sources. It entails a willingness to consider evidence which contradicts the thesis which is being maintained; one of the dangers in books which are as blatantly polemical and programmed as Barnett's is that a writer runs a grave danger of ignoring awkward sources which contradict or qualify the proposition which is being advanced. There is an evangelical urgency about the Barnett thesis which may appeal to us as citizens but which detracts from the degree of detachment and dispassionate analysis which a historian ought to aim at.

Before and after Gibbon, the decline and fall of empires has had a recurring attraction for historians. British Culture v. British Industry derives its sharpness as a theme from its bearing on British 'decline'. We would not be discussing it with such enthusiasm unless something was supposed to have gone badly wrong with the British economy. Indeed, Wiener has a chapter on 'the wrong path', though he places a question mark after it. That there has been a 'decline' seemed so self-evident to both authors that they did not linger long in defining what they mean by this term. Yet it is of critical importance to do so if we are bent on distinguishing between 'illusion' and 'reality'.

Chronology and Scale

Two elements are very significant in talking about the link between culture and industry: chronology and scale. If we restrict ourselves to British domestic history, neither of the pace-setters in this debate give us much help in determining precisely when the alleged switch from dynamism to decline took place. Wiener begins his account explicitly at mid-century. He tells us that 'Nineteenth-century Britain was a pioneer of modernization' but nowhere do we learn much in his account about how that 'modernization' had come about and what it really amounted to. Since we nowhere learn how an 'industrial revolution' had occurred in Britain (over perhaps the previous century?), and what kind of individuals had been prominent in bringing it about, it is difficult to establish our bearings. Was culture at this initial stage particularly conducive to the pioneering spirit? On the other hand, 'pioneering' may have occurred in a cultural context which was as ambivalent, if not hostile, to 'industry' as it allegedly became subsequently. The 'snobbish' attitude towards business, of which Wiener finds many examples, may not have been either very new or very important. It was neither very significant in the 'rise' of the industrial spirit nor in its decline. Indeed, Donald Coleman has noted that ambivalent or hostile attitudes towards merchants were commonplace before the advent of the industrial era. 'The coming of industrialization did not bring radical change to contemporary comments on the businessman. They retained their variable and ambivalent nature. Their targets came inevitably to include more manufacturers than merchants.'[3] Barnett is no more explicit on the human ingredients involved in the growth of Britain as an industrial country. He is much more interested in the grasping moral designs of the products of Victorian and Edwardian public schools who averted their gaze 'from the muddy topics of the contemporary world and real human nature, and neglected science in favour of the moral precepts, the chivalric code and the ideal humanity enshrined in religion and the classics' and were thus, implicitly or explicitly, moving into positions in which they would be able to sabotage the industrial future of the country as a result of their absurd preoccupations.[4] Leaving aside, for a moment, whether this is anything more than a cameo caricature, it tells us nothing about the organization and composition of industry prior to the rise to power of the tender-hearted and high-minded. Is it not a little surprising that 'real human nature' should have proved so feeble in the face of this moral onslaught launched by the awful Dr Arnold?

We are therefore confronted, by both authors, with a hazy picture of a country which must have been dynamic, innovative and modernizing at some undefined point and for some undefined period but which then succumbed to some kind of romantic nostalgia or religious fervour and plunged into 'decline'. In neither instance do we have any way of telling whether there has really been a decline, say from 1850 to 1980, because we have been given no hint about when a comparable rise happened. Is it from 1700 to 1850? Now, it may be possible to draw up a cultural balance sheet 'before' and 'after' which would indicate some fundamental cleavages in attitudes to industry and industrialists, but that has not been done.

It is not only the chronology of 'decline' which is vague, so is the scale of decline. Here we encounter a difficulty with which many economic historians have wrestled from their particular perspective. How is 'decline' to be identified and measured? No economy is ever totally static and it scarcely needs to be said that its overall expansion or decline frequently entails quite different patterns within particular sectors. Indeed, it may be necessary for certain sectors to decline in order to release resources for another sector. Measurement of health therefore contains both objective statistical elements and subjective assessments of size in relation to the overall shape of the economy. A particular product may, as it were, outstay its welcome, and what may at the time appear to be an industry which is still expanding may subsequently be identified as a cause of decline over a longer term. Judgment frequently depends upon the point in time at which it is made. Obviously, assessing patterns correctly at the appropriate time is central to business but it is never self-evident what the outcomes are going to be. This uncertainty principle is inescapable, but the hazards do not seem to be sufficiently appreciated by our authors. If we take the entire period from 1850 to 1980 it would seem difficult to apply *tout court* the term 'decline' in the case of the British economy as a whole. We may think of certain specific shortcomings and failures in particular areas but we can also point to successes in others. Are we to measure solely profitability or must we also consider volumes or levels of employment? In some instances we might wish to combine them in an assessment whilst at other times these individual indicators might seem to point in contrary directions.

The suggestion need not be laboured any further, except to draw attention to the obvious corollary that a sophisticated analysis of varied 'growth' and 'decline' makes it hard to apply 'cultural' factors across the board. One might expect industry to be uniformly in decline if the cultural climate in which it operated was also uniform. Of course, there have been periods when it is plausible to see industry as a whole labouring under common difficulties but the world of industry is no more homogeneous than the culture in which it necessarily operates.

A Dose of Industrial Spirit

It is a difficulty that we are dealing, in Wiener's case, with something as nebulous as 'the industrial spirit'. Perhaps inevitably, he nowhere defines what it is and how it is acquired. He is, of course, more forthcoming on the gentrification of the industrialist. He provides many examples and we need not dispute the potency of the 'gentlemanly ideal'. On the other hand, we should guard against the assumption that its attractiveness was universal. There is a danger that we overlook those businessmen who did not to send their children to public schools and the ancient universities of England, and who chose themselves to live prosperously without becoming country squires. If they did also acquire expensive tastes it has to be established that these tastes were necessarily to the detriment of their commitment to business. Perhaps what needs to be stressed at this juncture in the debate is the sheer variety of human motives and conduct.[5]

It may also be misleading to suppose that a clear national pattern exists. Barnett speaks of 'the powerful resistance throughout society to the changes essential for the achievement of maximum success as an industrial nation'.[6] He writes about 'the British people', though he expresses the hope that 'England may yet prove stronger than the storms'. Wiener uses 'English culture' in his title but writes of 'British' businessmen. He does not appear to notice that there might be other cultures in Britain

besides that of the English which need to be taken account of.[7]
A not insignificant part of British nineteenth-century industry
was located in the West of Scotland. Its development was extraordinarily rapid and diverse. The great majority of the leaders
in shipbuilding and heavy engineering on Clydeside came from
the area and remained rooted in it. Some did seek careers in
England, but they were a minority. The majority continued to
be closely linked with a city in which they still lived. Many of
them lived in style and comfort, but it is difficult to see much
evidence that they were infected by a culture which was hostile
to business. They did not hanker for an English-style thatched
cottage or manor house. Lords Maclay and Weir of Eastwood,
for example, both prominent in the interface between British
business and politics in the mid-twentieth century, were put to
work by their prosperous fathers in their respective businesses
at an early age without being exposed to higher education. It
is dangerous to build too much upon a couple of examples drawn
from a particular region in Britain but these illustrations should
make us on our guard against believing that the rural idylls of
English poets were universally seductive throughout Britain.

It remains to be considered whether the 'haemorrhage of talent'
out of industry, supposing it did take place, was in itself harmful.
Again, we are dealing with mysterious elements. The attraction
of business, for some entrepreneurs, has always been that it
offered the opportunity to make money as a springboard for
some other activity – charitable work, politics or merely to enjoy
a leisured existence. Looked at from the standpoint of the community at large, the release of such talent into other spheres
might be beneficial. That might, however, still mean that the
loss of such men (and perhaps their children) from industry was
serious for its prosperity and management. On the other hand,
it could be argued that the regular withdrawal of a proportion
of hitherto dynamic entrepreneurs was beneficial. It made room
for promotion of younger men. It prevented undue ossification.
By the same token, the failure to maintain dynasties is not in
itself a source of regret. Some firms failed because sons and grandsons did not take up the role of rentier country gentleman but
insisted upon playing an active part in a business for which they
were not suited. It has often been remarked that British industry
was open to 'outsiders' from other countries. Such aliens could
make their mark upon British industry very quickly. Without
a certain element of suspicion towards industry in the indigenous

culture (if we grant that this does indeed exist) foreigners would not have been able to make their dynamic presence felt so easily. Was that gain or loss?

Education and Enterprise

It is in the sphere of education that the 'anti-industrial' bias of British culture has been most firmly identified. The indictment does seem at first sight to be solidly based. Almost without exception, the great English public schools were located in rural surroundings in Southern England, well away from the conspicuous signs of industry. An attitude of contempt towards 'mere money-making' was rife. Wiener suggests that these schools gradually relaxed their entrance barriers which had formerly kept out the offspring of those who had the misfortune to be 'in trade'. He adds, however, that they were admitted 'only if they disavowed their backgrounds and their class'. Public schools concentrated on educating their pupils for careers coloured by the aristocratic ideals of honour and public leadership – the armed forces, the law, the civil service and politics, in particular. He comments that public school boys made excellent administrators of a far-flung empire but their training for that task made them ill fitted for economic leadership. Such few businessmen as emerged from these schools were only of the 'civilized' kind, that is to say they did not pursue production and profit single-mindedly. The same attitudes towards business and 'science' were also prevalent in the two English ancient universities. Sheldon Rothblatt went so far as to say that in the eyes of the dons almost no subject which could be turned to the benefit of business deserved university recognition. The disdain of *homo oeconomicus* was virtually complete. It is further argued that these attitudes permeated the political elite and reinforced an indifference to the world of business already powerfully entrenched there. In addition, while most Englishmen did not go to public schools, the values inculcated in them also spread through the state system.

The broad picture is familiar enough. It can be filled out in sufficient detail to make it generally persuasive, though there is still room for further research on the career patterns of both schoolboys and university students. It is easy to transmit the image of hostility from book to book without considering the element of exaggeration that may be entering in. For example, it may well be too strong to suggest that boys from business backgrounds were required to 'disavow' their backgrounds – as though some formal ceremony was required. The argument is also a little circular. There might be more cause for complaint if public school boys 'ill fitted for economic leadership' had gone into leading positions in industry. If they did indeed make excellent administrators of a far-flung empire, why complain? Of course, it may have been a ghastly mistake ever to have got mixed up with an empire which offered so many young men a challenging and somewhat exotic career. It is easy, but facile and futile, to look back on Victorian Britain from a post-imperial age and criticize its politicians and educators for making sure that they did have the kind of manpower they thought they needed for the kind of tasks they knew they had.

In any event, it is a mistake to concentrate so exclusively on both the public schools and the ancient English universities as the source of all ills. Michael Sanderson has powerfully argued that insufficient attention has been given to the English civic universities. He points out that as early as 1914 only a minority (say 42%) of students in England were at Oxford and Cambridge. Some 22% attended London University and the remainder attended the new institutions established in cities in the South, the Midlands and the North of England. While their conception of their function varied somewhat in the light of the wishes of their benefactors, there was no suggestion that they despised industry. Many of their benefactors were themselves industrialists who looked to a continuing relationship between industry and the universities. 'Between 1880 and 1914' Sanderson argued, 'the symbiotic relationship of civic university technology departments and industrial firms was closer than ever before or since.' It is hard to detect an anti-industrial ethos when so many of the students came from industrial backgrounds and had industrial careers. For example, a third of Birmingham and Bristol graduates went into industry in the late nineteenth century and a half of the Newcastle graduates. In these universities at this time it was not 'anti-industrial attitudes' that were a matter for concern as the fact that industry showed insufficient interest in applying the discoveries of science departments.[8] It should also be mentioned that Sanderson's article pays no attention to the graduates of Scottish universities – Professor Wiener likewise ignores their not inconsiderable contribution to British industrial manpower.

Of course, to draw attention to the British university system as a whole rather than to look simply at Oxford and Cambridge is not to suggest that all institutions and their products were equal in social esteem. What existed in this sector was to some extent a continuation of the assumptions implicit in the education system as a whole. Thirty years ago Lord Ashby pointed out that British artisans owed little of their skill and knowledge to formal schooling. Mechanics' institutes were the main resource of those seeking to improve their understanding. Much faith continued to be placed in apprenticeship schemes and the transmission of techniques (and their improvement) 'on the job'. From 1860 onwards, there was limited government assistance in sponsoring classes in science, though there was much doubt about the value of what was on offer.[9] From a later perspective these efforts look unsatisfactory but the failure to do more sprang not from a deep-seated anti-industrialism but from a belief (shared by the work force itself) that traditional ways of imparting skills were still quite adequate. It was plausibly if arrogantly suggested that it was countries without such work forces that had to devise formal methods of instruction.

Political Success and Commercial Failure ?

One alternative description of this attitude would be to describe it as unbearably smug. Again, in retrospect, it may so appear but historians too readily gloat in their superior knowledge. It is not difficult, at the end of the nineteenth century, to find prophets of doom. The load the weary Titan had to carry was too great. The miracle of the nineteenth century was at an end. On the other hand, in its totality, the British achievement still appeared remarkable to most contemporaries. There was no incentive to 'modernize' the content of education in England, Wales and Scotland in a dramatic fashion stemming from a manifest public sense that 'we cannot go on as we are'. It is just such an underlying conviction that a government based to some degree at least upon consent requires before it can act. Here we come to the heart of what some see as the British dilemma. As Wiener himself admits, the way in which political change took place in nineteenth-century Britain was widely admired, both within the country and beyond. The franchise was extended and the political nation expanded within a framework which appeared to maintain institutional continuity. There was no revolution and no civil war. If there was in this process a 'gentrification' of 'the middle class' so there was also a 'bourgeoisification' of 'the aristocracy'. Of course, this fusion was neither complete nor everywhere prevalent: social distance remained a reality. However, the governing elite, if we have to use such a term, was a fluid entity and we cannot assume that its culture was unambiguously anti-industrial. Do we think of Sir Robert Peel or William Gladstone as hostile to commerce? It is true, however, that there was no capture of the commanding heights of the country by a middle class commercial party. Cobden and Bright had hoped, in mid-century, that such an ambition was feasible, but their expectations were grievously disappointed. However, Lord Salisbury did become a director of a railway company and so did Sir Edward Grey.[10] When Andrew Bonar Law succeeded Arthur Balfour as leader of the Conservative Party in 1911 this was widely taken to be symbolic of a transition from 'land' to 'industry' in its affairs, but this was an over-simplification.

Indeed, we may go further and suggest that Britain has lacked a political/business class which has played a directing role in its affairs either in the nineteenth century or since. Its political culture has not been 'anti-industrial' but the nature of the political system has been such that national politics has been an all-engrossing activity. 'Business' was represented substantially in the House of Commons and inevitably there is always an interface between business and politics, sometimes accompanied by a whiff of scandal and corruption, but businessmen as such have never directed government.[11] The route to Number 10 normally requires a long arduous apprenticeship in the House of Commons, and this is also true of the major offices of state. Such a career is not compatible with controlling a major industry, though it does not preclude directorships which can give some insight at first hand. From time to time, particularly in wartime, businessmen with specialist knowledge have been brought in to deal with particular problems, but even though the granting of a peerage enables such men to be appointed without difficulty, it has not been the case that businessmen have travelled this path frequently. There have been occasional individuals, like Lord Woolton, who have pursued successful business careers and have then succeeded in politics, but they have been rare and they have not been pursued simultaneously. From time to time, there have been attempts to fill the language of politics with 'business talk', as for example at the beginning of the century in discussion of 'National Efficiency' or subsequent enthusiasm for 'Great Britain Ltd', but these have proved evanescent. From one point of view, it might be thought highly significant that Mrs Thatcher is the first British Prime Minister to be a science graduate but from another it is quite irrelevant. Her early career as an industrial chemist had no bearing on her subsequent political rise.

The intensely political character of British politics has been frequently deplored. The increasing professionalization of political life – the payment of MPs in 1911 being both a symbol and cause of this development – has tended to produce a political class which has little first-hand experience of anything except politics. Outside commentators have frequently deplored this condition and advocated all sorts of remedies which would make available 'expertise' at the heart of the political process. Such criticisms have also extended to a more fundamental assault on the political system as it has developed in the twentieth century in particular.

Visible and Invisible Hands

It is sometimes suggested that it is not British culture which is hostile to British industry but the way in which politics is carried on which inhibits the effective articulation of both 'culture' and 'industry'. It has proved quite impossible to devise a 'national plan' which, its advocates suggest, would harmonize and, at least to some extent, 'depoliticize' the industrial objectives which all should share. Elbaum and Lazonick (1986), for example, attribute the decline of the British economy in the twentieth century to the fact that in their view 'economic decision-makers, lacking the individual or collective means to alter existing constraints, in effect took them as "given"'. Britain's problems derived not from its cultural values as such, nor from substantial individual entrepreneurial incompetence, but from a 'matrix of rigid institutional structures that reinforced these values and obstructed individualistic as well as collective economic efforts at economic renovation'. The British did not respond in the way a neoclassical model of competition suggests they should have. In a period of contraction the market mechanism was not an efficient allocation mechanism. The rationalization proposals of the inter-war period were half-hearted and of limited effectiveness. At this time, and in the post-war period, the tight work rules of the British trade unions inhibited structural reorganization. 'What British industry in general required', they conclude, 'was the visible hand of co-ordinated control, not the invisible hand of the self-regulating market'. They exonerate 'state activism' as attempted after 1945 from any substantial responsibility for continuing decline.[12]

Economic historians will no doubt continue to argue whether indeed that is what 'historical perspective' suggests. However, the role of the state in these matters is ultimately a question of political choice. Even if some of them pine for the visible hand, the 'co-ordinated control' such a government would need to possess cannot be without other 'non-economic' political and social consequences. There are no economic solutions which do not have political ramifications. Even supposing that the 'visible hand' did offer the only realistic opportunity of halting or reversing decline, it might only be able to do so at the cost of restricting individual liberty to an unacceptable degree. These are large issues which have been and still are vigorously debated. If it is indeed the case that 'a distinctive feature of British state policy throughout recent history has been its reluctance to break from *laissez-faire* traditions' it might also be claimed that there has been a reluctance to break from a certain notion of freedom that has accompanied it.

This line of discussion suggests that there are issues of belief and value which are inescapably bound up with democratic politics as these have come to be understood in twentieth-century Britain. In *The Audit of War* Barnett is not reticent or tentative in his judgement. 'The wartime coalition government' he writes, 'therefore failed across the whole field of industrial and educational policy to evolve coherent medium- or long-term strategies capable of transforming Britain's obsolete industrial culture, and thereby working a British economic miracle. Instead all the boldness of vision, all the radical planning, all the lavishing of resources, had gone towards working the *social* miracle of New Jerusalem'. In his view, too, 'The Labour Party's commitment to "nationalisation" in no sense represented a real-world operational blueprint for radical industrial change, but, as is now notorious, was merely an empty, if long-revered, New Jerusalem slogan'.[13] Such scathing criticisms may now appear self-evident, but it still remains to be explained why 'illusions' were so generally preferred when 'reality' was on offer.

It was not apparent to a British electorate in 1945 that the choice confronting the country was between the achievement of an economic miracle in the longer term and the achievement of a social miracle in the short-term. Long-term economic miracles have a habit of failing to arrive. The electorate wanted both economic recovery and social transformation. That is not very unusual in electorates, though no doubt very undesirable. However, fulminating against the 'moralising' of secular or clerical prophets seeking 'New Jerusalem' does not alter the fact that 'ordinary' electors wanted to see swift changes in their own housing and health care. They wanted it and they wanted it now. The 'climate of expectation' was in part stimulated by such 'economic incompetents' as William Beveridge and William Temple but they were also responding to a political and ethical demand which they did not invent. As he got older, Temple showed more humility concerning an acceptable organization of industry than he had shown as a young man.[14] In any case, the generalizations of Barnett about the relationship between religion and business in Britain do no more than skim the surface. It is only very recently that serious work in this area has begun. It is already apparent, however, that attitudes to the generation and use of wealth amongst Christians have varied very widely, as they have done throughout Christian history. There is a certain irony in the fact that the only Anglican dean with a degree in engineering, and a business background – Dr Hewlett Johnson of Canterbury – became famous as the 'Red Dean' and arch-opponent of capitalism. However, it would be rash to build many generalizations upon his idiosyncratic career.[15]

In any event an 'economic miracle' is not a permanent 'steady-state' phenomenon capable of once-for-all achievement to be followed by a rationally determined allocation of its social benefits. Any economic miracle contains within it the seeds of its own destruction as consumers seek to extract the maximum individual benefit from its accomplishment. It may be suggested that British history since 1945 has experienced fluctuating trade-offs between 'economic' and 'social' miracles according to the inevitably uninformed judgement of a mass electorate. It is in this tension that we are likely to locate some of the sources of the 'British disease'.

The Outside World

In 1985 Mr Aubrey Jones, a believer in the death of Socialism and Private Enterprise and arch-exponent of 'planning by dialogue' turned his attention to uncovering the roots of stagnation in the British economy. 'I have come to realise' he writes 'that I was born the citizen of a country in relative decline; in the years that remain to me the relative may be turning into the absolute.'[16] Whatever the future may hold, what has sparked off the protracted analysis of the British condition has been a perception of Britain's performance as compared with that of other countries. Other countries have been conspicuously more successful and it is this relative decline which has attracted attention. Jones is among those writers who envisage a situation in which Britain will drop out of the league altogether. Failure will become absolute. On the other hand, Carlo Cippola suggests that, except when entire societies cease to exist, all cases of decline turn out eventually to be cases of relative decline.[17]

If we therefore turn our attention to the world environment in which Britain existed we are immediately confronted by the problem of determining which comparisons are valid. It is undoubtedly true that if we compare the 1880s with the 1980s, the United Kingdom's share of world exports of manufactures has fallen sharply, a sharper decline than any other industrial country has experienced, roughly from some 40% to under 10%. The German, French and Italian percentages over the same period have fluctuated over a much shorter range. Japan has shown the most startling growth and come from 'nowhere' in 1880 to a position where its percentage comfortably exceeded that of the United Kingdom in 1980. In the period since 1950 the percentage shares of the Federal Republic of Germany and the United Kingdom have been approximately reversed. Such blunt figures do not tell the full story and there are always statistical problems in comparing performances over time, nevertheless we must accept the basic picture that is disclosed by such information. Other indices would show a similar reversal of fortune.

Yet it is not clear what lessons should be drawn from such statistics. Do we need to embark on a lengthy analysis of the British 'failure' and seek to identify scapegoats, cultural or otherwise? The relative decline in the British position comes as no surprise, because it was just what one might reasonably have expected to occur. Only if relative decline had not occurred would there be a need to find an explanation for a remarkable retention of manufacturing share. However we understand the 'Industrial Revolution' in Britain, the early lead which Britain established could not be maintained indefinitely. The circumstances which gave rise to it may have been unique, but other countries could learn from the British example. That notion of replication is too simple to describe the pattern of industrialization worldwide, but there was no fundamental obstacle to the application elsewhere of techniques pioneered in Britain. Indeed, it was possible to by-pass some stages and to begin with more advanced machinery. On this argument, by the First World War, British industry was a victim to 'ageing'. Innovative dynamism had been replaced by conservative routinization. Some observers have professed to see signs of a comparable rigidity in the recent history of the United States and even of Japan as the torch of expansion passes to other East Asian economies. The 'British disease' on this analysis is likely to afflict other economies in time and owes little to specifically British cultural factors. On the other hand, the knowledge that a loss of drive can happen can lead to specific steps being taken in order to try to prevent, for example, a kind of national Japanese 'gentrification'.

In making comparisons with other countries it is also necessary to seek to do this much more systematically than is normally attempted. This book tries to make just such a contribution. Is it really the case that those elements in British culture allegedly so hostile to industry are virtually absent from other countries, at least from other European countries? Lord Annan, Neil McKendrick and many other writers have written persuasively on the attitudes towards business and money-making to be found amongst English writers in the nineteenth and twentieth centuries.[18] The image purveyed is preponderantly a negative one. There was a comparably strong hostility towards life in big cities and a yearning for the alleged delights of simple country living. Rural nostalgia finds a place in the English consciousness in many places. Of course, there are exceptions, but we may think the case for a pervasive dislike of industrialization and urbanization has been made. Yet it is not altogether clear what significance ought to be attached to this mood. We might say that this distaste among men and women of 'cultivated taste' is just what one would expect. It has been handed on from generation to generation, though in each decade since the early nineteenth century writers seem to think that they are making some epic discovery. The 'British disease' itself can be seen as a kind of British tradition.

Two questions need to be asked. Is the degree of mutual hostility between the worlds of 'business' and 'the arts' simply a British phenomenon without significant parallel anywhere else? Or is it merely a particular expression which exists powerfully in other European countries too? If the former is nearer the truth, then it would strengthen the argument that British culture is a major factor in explaining British industrial retardation. If the latter is nearer the truth then the argument is correspondingly weakened. Perhaps we also need to ask how much what Bloomsbury or F.R.Leavis think actually matters in the 'real world'. It is in the nature of intellectuals to feel resentment at their condition of dependence on values and activities of which they disapprove. Contempt for business in literary circles may well have prevented some of the 'best' brains from following business careers, though it is by no means clear that the 'best' minds would be best in business.

Similarly we need to pursue more thoroughly those other aspects of British culture which one might also expect to find elsewhere in a fashion by no means totally dissimilar. Again, on examination, attitudes to the past, to 'tradition', to work and to wealth, to the city and to the country, to name only a few relevant areas, may not be so conspicuously and completely different as to bear the weight of 'cultural' explanation placed upon them. Such cross-national comparisons are notoriously difficult to make and assess but without them it is only too easy to see Britain as a very odd country when in fact it may be no more odd in its cultural values than other and more industrially successful societies.

It is also necessary to place due weight upon the general experience of Britain internationally. A central consideration in this respect is the significance of the British Empire. When we compare the Britain of 1880 with the Britain of 1980 we are comparing very different entities. The *Expansion of England* to take the title of Seeley's book published in 1883 was not a treatise on economic growth but on the global impact of the British people. The extraordinary ramifications of British power across the seas produced an empire of great complexity and, at least superficially, great resources. By 1980 that empire had disappeared, with the exception of small scattered outposts.

Decolonization had taken place at a great pace in the decades after the end of the Second World War. Historians are only now trying to come to terms with the totality of that experience. It is, however, still possible, to read books which neglect it entirely as an issue which is relevant to the problem of 'decline'. Once again, it is a matter of finding the right perspective.[19]

British Imperialism was controversial throughout its existence and has remained disputed amongst historians. Some have long argued that British industrialization depended in considerable measure upon the proceeds of mercantilism. Others have believed this to be inherently implausible. Some have argued that the empire throughout its history rested upon exploitation and that, as a whole, it was a 'profitable' concern. If that is the case, then it follows that the downfall of empire would be bound to have serious consequences for the British economy. Others have argued that the empire as a whole was never profitable, though certain parts of it were for certain periods for certain companies. If it was never profitable, then its 'loss' was not very significant, looked at simply in economic terms. These bold questions, however, are very difficult to answer. Nineteenth-century economists and historians disputed these issues amongst themselves. Their successors, stimulated in some cases by the work of L.E.Davis and R.Huttenback, *Mammon and the Pursuit of Empire*, have been attempting to draw up a balance sheet on the costs and benefits of British imperialism. Scholars have sought to speculate on what might have happened to British exports, visible and invisible, to its imports, to flows of capital and labour, to levels of taxation, to the defence budget – to name only some of the relevant areas of enquiry – if the dominions and colonies had become independent polities from the middle of the nineteenth century onwards.[20] Such counterfactual questions are certainly stimulating and a recent article by O'Brien produces some fascinating conclusions. He has returned to some traditional nineteenth-century arguments and investigated them on the basis of twentieth-century knowledge and sophistication. He examines such matters as the emigration of British labour overseas; the profitability of investing money to support capital formation in the empire; the potential gains from sustaining and using imperial political ties to further trade and commerce; and finally the cost of security and defence. The complexity of the topic does not admit of any facile summary, but the 'balance sheet' O'Brien seeks to establish repays close study.[21] He is only concerned, however, with the period up to 1914. A comparable analysis carried out from 1914 to the 1960s would be equally relevant.

Yet, whatever may be thought of such a balance sheet it still does not take into account less quantifiable aspects of the imperial experience. If British culture was at loggerheads with British industry it was an imperial culture which was so engaged. The empire penetrated the emotions of millions. It gave Britain its position among the nations and confirmed a pervasive sense of national not to say racial superiority. Taken together with Britain's insularity, the empire marked out the 'island race' as a people set apart, with connections across the globe matched by no other state. 'British culture' had in these respects a psychological dimension shared by no other European state, not even by France. If we accept these suggestions, the unravelling of the empire was bound to be a difficult process and one which would be harmful to national self-confidence and pride. It is not given to many countries to 'lose' the kind of empire Britain had 'possessed'. We have to look to a 'loss of nerve' as a persuasive reason for economic decline.[22]

Such an emphasis, however, may not correlate very well with specific economic trends. We also have to consider how and why the empire was 'lost'. Some writers have stressed how reluctant even a Labour government after 1945 was to contemplate its abandonment. However, in the end, it was felt that there was no alternative. Britain's experiences during the Second World War in Asia made it impossible to think of staying on indefinitely. Even so, successive governments were determined to control the pace of change themselves and not be rushed into withdrawal by pressure from the United Nations, the United States or the Soviet Union. The creation of the Commonwealth is taken to be a sign that Britain still had a deep sentimental attachment to its former colonies. On the other hand, it is sometimes suggested that by 1945 the empire had come to be seen as an enormous incubus. It was a burden which should no longer be carried. So long as withdrawal could be carried out in reasonable order it would be better to achieve it within a short time scale. That would liberate Britain and enable the country to make a fresh start unhindered by an irrelevant legacy from the past. On this reading of events, the decline of an imperial power was not really a decline at all. At least in the twentieth century, and quite possibly earlier, the empire had been a contributor to national decline rather than a source of national strength. It was time to forget the Commonwealth as a concept and come to terms with Britain's proper role in a vigorous new Europe.

This argument is still open and continues to have contemporary political resonance. Whichever opinion is favoured, we might suggest that the direction which Britain should take in international affairs has been a major problem, at least in the twentieth century, and has had implications in many areas of national life. This uncertainty has been most conspicuous in the decades before both world wars and in relation to the European Economic Community. There is room for much counter-factual speculation on what Britain would be like in 1980 if the country had not participated in either world war – always assuming that there would be any country at all as a consequence of abstention! Likewise, it is sometimes suggested that after 1945 Britain 'missed the bus' in its attitude to European economic integration. If very different policies had been followed at this juncture, it is alleged, the problems experienced by the British economy would not have been so severe. Emphasis on these points suggests that policy decisions have got to be taken into account, as well as structural conditions. The capacity and performance of British industry both contributed to policy outcomes and suffered or benefited from them.

The conclusion seems to be that 'British Culture versus British Industry' is indeed an element in the history of British 'decline', but the thesis needs both to be explored further comparatively and also treated with reservation if presented as *the* major cause of that experience. The attractiveness of the analysis lies in its monocausal simplicity. Acceptance of the claim seems to lead to an equally simple conclusion: if you want to reverse the decline of British industry you have got to change the culture – a difficult but possibly realizable goal and one which will be greeted with anguish by those elements in that culture which will suffer in the process. On the other hand, if we are inclined to say that there is 'something' in the thesis but that it is not the entire story, cultural adaptation may be less important than is sometimes claimed. The essays that follow should help readers to make up their own minds.

NOTES

1. M. J. Wiener, *English Culture and the Decline of the Industrial Spirit 1850–1980* (Cambridge, 1981; pbk. edn used, Harmondsworth,

1985). M. Mathieson and G. Bernbaum, 'The British Disease: A British Tradition?', *British Journal of Educational Studies*, Vol. XXXVI No. 2 (July 1988) argue that many of the critics of contemporary British education are only repeating long-standing anxieties about its nature and organization.

2. C. Barnett, *The Audit of War* (London: Macmillan, 1986).

3. D. C. Coleman, 'Historians and Businessmen' in D. C. Coleman and Peter Mathias, eds., *Enterprise and History: essays in honour of Charles Wilson* (Cambridge: CUP, 1984) pp. 38–40.

4. Barnett, *Audit*, p. 14.

5. A view likely to be confirmed by perusal of D. J. Jeremy and C. Shaw, eds., *Dictionary of Business Biography* (London: Butterworth, 1984–86) and A. Slaven and S. G. Checkland, eds., *Dictionary of Scottish Business Biography* (Aberdeen, 1986).

6. Barnett, *Audit*, p. xii.

7. Some of the problems inherent in the notion of a British culture are explored in K. G. Robbins, *Nineteenth-Century Britain: Integration and Diversity* (Oxford: OUP, 1988).

8. M. Sanderson, 'The English Civic Universities and the "Industrial Spirit", 1870–1914', *Historical Research* Vol. 61 No. 144 (February, 1988) p. 99.

9. G. Roderick and M. Stephens, *Where did we go wrong?* (Falmer, 1981); J. Wrigley, 'Technical Education and Industry in the 19th Century' in B. Elbaum and W. Lazonick, *The Decline of the British Economy* (Oxford: OUP, 1986).

10. Both Cobden and Bright were 'businessmen in politics' but the former was not a very successful businessman and the latter emphatically subordinated his business career to his political ambitions: N. C. Edsall, *Richard Cobden: Independent Radical* (London: 1986: Harvard: UP, 1987); K. G. Robbins, *John Bright* (London: Routledge, 1979); K. G. Robbins, 'John Bright and the Middle Class in Politics' in J. Garrard et al., eds., *The Middle Class in Politics* (Farnborough: Saxon House, 1978). For Salisbury see T. C. Barker, 'Lord Salisbury, Chairman of the Great Eastern Railway 1868–72' in S. Marriner, ed., *Business and Businessmen* (Liverpool: LUP, 1978). For Grey see K. G. Robbins, *Sir Edward Grey* (London, 1971). See also J. V. Beckett, *The Aristocracy in England 1660–1914* (Oxford: OUP, 1986).

11. J. Turner, ed., *Businessmen and Politics* (London, 1984); G. Searle, *Corruption in British Politics 1895–1930* (Oxford: OUP, 1987).

12. Editorial opening chapter 'An Institutional Perspective on British Decline' in B. Elbaum and W. Lazonick, *The Decline of the British Economy* (Oxford: OUP, 1986).

13. Barnett, *Audit*, pp. 304 and 275n.

14. A. M. Suggate, *William Temple and Christian Social Ethics Today* (Edinburgh: T. & T. Clark, 1987); E. R. Norman, *Church and Society in England, 1770–1970* (Oxford: OUP, 1979).

15. D. J. Jeremy, ed., *Business and Religion in Britain* (Aldershot: Gower, 1988); B. Hilton, *The Age of Atonement: the Influence of Evangelical*

Social and Economic Thought 1785–1965 (Oxford: OUP, 1988); R. Hughes, *The Red Dean* (Worthing: Churchman, 1987); W. J. Sheils and D. Wood, eds., *The Church and Wealth* (Oxford: Blackwell, 1987).

16. A. Jones, *Britain's Economy: the Roots of Stagnation* (Cambridge: CUP, 1985), p. 2.
17. C. M. Cippola, ed., *The Economic Decline of Empires* (London, 1970).
18. See the excellent clutch of editorial introductions written by McKendrick to the following volumes: R. J. Overy, *William Morris, Viscount Nuffield* (London: Europa, 1976); C. Trebilcock, *The Vickers Brothers* (London: Europa, 1977); P. N. Davies, *Sir Alfred Jones* (London: Europa, 1978); R. Church, *Herbert Austin* (London: Europa, 1979).
19. I eschewed the word 'decline' and settled for a less severe alternative in *Modern Britain: The Eclipse of a Great Power 1870–1975* (London: Longman, 1983). See also A. Sked, *Britain's Decline* (Oxford: Basil Blackwell, 1987).
20. L. E. Davies and R. Huttenback, *Mammon and the Pursuit of Empire* (Cambridge: CUP, 1986). See also their 'The political economy of British imperialism: measures of benefits and support', *Journal of Economic History* 42 (1982), pp. 119–30.
21. P. O'Brien, 'The Costs and Benefits of British Imperialism 1846–1914', *Past and Present* No. 120 (August 1988).
22. M. Kahler, *Decolonization in Britain and France* (Princeton: UP, 1984). M. E. Chamberlain, *Decolonization: the fall of the European Empires* (Oxford: Blackwell, 1985). R. F. Holland, *European Decolonization 1918–1981: an introductory survey* (London: Macmillan, 1985).

Peter L. Payne

Entrepreneurship and British Economic Decline

'It is now conventional wisdom that, for some hundred years or so, British growth and especially productivity performance have been deeply disappointing when compared with that of other advanced countries. More contentious, but nevertheless widely held, is the belief that the failures of the post war economy are deeply rooted in the past, presenting successive governments both with an unenviable legacy and a most daunting task in their aspiration to remedy Britain's relative economic decline.'[1] With these words, Nick Crafts introduces a valuable collection of articles concerned with the long-run economic performance of the economy of the United Kingdom. If they do nothing else, these papers reveal the sheer complexity of the causes of Britain's relative economic decline. The object of this essay is to examine just one of the inter-related factors involved: the role of entrepreneurship, but in discussing this factor a conscious attempt has been made to consider a number of cultural and institutional influences bearing upon it.

I

Let us be quite clear at the outset, criticism of the British entrepreneur is no new phenomenon: it goes back to the closing decades of the last century when Britain's international economic dominance, once so obvious, especially in manufacturing, was seen to be passing to the United States and to Germany. But the modern debate, and its relevance to explaining the *relative* decline of Britain's rate of economic growth, essentially dates back to the appearance of David Landes' paper on 'Entrepreneurship in Advanced Industrial Countries: The Anglo-German Rivalry', which was presented at a conference at Harvard in November, 1954, and which, extended and elaborated, was reborn as his contribution to the sixth volume of the *Cambridge Economic History of Europe* in 1965.[2] Meanwhile, there had appeared Habakkuk's seminal essay on *America and British Technology* in 1962, and Derek Aldcroft's essay on 'The Entrepreneur and the British Economy, 1870–1914'. This was published in the *Economic History Review* in 1964, and it provoked a counterblast by Charles Wilson in the following year.[3]

There followed a number of general assessments of entrepreneurial performance, of which perhaps the most well known is A. L. Levine's *Industrial Retardation in Britain, 1880–1914* (1967). There was also the curiously neglected essay by Eric Sigsworth, 'Some Problems in Business History, 1870–1914' (1969), a remarkably perceptive synthesis which, like Francois Crouzet's much later study on *The Victorian Economy* (1982), made considerable use of the collection of essays assembled by Derek Aldcroft on the responses of a wide variety of British industries to foreign competition between 1875 and 1914.[4] Not the least interesting of the findings which emerged from these essays – the commissioning of which, it was always understood, was to give greater credence to Aldcroft's criticisms of the British entrepreneur – was that the various authors found all too little to condemn. Furthermore, additional industrial studies, like those of Roy Church (on boots and shoes) and A. E. Harrison (cycles, 1969), reached similar conclusions, as did the papers presented to the Mathematical Social Science Board Conference on the New Economic History of Britain held at Harvard University in 1970 and Theo Barker's contribution to *The Twentieth Century Mind*.[5]

But these were, essentially, negative findings: the majority of British authors of case studies of industries and individual firms – ever growing in number and sophistication – could find little or no *evidence* of entrepreneurial failure. Their conclusions were unsatisfactory to a number of American econometric historians. To them, the measures of performance previously employed were inadequate on theoretical and methodological grounds. To Donald McCloskey and Lars Sandberg, foremost among the American cliometricians, the only legitimate way to arrive at a proper conclusion concerning the relative importance of entrepreneurial failure – if such proved to exist – was by quantitative methods, the selection of which should be determined by the application of explicit economic models.[6] Utilizing this more rigorous approach, McCloskey found that British iron and steel masters exploited the potentialities of world technology before the First World War as well as, if not better than, their much lauded American competitors: 'Late nineteenth-century entrepreneurs in iron and steel did not fail. By any cogent measure of performance, in fact, they did very well indeed'.[7] Similarly, Sandberg, after examining Britain's lag in adopting ring-spinning and in installing automatic looms in cotton manufacture, concluded that 'under the conditions then prevailing with regard to factor costs, as well as the technical capabilities of the ring spindles then being built, the British may well have been acting rationally'. He could, moreover, find no evidence that firms installing automatic looms at the time the cotton industry was beginning to be criticised for ignoring them expanded faster or made larger profits than their more conservative competitors'.[8] On the basis of these and other studies, McCloskey expressed the belief that there was 'little left of the dismal picture of British failure painted by historians'.[9]

Essentially, this seemed to represent the state of play, especially concerning what I labelled 'the critical period' between 1870 and 1913, when I attempted to survey the debate on British entrepreneurship from *c*1815 to 1970 for the seventh volume of the *Cambridge Economic History* and, a little later, for the nineteenth century alone, for the pamphlet series of the Economic History Society.[10] Yet, however convincing the evidence for abandoning the concept of entrepreneurial failure (and hence the relevance of this possible explanation of British economic decline), I could not resist expressing certain doubts, imprecise and imperfectly articulated though they were.[11] To obscure my ignorance, I adopted the craven – though academically respectable – tactic of posing a series of questions to which further answers were required. These included the yardsticks necessary for the measurement of success or failure, and the desirability of determining the significance of the entrepreneurial factor in

Britain's manifestly accelerating relative decline *since* the First
World War.

II

In the last ten years or so, much new material has appeared
and, partly as a consequence, it has been possible more clearly
to interpret evidence that even by the mid-seventies was already
available but whose significance had wholly or partially escaped
me. It is unnecessary, indeed impossible, comprehensively to survey the new information. I must confine myself to touching upon
a number of relevant issues.

Let me begin by confessing that in observing that the authors
who contributed to Derek Aldcroft's collection of essays had
discovered little hard evidence of British entrepreneurial failure
in the half century preceding the First World War, I was greatly
influenced by my own belief that it was extremely difficult to
perceive glaring errors from the records of individual firms. It
can be done, of course. Roy Church has demonstrated as much
by his masterly investigation of Kenricks;[12] but all too often
the inquirer is forced to conclude that, with the information
apparently available to the firms themselves, major decisions
seem to have been perfectly *rational* in the context of future
profitability, although the attainment of such an objective was
frequently tempered – even compromised – by social considerations, a point most recently emphasized by Jonathan Boswell
and Harold Perkin.[13]

I have always believed that the correctness or ineptitude of
entrepreneurial decisions must be assessed within the context
of the firm. This means that if, for example, innovations 'do
not yield reductions in average unit costs, then it would be
irrational for a businessman to introduce them even if the innovations would benefit the future growth of the economy'.[14] It
also means that decisions are sometimes arrived at which deliberately eschew maximum profitability because of a conscious
awareness that the social cost would be too great; that, in Samuel
Courtauld's words, 'the highest rate of profit should not be the
over-riding consideration'.[15]

It will be clear that, like McCloskey and Sandberg, I have
envisaged businessmen as neo-classical managers optimizing profits subject to given constraints. Not surprisingly, as Leslie Han-

nah has observed, it has not been difficult to give them 'a clean bill of health'.[16] And yet, as he says, one cannot ignore the fact that between, say, the 1880s and the inter-war years Britain's rate of economic growth was relatively slow[17] and that her international position was deteriorating, mainly because other nations were either making more efficient use of existing resources or shifting resources into new industries and new markets when we remained wedded to well-tried ways in old industries.

In explaining this failure, Lazonick has appealed to us to abandon neo-classical concepts and to embrace a Schumpeterian definition of the entrepreneur as one who fundamentally changes his industrial environment by bursting out of the organizational constraints that narrow his feasible technological choices and profitable opportunities.[18] Looked at in this way, clearly there was – and still is – entrepreneurial failure. Taking Lazonick's own field of research, for example, 'the vast majority of businessmen in the British cotton industry ... had neither the incentive to participate nor the ability to lead in the internal transformation of their industry. The competitive and specialized organization of the industry had developed a breed of managers with specialized skills and individualistic attitudes who were not only ill-suited for involvement in a transition from competitive to corporate capitalism but also by their very presence obstructed such a transition ... The result was prolonged technological backwardness and industrial decline'.[19]

In this, as in the other industries considered by Elbaum, Lazonick and their associates, British businessmen are accused of entrepreneurial failure because they failed 'to confront institutional constraints innovatively'.[20] Only by the replacement of the atomistic, competitive organization of British industry by a corporate, concentrated, managerial structure capable of superseding the market as an allocative mechanism could British decline be halted or even reversed. Adam Smith had to give way to Alfred Chandler: the invisible hand of the self-regulating market to the visible hand of co-ordinated control.[21] Leaving aside the major question of whether this *would* have achieved a higher rate of economic growth, why did this not occur? Elbaum and Lazonick feel that it cannot be adequately explained by reference to 'cultural conservatism'; more significant was the matrix of rigid institutional structures that 'obstructed individualistic as well as collective efforts of economic renovation ... Entrenched institutional structures – in industrial relations, enterprise and market organizations, education, finance, international trade, and state-enterprise relations – constrained the transformation of Britain's productive system'.[22] All economic historians are indebted to Elbaum and Lazonick for focusing attention on the question of institutional adaptation. They have, in effect, given substance to the generalities of Mancur Olsen,[23] and one cannot help believing that much future work will necessarily be involved with illustrating, refining and assessing their approach, which represents a major advance in understanding Britain's relative economic decline.

Just how far it will further our knowledge of the role of the entrepreneur in this decline, I remain uncertain. It seems to me that on this score, their arguments and the definitions they employ – however convincing their case for clarification in this regard – take us less further forward than my initial exposure to their ideas led me to believe. If neo-classical theory is inappropriate in the assessment of entrepreneurship, the use of Schumpeterian concepts also contain a definitionally determined answer.[24] Let me ask a question. In the current take-over mania, there can be little question that institutional rigidities are being seriously eroded. Are we then witnessing a belated upsurge in British entrepreneurship? Will British industry be revitalized by the massive restructuring currently underway? It remains to be seen, but it requires the exercise of considerable optimism to believe that the present ferment of leveraged buy-outs, 'junk bonds' and unbundling will necessarily lead to the regeneration of the British economy. To achieve this, the visible hand requires to be actuated by a Schumpeterian brain, not one motivated simply by the desire to achieve short-term financial advantage.

One cannot but be concerned by the evidence that only rarely do mergers lead to increased efficiency (and hence real economic growth).[25] Lazonick's belief in the beneficial consequences of the large corporation – while receiving some support from Hannah – seems to ignore the danger implicit in the larger firm that bureaucratization and adherence to routine and tradition might stifle – rather than promote – innovation.[26] It is indeed part of the folklore of monopoly capitalism that patents have sometimes been purchased and suppressed: the visible hand may throttle the goose that lays the golden eggs. Big is *not necessarily* beautiful (or growth-inducing), a point to which I drew attention in 1978.[27] In the context of my present argument, it might be added that if the growth of the firm has been achieved by acquisition by shares, the share price has to be maintained, and for this reason there is a tendency to disperse profits rather than retain them within the enterprise.[28] Furthermore, there is growing evidence that mergers do not result in synergistic increases in profitability, but have an averaging effect: companies with above normal profits have their profits lowered by mergers; companies with initially sub-normal profits have them raised. The consequence may or may not be increased net real investment.[29] The post-merger structure of a giant firm or of an industry may have Schumpeterian *potential* but only time will reveal whether that potential is exploited: the example of GEC under Lord Weinstock is not encouraging.[30]

III

Be that as it may, if the work of Elbaum and Lazonick and the authors assembled by them represents a major contribution to the continuing debate on British entrepreneurship, perhaps the most interesting, certainly the most eloquent, of the recent explorations of the causes of British industrial decline has been that by Martin Wiener.[31] He argues that from the middle of the nineteenth century 'Businessmen increasingly shunned the role of industrial entrepreneur for the more socially rewarding role of gentleman (landed if possible)', and that the consequence was a dampening of industrial energies. 'Social prestige and moral approbation were to be found by using the wealth acquired in industry to escape it'. By returning to an older, pre-industrial, agricultural and craft-based countryside, the industrialist became gentrified, thus 'discouraging commitment to a wholehearted pursuit of economic growth'.[32] In turn, his children, educated in revivified public schools and ancient universities, were dissuaded from following in father's footsteps. Instead, they found employment in the civil service, the army, the church and the liberal professions, resulting in a haemorrhage of talent – often to the empire – from which the British economy was never to recover.

Wiener's beautifully written thesis is extremely seductive but basically flawed. It is not that the evidence that he has marshalled is wrong, it is partial and inadequate. His explanation of British economic decline has achieved a remarkable popularity because it tells people what they want to hear. By clutching at the belief that Britain's decline can be ascribed to some general cultural miasma and the diminution of 'the industrial spirit', businessmen, politicians and trade unionists can each evade blame for Britain's poor economic performance, for this was due to some intangible factor beyond their control. As Coleman has said, such a notion has all the fascination of Max Weber's 'spirit of capitalism' and only a little more evidence that it exists.[33]

A number of specific criticisms may be outlined. The first is concerned with Wiener's chronology. 'There is ample evidence of hostile attitudes towards businessmen in the later eighteenth century. They can be found not simply in those well-known rude remarks by Adam Smith but much more widely in novels, stories, moral tales and other sorts of popular fiction'[34] current, it is worth noting, during the very period during which the industrial revolution occurred.[35] As Professor T. S. Ashton observed in the very first issue of the journal *Business History*, 'The businessman has never been a popular figure. Dislike of him runs, a continuous thread, through nineteenth century literature, showing up most strongly in the writings of Ruskin and his followers, but visible also in those novelists and essayists, who much preferred the ways of gypsies and tramps'. Not the least of the reasons for the widespread acceptance of such ideas was that 'the business-man has not had much to say for himself. His taciturnity is, indeed, one of the counts against him: evidently he must have a good deal to be silent about'.[36]

But while it is possible to accept the argument that the social prestige of business was low during the nineteenth century, there is no evidence that it *declined* after 1850. The social prestige of business has been, and continues to be very low. For re-emphasizing this 'central truth' – to use Leslie Hannah's words[37] – Martin Wiener has placed us all in his debt. And perhaps too Wiener should be thanked for provoking others, such as Neil McKendrick, to look anew at the evidence which suggests 'a far more complex and subtle interaction of business, literature and society than a simple graph of the rise and fall of literary Luddism'.[38] To McKendrick, the economic consequences of cultural responses to industry require much more careful treatment. Peaks of hostility to the businessman could reflect times when his place in society, his power and his influence are seen to be at their zenith; troughs of apparent indifference, times when his power and influence are in eclipse. Wiener's lack of attention to the implications of the relative literary neglect of businessmen in the last fifty years, it is argued, further weakens his case.[39]

But there are other problems too with Wiener's aetiology. As Harold Perkin has recently emphasized, Wiener is incorrect in assuming – albeit with a wealth of superficially convincing examples – that aristocratic values were in fact anti-industrial. A veritable library of monographs reveals that the British aristocracy and gentry during the industrial revolution were the most economically progressive and profit-oriented ruling class in Europe. 'They invested eagerly in agricultural improvement and enclosure, in trading ventures, mining, roads, river navigation and canals, docks, early railways, urban development and even, where circumstances permitted, in manufacturing such as brick-making, iron-founding, and textiles'.[40] They may not always have managed such enterprises directly, but the vast majority encouraged the exploitation of the resources to be found on, near, or under, their estates. And they continued to do so throughout the nineteenth century and beyond.

And what of those early middle class industrialists, traders, financiers and bankers who, being successful in their original pursuits, sought to secure acceptance into upper class society by the acquisition of a landed estate, the purchase or the building of a great house, the pursuit (as Coleman has commented) of foxes instead of profits? Did this buccolic emulation portend the beginning of the end of the British economy? Of course not. It was always so, before, during and after the Industrial Revolution.[41] Certainly, it was not a phenomenon peculiar to the period after 1850. The pursuit of non-economic ends did not involve any *net* haemorrhage of entrepreneurial talent. Quite the reverse. Many new thrusting firms would not have come into existence, or small established companies grown, had not their founders or owners seen or been aware of the tangible results of commercial or industrial success.[42] What was wrong with British industry after (indeed, before) 1850 was not a poverty of entrepreneurial (or industrial) spirit, but a surfeit. There were *too many* fiercely independent, aggressively competitive firms coming into existence,[43] hence the domestic industrial structure of which Lazonick properly complains, and the proprietors of the great majority of them were totally unaffected by public schools and classical liberal education. Furthermore, there is no evidence that the sons of businessmen were *increasingly* deflected to the lifestyle of the landed gentry. Nor, for that matter, 'is it clear that the traditional professions absorbed an *increasing* proportion of the labour force'.[44]

One last, more speculative point may be made. What Wiener has discovered is not so much a decline in industrial spirit as a reaffirmation of the stratified and hierarchial nature of British society. From an economic point of view, the significance of this is that the market confronting British manufacturers was similarly stratified. Recognizing this, many of them established themselves and survived by exploiting these differences and, by concentrating on lines that exhibited craftsmanship and individual character, consciously differentiated their products in order to secure a degree of monopoly power which permitted them to reap high profits on a relatively small capital and turnover.[45] This, in turn, strengthened their resolve not to increase the scale of their operations beyond that which would have involved the recruitment of managerial talent and financial resources outside the family circle. This policy of product differentiation, sustained as it was by the lack of homogeneity in the domestic market, depressed the national rate of economic growth and was partially responsible for the longevity of the small family firm and the slow adoption of corporate capitalism 'characterized by industrial oligopoly, hierarchical managerial bureaucracy, vertical integration of production and distribution, managerial control over job content and production standards, the integration of financial and industrial capital, and systematic research and development'.[46]

But even when it appeared that British companies were on the same evolutionary trajectory as the great American corporations; even when British firms – advised by such management consultants as McKinsley & Co – seem to have adopted the multi-divisional form of organization apparently required for the diversification of corporate strategy by region and/or by product, something was lacking. The giant British firms hesitated to embrace *all* the features of the American model.[47] Such deviations may have been the result of a characteristic British slowness to accept an important innovation and hence to employ it properly. Alternatively, they may reflect a rational response to a different economic and social environment.

Certainly, Chandler himself explains the gradual nature of organizational change in Britain in these terms. By the time the United States had entered the First World War, management decisions had already replaced co-ordination by market forces in many of the most critical sectors of the economy, but in Britain – where existing market mechanisms were more efficient than in the United States – businessmen were under far less pressure to integrate forward and backwards, to create managerial hierarchies and to centralize their administrations.[48] Many British firms may have grown to impressive size, usually by merger, but the holding company form of organization which almost invariably was adopted simply permitted the perpetuation of family firms, albeit now loosely grouped into federations.[49] Derek F. Channon, who investigated the post-Second World War strategy and structure of British enterprise found that although the number of family controlled companies fell between 1950 and 1970, just over one third of the hundred largest manufacturing firms in Britain still possessed significant elements of family control by the latter date.[50] Such companies were consistently less diversified than the others and were more reluctant to adopt the multi-divisional form. But even those British companies that had re-structured themselves on the American pattern possessed less sophisticated overall control and planning mechanisms and procedures than their transatlantic counterparts.[51] For the multi-divisional form to be effective, 'it is essential that all divisions adopt a uniform set of accounting conventions in order to generate comparable cost and revenue data. By this criterion, multi-divisionalization in Britain was, with some major exceptions, only marginally effective and certainly different from the USA in the 1960s and early 1970s'.[52] There are further differences. Many British holding companies adopting the multi-divisional form 'often did little more than insert another layer of management between the operating units/subsidiaries and central functions, thus making a cosmetic rather than a fundamental change in their internal organisation'.[53]

As Channon found, 'many of the internal characteristics of the corporations adopting a multi-divisional structure reflected prior structural forms. In particular there was little evidence of change in the reward system, especially as a mechanism to apply *internal* competition for divisional performance'.[54] And Lazonick, in an exceptionally valuable paper, concluded that:

the implementation of a bureaucratically integrated managerial structure in late postwar Britain may have faced severe institutional and cultural obstacles, such as (1) a system of higher education that had been shaped in part by the prevalence of bureaucratically segmented managerial structures, (2) the control of technology by shop-floor and shop-culture interest groups, and (3) the persistence of aristocratic values and social class distinctions in the hierarchical ordering of the managerial structure. In the face of these obstacles, insightful executives and experienced management consultants may not have been sufficient to transform the system of incentives, the lines of communication, and the loci of control within a large bureaucratic enterprise to permit managerial structure to make a success of the new organizational form.[55]

Lazonick clearly perceives the British inability fully to replicate American organizational practices as being yet another failure to confront institutional constraints innovatively, but Clark and Tann see it as a rational response conditioned by cultural differences between the two countries. To Clark, the British have appropriated from the Americans only those elements that are compatible with a distinctive British culture. Thus, he argues, in Britain there has been a persistent tendency towards loose-coupling – achieved by permitting a high degree of autonomy between sub-units of the enterprise and by a conscious decision not to preplan and specify the relationship between them – and the devolution of certain areas of decision-making. The consequence has been a considerable degree of that local autonomy which is deeply rooted in so many aspects of British society. Clark's emphasis is significant: 'high degrees of loose-coupling and of devolvement can be quite consistent with degrees of paternalism and with strong social control by a particular strata who themselves handle co-ordination in a personal way'.[56]

Wherever the truth may lie, it is impossible to ignore either the evidence that the largest British multi-divisional firms seem to have performed less well than their American counterparts in similar product markets,[57] or that the British subsidiaries of foreign multi-national companies have been more efficient and profitable than comparable indigenous enterprises.[58] These differences are not readily explicable, but it is difficult to avoid the suspicion that the quality of management was at least partially responsible.

This suggests a further important and relevant issue. The pioneering researches of Mira Wilkins on the multinational company have revealed that although there were many British multinationals operating in the same way as their American counterparts before the First World War, there were, in addition, 'thousands of companies registered in England and Scotland to conduct business overseas, most of which, unlike the American model, did *not* grow out of the domestic operations of existing enterprises that had their headquarters in Britain ... most were what [Wilkins has] called free-standing companies'.

The limited size of the typical head office was ultimately the crucial feature that distinguished these companies from contemporary US multinationals. American businessmen of this era learned at home about multi-regional operations over the vastness of the United States; American companies became large, multi-functional, multi-regional enterprises that developed management talents. Domestic business was a training ground for multinational enterprise, whereas the compact, geographically small domestic market in Britain provided an unsuitable basis for developing skills in business administration comparable with those learned by American managers. The free-standing company, therefore, served as an alternative in many instances to the extension of the British home-based operating enterprises abroad, though the need to manage the business overseas was still there and provided a formidable challenge, and one that the free-standing companies often failed to meet.[59]

There is little question that the mortality rate of these overseas companies greatly exceeded that of their purely domestic counterparts largely because they failed to create satisfactory managerial organizations. The consequence was that in many cases the holders of the companies' securities suffered losses and the firms were either formally wound up or were simply allowed to wither away.[60] Once again, the root cause of such failures appears to have been the paucity of effective managerial skills and this was, Wilkins implies, a function of the persistence in Britain of the family firm.[61]

IV

The foregoing discussion indicates that while the *central* thrust of Wiener's argument is erroneous, it would be foolish to ignore the importance of certain cultural elements in Britain's relative economic decline, however difficult it may be to determine their exact significance or the manner in which they have operated.[62] Let us return to fundamentals. Many of those who have sought to diagnose the basic cause of Britain's economic malaise have concluded that it stems largely from productivity problems.[63] For decades the rate of productivity growth has lagged behind that of most other countries.[64] There have been several hypotheses put forward to explain this disquieting phenomenon. Crude explanations focused upon the greater productivity potential of manufacturing as compared with agricultural activities, with the corollary that where Britain had led others could follow (while avoiding Britain's 'mistakes'), and have been superseded by increasingly sophisticated interpretations dependent upon the analysis of statistical data, the range and variety of which were only recently undreamed of.

What is intriguing here is that several of the factors that have been identified as major influences on Britain's relatively low and slow-growing productivity possess a cultural component. A number of the more simplistic of these may rapidly be discounted, if only because they are mutually inconsistent. Richard Caves provides illustrations:

Britain's productivity is said to be low because an elaborate class structure with wide income disparities denies economic harmony – and because egalitarian measures to redistribute income have dampened the incentives of managers and savers ... Growth and productivity may be stalled by institutions that are too resistant to change – or by public policies that change all too often as the party in power embraces a new policy fad, or a party newly in power jettisons its opponents' pet devices to install its own.[65]

Nevertheless, it is impossible to deny the baneful effects on productivity of British industrial relations and work practices.

The influence of the trade unions on the introduction of new, productivity-enhancing techniques is a much debated topic. The evidence is overwhelming that from the very onset of industrialization the members of the labour force regarded the adoption of new inventions with acute suspicion. New machines were thought of as a means of diminishing labour's bargaining power, reducing wages, eroding the status of those possessing craft skills, and adversely affecting established work patterns.[66] It may be conjectured that the fate of the handloom weavers made an indelible impression on employees in all branches of manufacturing, not simply those in textiles. The workers' conviction that new methods of organization and improvements in physical plant were detrimental to their interests was strengthened by the knowledge – originally surmised, but later in the nineteenth century partially confirmed by formal discussions among representatives of the employers and employees – that employers consistently regarded new techniques primarily as labour-saving devices. Indeed, it is arguable that many innovations were directly stimulated by the recalcitrance of the workers.

In the context of the present discussion, the significance of such attitudes is that much of the return on capital expenditure was offset by enhanced labour costs consequent upon the compromises necessary to secure the acceptance of new machines by the work-force. All too frequently this made itself manifest in overmanning and a far lower increase in labour productivity than was technically feasible. Case after case could be cited from the records of the Board of Conciliation and Arbitration for the Manufactured Steel Trade of the West of Scotland to illustrate this argument.[67] One will suffice. In 1902 Colvilles installed new, more powerful engines in their plate mills at the Dalzell Works. These greatly accelerated the speed of rolling, and the time taken to convert a ton of steel slabs into steel plates was considerably shortened. Ancillary equipment was also fitted in order to reduce the severity of the physical effort involved in moving these heavy products. Colvilles therefore appealed to the Board to permit them to reduce the men's wages, arguing that 'the earnings of the men have gone up, although the exertions from doing the work has gone down'.

The operatives saw things differently. Their statement to the Board emphasized that in accelerating the conversion process, the introduction of new rolling mill engines had so enhanced Colvilles' output that prices had fallen and hence their wages, regulated as they were by a sliding scale based on the selling price of ship plates. Furthermore:

The improvements referred to have changed the individual labour of the men, [making] their work more exacting and laborious and [involving] more exertion and strain, both physically and mentally ... The increased output and quick speed, coupled with the thinness of the gauges and larger lengths and wider widths require much greater vigilance and more intense mental strain on the men than formerly. If [the employers'] claim is admitted by the Board, it means that the more a workman produces by his extra vigilance, skill and exertion the less remuneration will he receive. The increased output is equally good for Employer and workman, but is no reason for reducing the wages of the men on the one hand, while increasing the profits of the Employers on the other hand. The present wages do not give adequate remuneration for work performed.

Lengthy discussion of these issues led to a complete deadlock and the case went to arbitration. The arbiter was Sheriff Davidson, the men's choice, part of whose lengthy statement of award reads:

The determination to adopt new machinery was the Employers', the cost was theirs and the risk ... I consider that, giving the workmen all that is fairly due to them for increased responsibility and the fact that they are dealing with material of greater value, and taking into account as well the gain to the Employers from increased output and a certain saving of labour, there is still a clear balance of earnings due in no way to the workmen themselves, but to the action of the Employers. I think, however, that the workmen are entitled to some portion of this balance. Where Employers and workmen come to a voluntary agreement such as was arrived at in 1884 in the Dalzell Steel Works, especially when a Sliding Scale is part of the agreement, it really means that a modified kind of profit-sharing or partnership is established between them, and an arbiter is bound to consider their respective positions in that light. Therefore I do not make the increase of output per day the measure of the reduction in wages, even after making allowance for the claims of the workmen ... The wages of the roller should, in my opinion, be reduced by 12.5 per cent on the present rate. Those of the breaker-down, chipper-in, and back of rolls men should be reduced by 7.5 per cent, and those of the winching-away man, sweeper, and screwer by 5 per cent.

The award gave rise to considerable argument. Certain facts were disputed, and the establishment of the principle of profit sharing and partnership was denounced by the employers. Nevertheless, the recommendations were accepted and the new rates came into effect.[68]

What is interesting about this case – and it is typical of many encountered in the iron and steel trades – was that it was settled reasonably amicably and that it appears not to have given rise to smouldering resentment. The men were conscious that the introduction of improved machinery and the minimization of costs were unavoidable if the industry was to survive the onslaught of competition from Germany, the United States and

Belgium. Yet their representatives tried always to get the best possible bargain for their constituents. As John Hodge, the secretary of the British Steel Smelters' Association, always claimed, his policy was to 'advise the men not to work against the machine ... provided we get a fair share of the plunder'.[69]

Now what is true of the iron and steel trades at the turn of the century is not necessarily true of other branches of industrial activity or of other periods. So much depended on the power of the workers and the determination of the employers to impose agreements upon their employees; and the relative influence of these factors varied over time. It has been suggested that the prevalence of restrictive practices ebbed and flowed with the trade cycle and the relative scarcity of skilled labour; that a general improvement was 'interrupted and reversed between the 1890s and 1920, and not continued in the post war period'.[70] Be that as it may, from the 1880s it is possible to detect a growing tolerance among masters and men, an increase in mutual accommodation. 'Ours wasn't a hating trade', one unionist said of his life-time in the steel industry,[71] and similar observations have been made by those in other industries. But the price paid by British industry for this social cohesion was a sub-optional exploitation of the technical possibilities of innovation, either because of an implicit acceptance of 'profit sharing' or because, as in the car industry, the employers surrendered their right to manage, believing themselves to be – as Lewchuk has so brilliantly demonstrated[72] – unable to convert labour time into labour effort. In such industries, the pace of work came to be determined by the work-force itself. In either case, the result was relatively low investment and low productivity.

How much significance may be attached to such factors is difficult to determine. Williams, Williams and Thomas[73] discuss some of the issues with great care without arriving at a definite conclusion. Suffice it here to say that it is arguable that until the 1970s the mutual accommodation between management and men evident in some branches of economic activity may have played an important role in Britain's sluggish productivity record. With the politics of confrontation associated with the Thatcher government, the absolute decline of manufacturing industry and a high level of unemployment, there has been a remarkable rise in labour productivity.[74] There has also been an ugly erosion of the tolerance once so characteristic of British society.

V

To return to the assessment of the role of entrepreneurship in Britain's economic decline. Recent explorations have strengthened my belief that it is difficult to condemn British businessmen for the way they behaved *within the context of their individual firms.* I would subscribe to Lazonick's verdict that on the whole they 'performed admirably as neo-classical managers – they took the conditions facing them as given and tried to do the best they could'.[75] I experience great difficulty in accepting his corollary that to merit the use of the appellation 'entrepreneur', they *should* have transformed their industrial environment. I ask myself how could they and equally, if not more important, why should they? Empirically to answer these questions involves a more intimate knowledge of many fields of economic activity than I possess. I can only say that my own researches into the Scottish iron and steel industry[76] suggest that the problems confronting those who tried – and I refer specifically to Sir John Craig – were all but insuperable, and the benefit from so doing was so long in arriving that had it been possible to foresee what restructuring the Scottish steel industry was to cost – in profits forgone and the horrendous physical and mental strain incurred – even Craig might have hesitated.[77] As it was, the attainment of his 'grand design' was made possible only by the intervention of Sir James Lithgow for whom – in this instance at least – private and public advantage coincided, a conjuncture which was quite fortuitous and, I would guess, extremely rare.[78] Even then, what was achieved fell short of what hindsight indicates should have been done, and even an ideal solution would have possessed but a limited term.

If I were to summarize what seems to be the current state of the debate on the British entrepreneur, I would be forced to say, albeit epigrammatically, that British entrepreneurs did not fail, but that there was a failure of industrial entrepreneurship.[79] It is undeniable that the rate of British economic growth would have been greatly enhanced had *more* businessmen developed new technologies or new industries possessing high potential levels of productivity.[80] One of the reasons why the British economy failed to generate this desirable response was, it has repeatedly been argued, not the fault of the entrepreneur as such, but stemmed from the British educational system. Certainly, this was the belief of Herbert Gray and Samuel Turner writing in

1916, and echoed most recently by Correlli Barnett and R.R.Locke.[81] By emphasizing the needs of technologically-based industries (and it was here that the British lagged so grievously[82]) and the nature of the new business organizations that the growth of the large-scale firm demanded, Locke shows that higher education in Germany – and to a lesser extent in the United States – met these requirements far more successfully than did the British and French systems.

There are a number of major difficulties involved in this important issue. Against Locke's highly persuasive argument must be set Sanderson's vigorous defence of British education[83] and Pollard's detailed comparative examination which reveals the remarkable 'capacity of the educational sector of the British economy to respond to the challenges facing it' in the period before the First World War.[84] Perhaps, after all, it was a question of demand? Sanderson is convinced that 'the more lasting problem was not so much the provision of technical education as the willingness of employers to receive its products'.[85] And, speaking of scientists, Pollard believes that there was 'no sign of unfilled need'. Even the decline of the Mechanics Institutes can be explained by a lack of demand.[86]

Certainly, there was little demand by the business community for educational provisions for professional management personnel. Lazonick ascribes this to the persistence in Britain of family firms and the reluctance of their owners to share control with qualified outsiders.[87] But there was more to it than this. The fact was that the vast majority of British businessmen were unaware of their own inadequacies and unconscious of the poverty of the information upon which they based their decisions. As Locke makes plain, British accountants – obsessed by the accuracy of the balance sheet and the profit and loss statement – provided little or no guidance for beleaguered management; British neo-classical economists despised and neglected the empirical study of the firm, their theories rarely had operational significance; British engineers knew little of economic realities.

In effect, the owners and directors of so many British firms did not realize what they were missing. It took the reports of itinerant productivity teams after the Second World War to bring home to them just how far the British were behind, just what could have been learned had the British business community shown even minimal interest in what had been going on in

Germany (let alone America), and had British academics made any attempt to understand, evaluate and disseminate the work of German business economists and cost accountants.

Meanwhile, training for management in Britain was, and to some extent still is, regarded as the responsibility of the firm itself. But, as Ackrill has observed:

Training is best suited to large companies who find it worthwhile to set up [appropriate] courses and whose organisation is big enough and diverse enough to provide recognisable pathways for its new recruits. The longer persistence of the family firms in Britain probably had something to do with a lesser provision of training since firms tended to be smaller in size than corporations in the United States, Germany and Japan, and also because it might be assumed that the sons and grandsons of the owners knew a good deal more about the general nature and indeed the particular details of a firm than outside entrants.[88]

No one knew this better than Lyndall Urwick, who observed in a paper to the Institute of Public Administration in 1927:

Broadly speaking, in ninety-nine hundredths of British industry there is no system of promotion. Family connections, ownership of capital, toadyism, seniority, inertia, or luck decide which men shall be selected to rule their fellows ... it is a fact that in the majority of our great enterprises there is no analysis of the factors which constitute 'fitness' for most of the managerial positions and no methods of measuring or assessing those factors whatever.

Indeed, Urwick reported that one speaker had only a few years ago told an Oxford business conference that 'the only principle of organization he had been able to discover in English industry was "myself, my father, my son, and my wife's sister's nephew"'; and that even more recently a 'friendly American' had written that 'In England the fact that you are the husband of the daughter of the Managing Director is apt to mean more than the fact that you have discovered a new process for smelting steel that cuts a quarter off the price of production'.[89]

Perhaps the most damaging consequence of the prevalence of these attitudes was that until very recently there was little or no 'pressure for the creation and expansion of social institutions for the development of professional managerial personnel'.[90] Is it merely chance that the more rapid growth of productivity in British industry has coincided with the preferment and growing seniority of the products of the feverishly created business schools and the postgraduate business courses mounted in British universities in the 1960s?

But if there was a paucity of training provisions for management, it is plausible that the British labour force was, paradoxically, too well trained (as opposed to too well educated), too disciplined and skilled to encourage their employers to abandon handicraft techniques, which in any case were consistent with the tactics of product differentiation.[91] The long-run economic significance of skilled labour, initially postulated by C.K.Harley,[92] has received powerful support from W.Lewchuk, who in his studies of the British motor vehicles industry has emphasized the importance of the associated tradition of labour independence on the shop floor which led British employers to exercise only partial control over labour effort. Instead, they depended upon motivation provided by piece rates to secure relatively high and acceptable profits despite low productivity, the malign consequences of which were not fully exposed until the 1960s.[93]

It was the skill of the British labour force, combined with the workers' appreciation of the 'rules of the game',[94] that inhibited and continues to inhibit innovation.[95] This, in turn, has contributed to the relatively low level of investment in Great Britain which, perhaps as much as any other factor, has retarded British economic growth.[96] But additional reasons for the low level of investment in *manufacturing* activity were undoubtedly the relative attractiveness of the service sector which, it is plain, did not fail to recruit new entrepreneurs,[97] and the fact, demonstrated by William Rubinstein, that money could be made so much more easily in finance than in industry.[98] Clive Lee's work shows that the expansion of the service sector *during the late Victorian period* possessed highly beneficial consequences for economic growth and that much of this expansion was neither directly nor in spatial terms immediately dependent upon manufacturing.[99] Thus, the movement into services, to which Charles Wilson drew attention in 1965,[100] provides positive evidence of entrepreneurial perspicacity and vigour in the closing decades of the nineteenth century, and this verdict has recently been strengthened by a number of specific illustrations, among the more notable of which have been those provided by Edwin Green and Michael Moss, T. R. Nevett, Asa Briggs, Clive Trebilcock and Charles Wilson himself.[101]

In the context of this exploration of entrepreneurship and

British economic decline, this movement into services is of the utmost importance. If the British entrepreneur is to be criticized for failing constructively to confront the organizational constraints that were progressively strangling him in the staple industries (industries which were so labour-intensive that Lee has described them collectively as the apogee of proto-industrialization, rather than the products of an Industrial Revolution); and if he is to be criticized for failing more vigorously to enter new manufacturing industries, then surely this same British entrepreneur deserves some praise for moving into the service sector, whose relatively rapid rate of output growth and high productivity, certainly between c 1870 and 1913, was so much superior to the old staples that its expansion provided what little buoyancy there was in Britain's aggregate economic growth?[102]

It was not until the twentieth century that the persistent movement into services could have become detrimental to aggregate economic growth. Why is this? The reason appears to reside in the fact that whereas productivity in the tertiary sector was initially greater than that of the waning staple industries, subsequent productivity in services may have increased only slowly, if at all.[103] It is admitted that there are innumerable problems of measurement and interpretation of service output change,[104] but it would seem probable that since the turn of the century higher rates of economic growth might have been achieved by manufacturing *goods*, particularly articles embodying a high technological and scientific component; the products of the sort of industries that Locke has argued that the British – with their 'inferior' or inappropriate educational system – were singularly unfitted to develop.[105] Having belatedly recognized the cost of this neglect – made particularly manifest, as Correlli Barnett has so strikingly revealed, during the Second World War[106] – those businessmen who sought to exploit previously neglected opportunities were confronted with a complex of difficulties. Many of these stemmed, first, from the inability of the British educational system to supply suitably trained middle management skills, applied scientists, production engineers and cost accountants; and second, from a labour force reluctant to accept and accommodate to change, the inevitable consequences of unimaginative labour-management relations over past decades, coupled with motivational problems apparently far greater than those confronting Britain's competitors in the United States and, later, in Japan.[107]

VI

Although several of the themes that have been touched upon in this brief survey undoubtedly deserve more intensive investigation, it should be apparent that some of the problems that have inhibited – and continue to inhibit – growth in the British economy are of a nature and magnitude that make them insoluble by entrepreneurial initiatives alone. An earlier version of Elbaum and Lazonick's argument, presented at the 1983 meeting of the Economic History Association,[108] seemed to point to necessity of state intervention, but as Lance E.Davis observed on that occasion, 'the African ground nut scheme, the Concorde, and the decision to "go with coal"',[109] do not inspire confidence in state ownership or state planning. Nor does the recent series of reflections by Aubrey Jones, who emphasizes that in his own experience as Minister of Fuel and Power and Minister of Supply, 'whatever the government's macro-economic policy, industrial structure was always the Cinderella'.[110] Certainly, governments cannot produce instant breakthroughs. The democratic state may take action which *may* accelerate the erosion of baneful institutional arrangements, but little more. As some of the growth-retarding factors are reduced in number and power (and it may be observed that the present government's attitude towards the universities reveals a lamentable ignorance of the significance of basic research in achieving this objective[111]), then a new generation of entrepreneurs, some of them graduates of the belatedly established business schools,[112] may contribute to the revival of the British economy, but the omens are not propitious.[113]

NOTES

1. Nick Crafts, 'The Assessment: British Economic Growth over the Long Run', in *Oxford Review of Economic Policy*, Vol. 4, No. 1 (Spring, 1988), p. i.
2. David Landes, 'Entrepreneurship in Advanced Industrial Countries: The Anglo-German Rivalry', in *Entrepreneurship and Economic Growth: Papers presented at a Conference sponsored jointly by the Committee on Economic Growth of the Social Science Research Council and the Harvard University Research Centre in Entrepreneurial History, Cambridge, Mass., November 12 & 13, 1954*; David Landes,

'Technological Change and Development in Western Europe, 1750–1914', in *The Cambridge Economic History of Europe*, VI, *The Industrial Revolution and After*, Part 1, edited by H. J. Habakkuk and M. M. Postan (Cambridge: CUP, 1965); subsequently reprinted and extended as *The Unbound Prometheus* (Cambridge: CUP, 1969).

3. H. J. Habakkuk, *American and British Technology in the Nineteenth Century* (Cambridge: CUP, 1962); Derek H. Aldcroft, 'The Entrepreneur and the British Economy: 1870–1914', *Economic History Review*, 2nd series, xvii (1964); Charles Wilson, 'Economy and Society in Late Victorian Britain', *Economic History Review*, 2nd ser., xviii (1965).

4. A. L. Levine, *Industrial Retardation in Britain, 1880–1914* (London: Weidenfeld & Nicolson, 1967); Eric Sigsworth, 'Some Problems in Business History, 1870–1914', in *Papers of the Sixteenth Business History Conference* (ed.) Charles J. Kennedy (Lincoln, Nebraska: University of Nebraska, 1969); Francois Crouzet, *The Victorian Economy* (London: Methuen, 1982); Derek H. Aldcroft (ed.), *The Development of British Industry and Foreign Competition, 1875–1914* (London: Allen & Unwin, 1968).

5. Roy Church, 'The Effect of the American Export Invasion on the British Boot and Shoe Industry, 1885–1914', *Journal of Economic History*, xxviii (1968); A. E. Harrison, 'The Competitiveness of the British Cycle Industry, 1890–1914', *Economic History Review*, 2nd ser., xxii (1969); D. N. McCloskey (ed.), *Essays on a Mature Economy: Britain After 1840, Papers and Proceedings of the MSSB Conference on the New Economic History of Britain, 1840–1930* (London: Methuen, 1971); T. C. Barker, 'History: Economic and Social', in C. B. Cox & A. E. Dyson (eds.), *The Twentieth Century Mind, Vol. 1: 1900–1918* (Oxford: OUP, 1972).

6. Donald N. McCloskey and Lars G. Sandberg, 'From Damnation to Redemption: Judgments on the Late Victorian Entrepreneur', *Explorations in Economic History*, ix (1971).

7. Donald N. McCloskey, *Economic Maturity and Entrepreneurial Decline: British Iron and Steel, 1870–1913* (Cambridge, Mass.: Harvard UP, 1973), p. 127.

8. Lars Sandberg, *Lancashire in Decline* (Columbus, Ohio: Ohio State University Press, 1974), pp. 82–4.

9. Donald N. McCloskey, 'Did Victorian Britain Fail?', *Economic History Review*, 2nd ser., xxiii (1970), p. 459.

10. P. L. Payne, 'Industrial Entrepreneurship and Management in Great Britain, c 1760–1970', in *The Cambridge Economic History of Europe*, VII, *The Industrial Economies: Capital, Labour and Enterprise*, Part I, ed. Peter Mathias and M. M. Postan (Cambridge: CUP, 1978); *British Entrepreneurship in the Nineteenth Century* (London: Macmillan, 1974).

11. See for example, Payne, *Entrepreneurship*, p. 50. For a critical evaluation of the cliometric revision, see R. R. Locke, 'New Insights from Cost Accounting into British Entrepreneurial Performance, *circa* 1914', *The Accounting Historians Journal*, vi, Part I (1979); and

the same author's 'Cost Accounting: An Institutional Yardstick for measuring British Entrepreneurial Performance circa. 1914', *The Accounting Historians Journal*, VI, Part 2 (1979).

12. Roy Church, *Kenricks in Hardware: A Family Business, 1791–1966* (Newton Abbot: David & Charles, 1969).

13. P. S. Andrews and E. Brunner, *Capital Development in Steel* (Oxford: Blackwell, 1952), pp. 208, 362–3; D. C. Coleman, *Courtaulds* (Oxford: Clarendon Press, 1969), Vol. II, p. 218; P. L. Payne, *Colvilles and the Scottish Steel Industry* (Oxford: Clarendon Press, 1979), p. 144; Jonathan Boswell, 'Hope, Inefficiency or Public Duty? The United Steel Companies and West Cumberland, 1918–39', *Business History*, xxii (1980); Jonathan Boswell, 'The Informal Social Control of Business in Britain, 1880–1939', *Business History Review*, LVII (Summer, 1983); Jonathan Boswell, *Business Policies in the Making* (London: Allen & Unwin, 1983); Harold Perkin, *The Rise of Professional Society. England since 1880* (London: Routledge, 1989), p. 364.

14. H. W. Richardson, in Aldcroft (ed.), *op. cit.*, p. 216.

15. Coleman, *Courtaulds*, II, p. 220.

16. Leslie Hannah, *Entrepreneurs and the Social Sciences: An Inaugural Lecture* (London: LSE, 1983), p. 12.

17. Growth in GDP per man-year was less than 1 per cent per annum in the period 1873–1924, lower than that of the first three-quarters of the nineteenth century, and subsequent periods: 1924–51, 1 per cent; 1951–1973, 2.4 per cent. R. C. O. Matthews, C. H. Feinstein and J. C. Odling-Smee, *British Economic Growth, 1856–1973* (Oxford: OUP, 1982), p. 22.

18. William Lazonick, 'Industrial Organisation and Technological Change: The Decline of the British Cotton Industry', *Business History Review*, LVII (Summer, 1983), pp. 230–6.

19. *Ibid.*, pp. 229–30. See also *Lancashire and Whitehall: The Diary of Sir Raymond Streat, 1931–1957*, ed. by Marguerite Dupree (Manchester: MUP, 1987).

20. Bernard Elbaum and William Lazonick (eds.), *The Decline of the British Economy* (Oxford: Clarendon Press, 1986), p. 2.

21. The work of Alfred Chandler is considered later.

22. Elbaum & Lazonick, *op. cit.*, p. 2.

23. Mancur Olson, *The Rise and Decline of Nations: Economic Growth, Stagflation, and Social Rigidities* (New Haven and London: Yale University Press, 1982), see especially pp. 77–87. Olsen stresses the importance of 'special interest' groups in reducing Britain's rate of growth. He cites Peter Murrell, 'The Comparative Structure of the Growth of West German and British Manufacturing Industry' in D. C. Mueller (ed.), *The Political Economy of Growth* (New Haven: Yale University Press, 1983.)

24. *cf.* Burton Klein: 'Even before he wrote *Socialism, Capitalism and Democracy*, Schumpeter had turned his entrepreneur into an innovator who put daring ideas into practices (as in the opening of the railroads). However, because he could not explain why some entrepre-

neurs acted upon a good idea and others did not, his theory became, in effect, a theory in which those who reached great success were destined to do so, which is to say, it became a more deterministic concept of entrepreneurship than the one set forth in his doctoral thesis'. Burton Klein, *Dynamic Economics* (Cambridge, Mass.: Harvard University Press, 1977), p. 135.

25. See K. Cowling, P. Stoneman et al., *Mergers and Economic Performance* (Cambridge: CUP, 1980). 'Any view that the alleged retardation of the British economy before 1914 was due to a lack of business concentration, while the subsequent improved growth performance in the interwar years and again after 1945, was due to increased merger activity, would clearly need to be qualified [by the conclusions of this book on the welfare cost of monopoly]. If the social cost of mergers was indeed high, then the sources of industrial growth would clearly need to be found elsewhere' (G. Jones reviewing the book in *Business History*, xxxiii (1981), p. 365).

26. W. J. Baumol & K. McLennan (eds.), *Productivity Growth and US Competitiveness* (New York: OUP, 1985), p. 203. See also Lance E. Davis and Susan Groth, 'Industrial Structure and Technological Change', *Caltech. Soc. Sci. Working Papers*, No. 57 (1974); Burton H. Klein, *Dynamic Economics*. In looking at invention Klein could find no case in which significant advances in relatively static industries came from major firms (p. 17), and Jacob Schmookler, 'The Size of Firm and the Growth of Knowledge', in his *Patents Inventions and Economic Change* (Cambridge, Mass.: Harvard UP, 1972), pp. 36–46, found that smaller firms 'used' more of their patents than larger firms (p. 39), quoting a report compiled at Harvard.

27. Payne, 'Industrial Entrepreneurship', p. 229. A recent study by George F. Ray, *The Diffusion of Mature Technologies* (Cambridge: CUP for the National Institute of Economic and Social Research, 1984), p. 90, concludes that 'size has less to do with the diffusion of new technologies in the mature phase than was believed some ten or twenty years ago. It is not denied that large companies have certain advantages ... Nevertheless, there are plenty of examples of medium-sized or smaller companies pioneering'.

28. Aubrey Jones, *Britain's Economy, The Roots of Stagnation* (Cambridge: CUP, 1985), p. 126.

29. Dennis C. Mueller, *Profits in the Long Run* (Cambridge: CUP, 1986).

30. The story of GEC told by John Williams, in Williams, Williams and Thomas, *Why are the British Bad at Manufacturing?* (London: RKP, 1983), pp. 133–78. 'The combination of a company having a billion pounds of free cash with a manufacturing output which has not expanded strongly seems obvious. At the least it provokes the suggestion that the company has not been successful in finding and seizing strategic opportunities in new processes, new products and new marketing arrangements where resources could be profitably and productively used' (p. 157). However, in discussing his recent bid, jointly with Siemens, for Plessey, Lord Weinstock observed 'We built a cash

mountain because we were efficient and we saw no justification for investing more than we have invested ... Had we had opportunities, we would have taken them but when we tried to use the money to buy other companies (EMI, British Aerospace, Plessey) we were not allowed to do it'. He also said: 'I keep reading surveys by learned academics, who presumably have never had to run businesses, in which they say there is overwhelming evidence that mergers do not produce any improvement in efficiency. My own experience with one small merger, two very large ones and a fairly large one is that we have enormously increased efficiency'. *The Times*, 5 August 1989, p. 19.

31. Martin J. Wiener, *English Culture and the Decline of the Industrial Spirit, 1850–1980* (Cambridge: CUP, 1981).
32. *Ibid.*, pp. 97, 127.
33. Donald Coleman, in a letter to the author, 14 January 1986; and see D. C. Coleman and Christine MacLeod, 'Attitudes to New Techniques: British Businessmen, 1800–1950', *Economic History Review*, 2nd series, Vol. xxxix, No. 4 (November, 1986), p. 599.
34. *Ibid.*, based on J. R. Raven, 'English Popular Literature and the Image of Business, 1760–1790' (Unpublished PhD thesis, Cambridge, 1985). See also, John McVeagh. *Tradeful Merchants. The Portrayal of the Capitalist in Literature* (London: RKP, 1981), and the stimulating essay by Neil McKendrick, '"Gentlemen and Players" revisited: the gentlemanly ideal, the business ideal and the professional ideal in English literary culture', in Neil McKendrick & R. B. Outhwaite, *Business Life and Public Policy* (Cambridge: CUP, 1986), pp. 98–136.
35. *cf.* Olsen, *op. cit.*, p. 78: '... until nearly the middle of the nineteenth [century], Britain was evidently the country with the *fastest* rate of economic growth ... This means that no explanation of Britain's relatively slow growth in recent times that revolves around some supposedly inherent or permanent feature of British character or society can possibly be correct ...'
36. T. S. Ashton, *Business History*, Vol. 1, No. 1 (December 1958), p. 1.
37. Hannah, *Inaugural*, p. 25.
38. Neil McKendrick, '"Gentlemen and Players" revisited', *loc. cit.*, p. 102.
39. J. M. Winter, 'Bernard Shaw, Bertold Brecht and the businessman in literature', in McKendrick & Outhwaite, *op. cit.*, pp. 185–204.
40. Perkin, *op. cit.*, pp. 365–6.
41. D. C. Coleman, 'Gentlemen and Players', *Economic History Review*, 2nd ser., xxvi (1973).
42. Payne, *Entrepreneurship*, pp. 25–6.
43. Again and again, this is emphasized by studies of individual industries. See, for example, Coleman and MacLeod, *op. cit.*, pp. 600–1, and appended notes 77–87; Correlli Barnett, *The Audit of War* (London: Macmillan, 1986), among others, assembles numerous examples. Taking two technological industries, the Report of the Official Sub-Committee on Post-War Resettlement of the Motor Industry, refers to the division of the industry into 'too many, often small-scale units,

each producing too many models' (CAB 87/15, R(1)(45)9, 21 March 1945), pp. 58, 274; on aircraft (cites Wier Papers 19/10–11, Aircraft Factories on Air Ministry Work, April 1935; and M. M. Postan, D. Hay and J. D. Scott, *Design and Development Weapons: Studies in Government and Industrial Organisation*, London: HMSO & Longmans, 1964, pp. 36–7), p. 130. For the cotton industry, Sir Raymond Streat's diaries are invaluable; see Marguerite Dupree (ed.), *Lancashire and Whitehall: The Diary of Sir Raymond Streat, 1931–1957* (Manchester: Manchester University Press, 1987).

44. Matthews, Feinstein and Odling-Smee, *op. cit.*, p. 115. See also David Jeremy, 'Anatomy of the British Business Elite', *Business History*, xxvi (1984), p. 20.

45. See Payne, *Entrepreneurship*, pp. 41–2. As Ackrill has pointed out, 'British managers knew that in Britain they faced differentiated markets, a fact borne out by the adverse experiences of German and US electrical firms which set up in Britain before 1914 but could not reap the same advantages of large-scale identical ordering on which success in their countries of origin had depended in large part'. Margaret Ackrill, 'Britain's Managers and the British Economy, 1870s to the 1980s', *Oxford Review of Economic Policy*, Vol. 4, No. 1 (Spring 1988), pp. 61, 64. It is significant that Mira Wilkins has found that 'the British ... excelled in trademarked consumer products', Mira Wilkins, 'European and North American Multinationals, 1870–1914; Comparisons and Contrasts', *Business History*, xxx (1988), p. 21.

46. Elbaum and Lazonick, in Elbaum and Lazonick (eds.), *op. cit.*, p. 4.

47. I am grateful to Dr Peter A. Clark, of the Work Organization Research Centre of Aston University, for first drawing my attention to certain implications of this point and for kindly supplying me with data. See Peter Clark, *Anglo-American Innovation* (Berlin: de Gruyter, 1987), p. 297.

48. A. D. Chandler, 'Introduction', in A. D. Chandler and Herman Daems (eds.), *Managerial Hierarchies* (Cambridge, Mass.: Harvard University Press, 1980), p. 6.

49. See P. L. Payne, 'The Emergence of the Large-scale Company in Great Britain', *Economic History Review*, 2nd Series, xx (1967), pp. 528–9, 533–5; L. Hannah, 'Visible and Invisible Hands in Great Britain', in Chandler & Daems, *op. cit.*, pp. 53, 55.

50. Derek F. Channon, *The Strategy and Structure of British Enterprise* (London: Macmillan, 1973), p. 76; see also P. L. Payne, 'Family Business in Britain: An Historical and Analytical Survey', in A. Okochi and S. Yasuoka (eds.), *Family Business in the Era of Industrial Growth* (Tokyo: Tokyo University Press, 1984), pp. 176–8.

51. A. D. Chandler, commenting on Channon's study, in 'The Development of Modern Management Structure in the US and UK', in Leslie Hannah (ed.), *Management Strategy and Business Development* (London: Macmillan, 1976), pp. 25–6. See also Peter Clark, *op. cit.*, pp. 306–40.

52. Peter Clark and Jennifer Tann, 'Cultures and Corporations: the

M-form in the USA and in Britain', Paper to the International Academy of Business, 1986, p. 18.

53. *Ibid.*
54. Channon, *op. cit.*, pp. 213–14.
55. W. Lazonick, 'Strategy, Structure, and Management Development in the United States and Britain', in K. Kobayashi and H. Morikawa (eds.), *Development of Managerial Enterprise* (Tokyo: Tokyo University Press, 1986), p. 139.
56. Clark, *Anglo-American Innovation*, p. 299.
57. Channon, *op. cit.*, p. 221.
58. See, for example, Neil Hood and Stephen Young, *Multinationals in Retreat. The Scottish Experience* (Edinburgh: Edinburgh University Press, 1982), pp. 11–13; Perkin, *op. cit.*, pp. 512–13.
59. Mira Wilkins, 'The free-standing company, 1870–1914': an important type of British foreign direct investment', *Economic History Review*, 2nd series, XLI (1988), pp. 261, 264.
60. P. L. Payne, *The Early Scottish Limited Companies, 1856–1898* (Edinburgh: Scottish Academic Press, 1980), Table 23, pp. 101*ff.*
61. Wilkins, 'The free-standing company', pp. 274–7.
62. Martin Daunton has come to similar conclusions. His discussion of '"Gentlemanly Capitalism" and British Industry, 1820–1914' forces him to accept Wiener's contention that 'the question of the causes of British economic decline remain beyond the sole grasp of the economists'. M. J. Daunton, *Past and Present*, No. 122 (February, 1989), p. 157, quoting Wiener, *op. cit.*, p. 170.
63. See, for example, Richard E. Caves and Lawrence B. Krause (eds.), *Britain's Economic Performance* (Washington, D.C.: The Brookings Institution, 1980), p. 19 and *passim.*
64. Many of the relevant statistics for the period 1870–1914 have been collected by Sidney Pollard, *Britain's Prime and Britain's Decline: The British Economy 1870–1914* (London: Arnold, 1989), pp. 8–17; for the same and for later periods, see Charles Feinstein, 'Economic Growth since 1870: Britain's Performance in International Perspective', in N. Crafts and D. Morris (eds.), 'Long Run Economic Performance in the UK', *Oxford Review of Economic Policy*, Vol. 4, No. 1 (Spring, 1988), pp. 1–3.
65. R. E. Caves in Caves and Krause, *op. cit.*, p. 139; based upon Samuel Brittan, 'How British is the British Sickness', *Journal of Law and Economics*, Vol. 21 (October, 1978), pp. 245–68.
66. For a recent compendium of evidence see Coleman and MacLeod, *op. cit.*, pp. 605*ff.* See also M. Berg (ed.), *Technology and Toil in Nineteenth Century Britain* (London: CSE Books, 1979).
67. *The Minute Books of the Board of Conciliation and Arbitration of the Manufactured Steel Trade of the West of Scotland* were discovered by the author in 1959 among the archives of the Steel Company of Scotland. These were subsequently deposited in the British Steel Corporation's Scottish Regional Records Centre. The general context

may be found in P. L. Payne, *Colvilles and the Scottish Steel Industry* (Oxford: OUP, 1979), pp. 103–15.

68. The 'Dalzell Plate Mill Case' formed the subject of several meetings of the Board between January and July 1902. The quotations are taken from this source.

69. John Hodge, *Workman's Cottage to Windsor Castle* (London: Sampson Low, Maston & Co., 1931).

70. Matthews, Feinstein and Odling-Smee, *op. cit.*, pp. 114–15.

71. Patrick McGeown, *Heat the Furnace Seven Times More* (London: Hutchinson, 1967), p. 116.

72. Wayne Lewchuk, *American Technology and the British Vehicle Industry* (Cambridge: CUP, 1987).

73. Karel Williams, John Williams and Dennis Thomas, *Why are the British bad at Manufacturing?* (London: RKP, 1983), pp. 34–47. They take as their starting point the article by Andrew Kilpatrick and Tony Lawson, 'On the nature of industrial decline in the UK', *Cambridge Journal of Economics*, Vol. 4 (1980), pp. 85–102, which argues that poor control of the labour process is a major contributory factor.

74. See C. Feinstein, 'Economic Growth since 1870: Britain's Performance in International Perspective', *Oxford Review of Economic Policy*, Vol. 4, No. 1, pp. 4–7.

75. Lazonick, 'Industrial Organisation', p. 236.

76. Payne, *Colvilles*, pp. 151–216.

77. *cf* Sir Eric Geddes on the superhuman difficulties confronting the founders of the Lancashire Cotton Corporation. Leslie Hannah, *The Rise of the Corporate Economy*, 2nd edition (London: Methuen, 1983), p. 76.

78. Steven Tolliday, *Business, Banking and Politics. The Case of British Steel, 1918–1939* (Cambridge, Mass.: Harvard University Press, 1987), pp. 111–23, puts a different interpretation on this episode, but the evidence – the whole of which I was unable to present in my *Colvilles* – does, I believe, support my case.

79. This is somewhat similar to the findings of Robert C. Allen, 'Entrepreneurship and Technical Progress in the Northeast Coast Pig Iron Industry: 1850–1913', in *Research in Economic History*, Vol. VI (1981), pp. 35–71.

80. A number of recent studies – some of them as yet unpublished – have revealed that technological innovation was not *invariably* sluggish (for example, Peter Wardley, 'Productivity, mechanization and the labour market in the Cleveland ironstone industry, 1873–1914', paper for the Cliometrics Congress, 1985; Gordon Boyce, 'The Development of the Cargo Fleet Iron Co., 1900–1914: A Study of Entrepreneurship, Planning and Production Costs in the Northeast Coast Basic Steel Industry', Mimeo, 1985), nor was there *always* a failure to attempt to exploit the new. See Payne, *The Early Scottish Limited Companies*.

81. H. B. Gray and Samuel Turner, *Eclipse or Empire?* (London: Nisbet, 1916); C. Barnett, *op. cit.*; R. R. Locke, *The End of the Practical*

Man: *Entrepreneurship and Higher Education in Germany, France and Great Britain, 1880–1940* (Greenwich, Conn. and London: JAI Press, 1984). See also Julia Wrigley, 'Technical Education and Industry in the Nineteenth Century', in Elbaum and Lazonick (eds.), *op. cit.*, pp. 162–88.

82. See, for example, William P. Kennedy, *Industrial structure, Capital Markets and the Origins of British Economic Decline* (Cambridge: CUP, 1987), pp. 6, 37, 57, *passim*.

83. Michael Sanderson, *The Universities and British Industry 1850–1970* (London: RKP, 1972); 'The Professor as Industrial Consultant: Oliver Arnold and the British Steel Industry, 1900–14', *Economic History Review*, 2nd ser., xxxl (1978); 'The English Civic Universities and the "Industrial Spirit", 1870–1914', *Historical Research*, LXI (1988), pp. 90–104; 'Education and Economic Decline, 1890–1980s', *Oxford Review of Economic Policy*, Vol. 4, No. 1 (Spring 1988), pp. 38–50.

84. Sidney Pollard, *Britain's Prime and Britain's Decline*, Chapter 3, pp. 115–213. The quotation is from p. 213.

85. Sanderson, 'Education and Economic Decline', p. 38; *cf.* his observation that 'the more insidious evil has not been anti-industrial attitudes in the universities so much as anti-intellectual, anti-academic attitudes in industry', 'The English Civic Universities', p. 102. See also Joan Woodward, *Industrial Organisation – Theory and Practice* (London: OUP, 1965), p. 14, and Michael D. Stephens in Michael D. Stephens (ed.), *Universities, Education and the National Economy* (London: RKP, 1989), pp. xiii, 129, 135.

86. Pollard, *Britain's Prime*, pp. 179, 198.

87. Lazonick, 'Management Development', p. 120.

88. Margaret Ackrill, 'British Managers and the British Economy, 1870s to 1980s', *Oxford Review of Economic Policy*, Vol. 4, No. 1 (Spring, 1988), p. 69.

89. L. Urwick, 'Promotion in Industry', *Public Administration*, Vol. V (1927), p. 185. I owe the reference to Lazonick, 'Management Development', pp. 121–2.

90. Lazonick, 'Management Development', p. 121. See also Robert Locke, 'Educational Traditions and the Development of Business Studies after 1945 (An Anglo-French-German Comparison)', *Business History*, XXX, No. 1 (January, 1988), pp. 88–103.

91. As Pollard has said 'The manual skill of the British workman was never in question; it was his attitude to innovation, his adaptability, and the use he might make of pure science, which were in doubt …' Pollard, *Britain's Prime*, p. 139.

92. C. K. Harley, 'Skilled Labour and the Choice of Technique in Edwardian Industry', *Explorations in Economic History*, xi, No. 4, (Summer, 1974), pp. 391–414.

93. W. Lewchuk, *American Technology*, especially Chapter 9, pp. 185–220; 'The Motor Vehicle Industry', in Elbaum and Lazonick (eds.), *op. cit.*, pp. 135–61, and 'The Return to Capital in the British Motor Vehicle Industry', in *Business History*, xxvii (1985), pp. 3–25.

See also J. Walker, 'Markets, Industrial Processes and Class Struggle: The Evolution of the Labour Process in the UK Engineering Industry', *Review of Radical Political Economy*, xii (1981), pp. 46–69; J. Zeitlin, 'From Labour History to the History of Industrial Relations', *Economic History Review*, 2nd ser., XL (1987), pp. 159–84. M. Edelstein, 'Realised Rates of Return on UK Home and Overseas ... Investment', *Explorations in Economic History*, xiii (1976), pp. 294, 304, 314, shows that such industries as mechanical equipment, coal, iron and steel, which have been criticized for their technological backwardness, were also among the most profitable.

94. Eric Hobsbawm's expression. See his 'Custom, Wages and Work-load in Nineteenth-century Industry', in *Labouring Men* (London: Weidenfeld & Nicolson, 1964), pp. 344–70.

95. D. C. Coleman and Christine MacLeod, *op. cit.*; William H. Lazonick, 'Production Relations, Labor Productivity and Choice of Technique: British and US Cotton Spinning', *Journal of Economic History*, XLI (1981), pp. 491–516. And see Correlli Barnett, *op. cit.*, pp. 66*ff.*

96. The importance of the level of capital investment to productivity growth has repeatedly been emphasized in such works as Baumol & McLennon, *op. cit.*, pp. vii–viii, 9, 36, 47, 67. Peter Wardley, in a forthcoming work, has estimated the (very low) capital/employee ratios for the largest (and invariably heavy) British industrial firms.

97. The importance of this recruitment was originally suggested by Charles Wilson, *op. cit.*

98. W. D. Rubinstein, 'The Victorian Middle Class: wealth, occupation and geography', *Economic History Review*, 2nd ser., xxx (1977), and 'Wealth, elites and the class structure of modern Britain', *Past and Present*, 76 (1977). The point has been vividly exemplified by R. P. T. Davenport-Hines in his masterly study, *Dudley Docker: The Life and Times of a Trade Warrior* (Cambridge: CUP, 1984); and in numerous entries in David J. Jeremy (ed.), *Dictionary of Business Biography*, 5 volumes (London: Butterworths, 1984–6). The overall picture will doubtless be clarified by the subsequent analysis of the data provided by the various authors and not fully utilized in their entries.

99. C. H. Lee, *The British Economy since 1700* (Cambridge: CUP, 1986), *passim*; 'The service sector, regional specialization, and economic growth in the Victorian economy', *Journal of Historical Geography*, x (1984), pp. 143, 148, 153; 'Growth and Productivity in Services in the Industrial Economies, 1870–1913', forthcoming.

100. Charles Wilson, *op. cit.*

101. Edwin Green and Michael Moss, *A Business of National Importance: The Royal Mail Shipping Group, 1902–1937* (London: Methuen 1982); T. R. Nevett, *Advertising in Britain: A History* (London: History of Advertising Trust, 1982); Asa Briggs, *Wine for Sale: Victoria Wine and the Liquor Trade, 1860–1984* (London: Batsford, 1985); Clive Trebilcock, *Pheonix Assurance and the Development of British Insurance*, Vol. I: *1782–1870* (Cambridge: CUP, 1986);

Charles Wilson, *First with the News: The History of W. H. Smith, 1792–1972* (London: Cape, 1985).

102. In addition to sources mentioned in note 99, see C. H. Lee, 'Regional Growth and Structural Change in Victorian Britain', *Economic History Review*, new series, xxxiv (1981), pp. 438–52; R. M. Hartwell, 'The Service Revolution: The Growth of Services in Modern Economy, 1700–1914', in Carlo M. Cipolla, *The Fontana Economic History of Europe*, Vol. 3 (London: Collins/Fontana, 1973), pp. 358–96. In the UK in 1870 manufacturing labour productivity was only 71 per cent of that in services, in 1913, only 46 per cent. Note too, although in 1913 service productivity in both Germany and the USA was higher than that in manufacturing, the *growth* of manufacturing productivity in both countries had been much greater (in Germany, double) than in services over the previous forty years. This characteristic was true of *only* Germany and the USA among the six countries considered by Lee, 'Growth and Productivity', Tables 1 and 2.

103. This is certainly an accepted view. An early and influential article is William J. Baumol, 'Macroeconomics of Unbalanced Growth', *American Economic Review*, Vol. 57, No. 3 (1967), pp. 415–26.

104. These problems have been surveyed by Anthony D. Smith, *The Measurement and Interpretation of Service Output Changes* (London: NEDO, 1972).

105. Locke, *The End of the Practical Man*, and his articles in the *Accounting Historians Journal*, see above, note 11.

106. C. Barnett, *The Audit of War, passim*.

107. Concerning this second group of difficulties, some telling examples are provided by Peter Pagnamenta and Richard Overy, *All our Working Lives* (London: British Broadcasting Corporation, 1984), *passim*. In a detailed analysis of the restraints on greater productivity related to problems of industrial relations in the United States, Robert McKersie and Janice A. Klein found 'worker or supervisor resistance to change' to be the area of greatest concern. See Baumol & McLennan, pp. 120*ff*. See also N. Crafts, *op. cit.*, p. ix.

108. B. Elbaum and William Lazonick, 'The Decline of the British Economy: An Institutional Perspective', *Journal of Economic History*, XLIV (1984).

109. Lance E. Davis, *ibid*, p. 597.

110. Aubrey Jones, *Britain's Economy: The Roots of Stagnation*, p. 79. While fiercely critical of the fuel industries – whose nationalization was, he feels, 'abundantly justified' – Aubrey Jones' observations on the nationalized coal, electricity, nuclear power and gas industries indicate their development to have been haphazard and unco-ordinated (pp. 64, 90). He remarks (p. 29) that when he was Minister of Fuel and Power (1955–56) 'the Ministry [lacked] technical expertise in all the industries sponsored by it, a lack which has continued to the present day'. In Scotland it is arguable that in intervening (often for the best of motives), the politicians and the State have all too often succeeded only in perpetuating many of the features of the Scot-

tish economy that stultify growth. See P. L. Payne, 'The Decline of the Scottish Heavy Industries, 1945–1983', in R. Saville (ed.), *The Economic Development of Modern Scotland* (Edinburgh: John Donald, 1985), pp. 79–113. See also Paul Hare, 'Planning a Market Economy: Problems and Lessons', *Royal Bank of Scotland Review*, No. 147 (September, 1985), pp. 46–50.

111. The importance of basic research is emphasized by Baumol and McLennan (eds.), *op. cit.*, pp. 198–200, and see the plea made by Tom Stonier, 'Technological Change and the Future', in Maxwell Gaskin (ed.), *The Political Economy of Tolerable Survival* (London: Croom Helm, 1981), pp. 140–51. See also Maurice Preston, 'Higher Education: Financial and Economic Aspects', *Bank of Scotland Review*, No. 148, December 1985: 'Higher education is, therefore, central to the process of economic advance.' (p. 17).

112. For the business schools, see Payne, *Cambridge Economic History*, VII, Part I, p. 224; Barnett, *op. cit.*, p. 294; Sanderson, *The Universities and British Industry*, p. 377; Hannah, *Inaugural Lecture*, p. 31. It is possible that the increasing number of non-executive directors being appointed to boards of quoted companies may have beneficial results, but even here the operation of the old-boy network may diminish the potential value of this promising development. See *Bank of England Quarterly Bulletin*, Vol. 19, No. 4 (December, 1979), pp. 392–3; Vol. 23, No. 1 (March, 1983), pp. 66–8; Vol. 25, No. 2 (June, 1985), pp. 233–6. And see *The Times*, 25 June 1986.

113. See, for example, the points recently made by Michael Heseltine, *The Challenge of Europe* (London: Weidenfeld & Nicolson, 1989). See also Sir Alan Cook on the industrial applications of scientific discoveries in universities, in Michael D. Stephens (ed.), *Universities, Education and the National Economy*, pp. 120–1; and C. Handy, *The Making of Managers* (London: NEDO, 1987), who reveals continuing gross deficiencies in management education.

W. D. Rubinstein

Cultural Explanations for Britain's Economic Decline: How True?

For almost as long as Britain's economic decline has been widely perceived, observers and historians have attempted to account for it; as it has progressed, these efforts have become more and more common, such that any academic library contains dozens of works, produced, it would seem, at a geometric rate of increase, to account for Britain's decline. Of all the explanations which have been offered, possibly none is as thoroughly explored as that which sees British culture as an enemy of British economic expansion and the culture-bound and determined quality of her post-1870 entrepreneurs as central to this decline. It would be pointless to mention more than a few highlights of this perspective, which have included the writings of D.C. Coleman, D.H. Aldcroft, David Ward, A.L. Levine, and William Kennedy among recent historians and Anthony Sampson and Correlli Barnett among well-known journalists and popularizers.[1] By the mid-1960s the notion of an effete British Establishment, utterly unable to compete in the international economy thanks to an educational system that was anti-industrial and virtually pre-modern, and a value system and ethos that revered the landed gentry and despised entrepreneurial effort, had become virtually ubiquitous in the informed popular mind. Although this interpretation was found surprisingly seldom when Britain was unquestioningly a world-class economic leader – how could British culture, at the time, be seen as inimicable to capitalism in the first nation to industrialize? – by the 1960s it formed part of virtually every informed critique of contemporary Britain.

Anthony Sampson's renowned *Anatomy of Britain* (first published in 1962) and its revised editions (published in 1965, 1971, and 1982) possibly did more than any other work to publicize and popularize the notion of the British Establishment – seemingly depicted by Sampson in unique detail and with extraordinary skill, frankness, and cogency – as reactionary, atavistic, thoroughly traditional, and unarguably inadequate to the late twentieth century. British entrepreneurs were seen in the main as fully a part of this sorry leadership elite, and certainly unable often to rise successfully above its limitations. The Establishment linkages, such as public school and university educations, of Britain's leading company chairmen are explored by Sampson in considerable detail. Strangely enough, frank depictions and 'anatomies' of the actual (or assumed) leaders of the British Establishment have been extremely rare in the kind of very superior journalism represented by Sampson, possibly because of the control of the British press and much of its publishing outlets by wealthy press lords, possibly because of Britain's stringent libel laws, and, previous to Sampson, perhaps the only twentieth-century predecessor was Simon Haxey's *Tory M.P.*, published by the Left Book Club in 1939, a work which is frankly and deliberately biased against the Conservative Party and its wealthy supporters. (Unlike Sampson, Haxey therefore ignores the influential organs of the left, like the trade unions).

Implicitly to Sampson and explicitly to many other observers of post-1960 British society, only thorough-going reform of much of the structure of British society, aimed above all at reforming or modernizing its pre-modern institutions like the House of Lords and the public schools, rejuvenating its educational sector and, in particular, its scientific and technological infrastructure, and greatly increasing investment in manufacturing industry, could bring Britain from its post-imperial economic miasma into a position where it could compete with Western Europe, America, and Japan. Yet, despite the fact that successive British governments between 1964 and 1979 at least had essentially identical goals to the advocates of forced modernization, Britain's economic decline was, seemingly, in no way halted; the latest (1982) edition of Sampson's *Anatomy* is the most pessimistic of the four editions of the work, written as it was at the height of the unemployment of the early Thatcher years.

Needless to say, innumerable editorial writers and commentators were, basically, in broad agreement with Sampson, as well as writers like the popular and influential historian Correlli Barnett who, in such works as *The Audit of War* spelled out the gross inadequacies of Britain's manufacturing sector to the challenges of the Second World War. Britain's victory over Germany, according to Barnett, was made possible only by the unlimited and thoroughly modern industrial base provided by the United States through Lend Lease or, after Pearl Harbor, directly to the Allied war effort. Barnett's work ends, too, with a familiar jeremiad against the 'hallucination' and 'fantasy' of Britain's great power pretences, held by Britain's political leaders and the governing Establishment. 'What was needed (and wholly was lacking) was a clear, cold vision' capable of 'transforming Britain's obsolete industrial culture, and thereby working a British economic miracle'.[2]

It is thus essentially clear that Professor Martin Wiener's important book has really only summarized and systematically brought together, with extensive historical evidence, what is by now an old viewpoint, with a pedigree of at least a generation and a half of enunciation. There is little question of the extremely fortuitous date of appearance of *English Culture and the Decline of the Industrial Spirit, 1850–1980* in 1981, when every factory closure and upward spiral of the unemployment index seemed to make it ever more plausible.

This paper presents a rather critical view of Professor Wiener's book and of the 'cultural thesis' of Britain's economic decline that is, in some respects, at variance with my own previous research.[3] It now seems extremely difficult to argue for the primacy of cultural factors in Britain's apparent economic decline as opposed to purely economic or simply fortuitous factors, though, clearly, there is more than enough substance to the thesis to warrant a very close examination. The cultural thesis fails, in my view, to devote sufficient attention to the peculiarities of the British economy or to deep-seated trends which began before 1870; it is not fully consistent with the actual chronology of change or, in some crucial aspects, with the true nature of British entrepreneurship; and it fails to present a persuasive nexus to account for the transmission of cultural values into economic behaviour and performance. Nevertheless, in a qualified form cultural factors may well be important in accounting for the type of society which Britain has become.

Before turning to the scope and significance of cultural explanations themselves, one might point to four very general and substructural facts about British business life and the British economy in the nineteenth century which are highly relevant to the question we are considering. These four should be highlighted in large part because they do not normally figure in the hallmarking of nineteenth-century British business life and entrepreneurship. Clearly, there are many other characteristics of British entrepreneurship which were just as significant, but which I am omitting to discuss here because of the attention they receive in most discussions of this subject. Among these other, widely discussed and highly obvious, significant features which marked British entrepreneurship in the nineteenth century were the family structure of most firms, the central fact of increasing competition from abroad, the almost uniquely small size of Britain's agricultural sector, the absence of revolutions or civil strife, and the universally-held tradition of the sanctity of property. All, obviously, are greatly important, but several other characteristics must be added to them. The four I shall discuss here are a rather miscellaneous group, but I think they curiously tend to point towards the same general conclusion.

The first of these is the relatively small size of peak British business fortunes compared with those in the United States (see figure 1). There was a difference of roughly ten times, on average, between the richest American businessmen and the richest British businessmen. It is very important to note that, so far as we can tell from the evidence, this vast difference was apparent even before or shortly after the American Civil War and America's industrial take-off. John Jacob Astor, fur trapper turned real estate tycoon, who died in 1848, was generally regarded as worth $25 million – £5 million, or richer in all likelihood, than any British businessman of the day – while Cornelius Vanderbilt (*d.* 1877), the railway magnate, was worth over $100 million at his death – that is, £20 million, far more than any British businessmen until after the First World War. By America's Gilded Age, the billion dollar fortunes of Rockefeller, Ford and Mellon obviously dwarfed anything ever seen before in history. The order of magnitude differences affect not only the very peaks of the wealth scale but, so far as current research can demonstrate, those lower down as well.

I have been unable cogently to explain this difference, and I am unable fully to explain this difference now. One can argue,

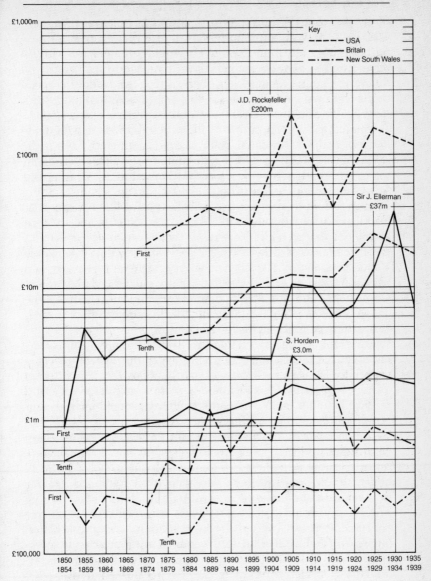

Figure 1: Peak Fortunes, United States, Britain and Ireland and New South Wales, 1850/4–1935/9

of course, that the reason American businessmen were so rich was that they were better businessmen than their British counterparts. Perhaps so. Up to a point, few would dispute that the ideology, legal system, and pervasive entrepreneurial spirit of nineteenth-century America probably favoured the development of the 'rational-capitalist personality' more even than in *laissez-faire* Britain. These important cultural differences may well have accounted for a portion of the difference. Very successful nineteenth-century American entrepreneurs may in truth have been, say, twice as able as their British counterparts, always assuming that such abilities may be objectively measured – a rather big 'if'. I am quite prepared to believe this. But ten times as able? Frankly, I find this impossible to believe, and I am certain that no historian of entrepreneurship could possibly believe it. Can it really be that men like Arkwright, Peel, Overstone, Rothschild, Leverhulme, or Northcliffe were only one-tenth as talented as Vanderbilt, Astor, Ford, Carnegie, or Morgan? The last two names in the series are instructive in the comparison, for Andrew Carnegie was born in Scotland, migrating to Pennsylvania at the age of thirteen, while J. P. Morgan, like his father Junius Spencer Morgan, lived much of his life in London, where he was a major figure in the world of city finance. And, more importantly perhaps, can these differences in ability which purportedly affected the relative size of British business fortunes possibly have affected all types of British businessmen equally – self-made men and *rentiers* by inheritance; virtually unlettered, rough-hewn, northern dissenters and suave Etonian merchant bankers; industrialists and financiers; northerners and southerners; Londoners and Mancunians and Glaswegians? It seems to me to be evidently unsupportable that these differences are due to sheer business ability rather than to some underlying yet ill-defined difference in the nature of the respective national economies, one resulting presumably from differences in factor endowments, in relative consumer demand, perhaps in the availability and price of land, and so on. If cultural influences accounted for much of this difference at all, it is difficult to believe that this was as significant a factor as straightforward economic ones in the narrow sense. These differences, moreover, seemingly emerged well before Britain's industrial supremacy began to vanish, and seemingly well before Britain's business class of entrepreneurs was absorbed into the Establishment via public school education and class merger with the landed aristocracy and older business elements.

The second factor which peculiarly affected the development of the British economy to which attention should be drawn is a trend shown in figure 2 which outlines the percentage of business and professional incomes assessed under Schedules D and E, plus the business portions of A, of the Income Tax, at roughly five-year intervals between 1806 and 1911/12. (There was no Income Tax between 1815 and 1842.) These figures measure all of the business and professional incomes of the middle classes, for only persons with annual incomes of £150 or more (£60 for the first Income Tax; £100 or more in 1856–73) were liable to pay Income Tax and only these are included here. The manuscript sources which detail the county-by-county totals have been arranged to show the percentage of the national totals assessed in London and the Home Counties (where many London businessmen and professionals lived), and many of the northern industrial counties.

It will be seen that the percentage of London in the national total rapidly declined after the Napoleonic period, bottoming in the 1850s and then, after about 1860, rapidly rose again, so that by the Edwardian period its overall percentage was again nearly half the national total and very similar to its place in the national total a century before. The northern industrial total, especially that of Lancashire, is roughly the inverse of this. So far as the British middle classes are concerned, it seems clear from this that the northern 'challenge' to the hegemony of London peaked around 1860 and that middle-class, disproportionately industrial and manufacturing income failed to increase its relative share among all middle-class income from about that date onwards. Although during the earlier nineteenth century the middle-class incomes of Lancashire were clearly growing disproportionately rapidly, thereafter, the largely commercial governmental, and service middle-class incomes of London and the south were growing relatively faster. It will also be seen that in the late 1840s and 1850s it was quite possible that middle-class incomes in the northern industrial counties might have as it were 'broken through' to overtake London and the south. This in fact, never happened, possibly because of the Cotton Famine of the American Civil War and the havoc this played with Lancashire's previously ascendant relative growth rate.[3]

Of the many general points which emerge from this data, attention should be drawn to two. One is the apparent continuing supremacy of the British middle classes as a whole as a mainly

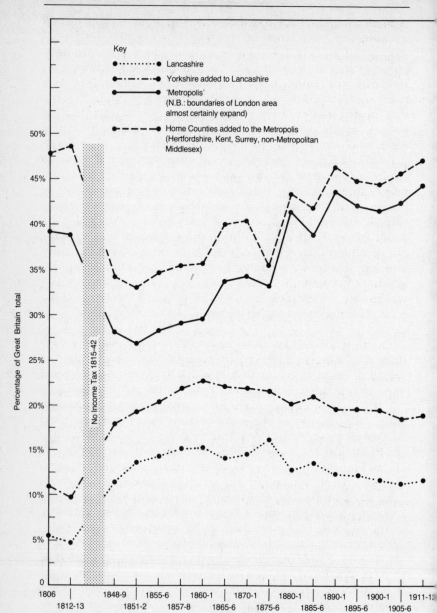

Key

- ● ·········· ● Lancashire
- ● ─·─·─·─ ● Yorkshire added to Lancashire
- ● ────── ● 'Metropolis' (N.B.: boundaries of London area almost certainly expand)
- ● ─ ─ ─ ─ ● Home Counties added to the Metropolis (Hertfordshire, Kent, Surrey, non-Metropolitan Middlesex)

Percentage of Great Britain total

No Income Tax 1815-42

Figure 2: Percentage of business and professional incomes (schedules D & E and business portions of A) of £100–£150 or more, by London and leading industrial counties, 1806–1911/12

commercial and service-based class, not an industrial and manufacturing one, even when Britain was pre-eminently the 'work-
shop of the world'. The other is an echo of the point we have
just encountered: the shift away from Lancashire and the north,
and back to London, fairly certainly began around 1860 and
not at some later date. Although the beginnings of foreign industrial rivalry may well be a major factor in this shift back, it
is surely insufficient to attribute the shift away from the industrial
north wholly or entirely to this factor, since the effects precede
the supposed cause; similarly, for the same reason, it seems quite
implausible to attribute this shift entirely to a 'haemorrhage of
talent' among industrial dynasties since, once again, the class
merger with the gentry via the public schools and successful
entrees into established society did not become a fully fledged
social fact until after 1870 – even if there was a 'haemorrhage
of talent' at all, something which I hope to discuss and qualify
later on. There is no doubt that the decades after 1860 saw
nothing to reverse this swing back to London and commercial
wealth, but its roots are to be found a decade before German
unification and five years before the North's victory in the American Civil War.

The third general factor to which attention should be drawn
does not concern this type of evidence but what might be
regarded as a stark economic fact which has in my view received
quite insufficient attention from those who suggest a primarily
cultural cause or causes for Britain's economic decline or, indeed,
either from those who favour a primarily economically-based
decline or those who believe that Britain was doing as well as
she could. The most important economic fact about late Victorian and Edwardian Britain which distinguished it from its main
industrial rivals was not, in my view, its factor endowment, its
early start, or the nature of its elites or educational system. The
most significant difference was that Britain, and British entrepreneurs, had no tariff protection while their foreign rivals did –
and, moreover, a tariff which was deliberately designed, in both
the American and German cases, with the systematic end in view
of increasing each country's industrial might and strength.

From the point of view of the cultural argument about British
economic decline, one ought to consider carefully the implications of this difference for the manner in which British entrepreneurship was internationally perceived: if German and
American businessmen and entrepreneurs were so superlatively

great at being entrepreneurs, why did they need high tariff walls to keep out their creampuff, backward, epicene British rivals? Of course most economists regard tariffs as invariably a bad thing which work directly against the interests of the country which erects them. Theoretical models can and have been constructed to demonstrate that Germany and America would have shown even more spectacular growth without them. Yet, frankly, it is very difficult to believe that the British economy would not have benefited most pronouncedly from erecting the wide-ranging system of Imperial Preference advocated by Chamberlain and the Tariff Reformers, who were largely motivated precisely by a cogent vision of Britain's impending economic decline, Britain compelled to fight against the foreign threat, as it were, with one hand tied behind its back. To take one obvious example, in 1913 Germany exported 1,053,000 metric tons of finished and semi-finished steel products to Britain and another 417,000 tons to the British Empire. In the same year the United States exported 239,000 tons of steel products to Britain and 1,440,000 tons to the British Empire, especially Canada. Britain exported 60,000 tons to Germany and 5,000 tons to the United States.[4] Other countries like Belgium and France also exported steel to Britain and the Empire. Germany's exports to Britain and the Empire represented about ten per cent of all of her steel output of all kinds, while the exports of Germany and the United States of finished and semi-finished steel alone to Britain and the Empire equalled fully 64 per cent of the total British output of crude steel.[5] It is not in my view fanciful to suggest that Imperial Preference might have captured at least 75 per cent of that total for British steel producers, making a substantial difference for the relative national statistics of steel output.

Moreover, such a tariff might well have directly stimulated the type of high-quality, modern steel manufacturing techniques at which Britain's performance after 1880 was especially lamentable. Thomas Brassey told an Edinburgh audience, 'Excluded from the principal manufacturing countries by a protectionist policy, it is to the colonies and to the half-civilized countries that we must look for the expansion of our trade'.[6] Banning most high-quality steel imports by outsiders to Britain and the Empire might well have stimulated British entrepreneurship in these fields. Tariff protection was an obvious and seemingly inevitable solution to Britain's seeming industrial decline; it was continuously rebuffed because of the pervasive strength of the ideology of Free Trade and because most workers, rightly or wrongly, believed that as enunciated by Chamberlain and his supporters it would lead directly to higher bread prices. As a result, Tariff Reform became a proven vote loser when it was presented by the Tories in 1906 and 1923. When systematic Tariff Reform was finally enacted in 1932 it was a major factor, in my view, in producing the considerable economic advance which occurred over the next six years.

The fourth peculiar factor which hallmarked the British economy in this period is again rather different from those we have discussed; it is also markedly less nationally specific than the other three. It is the extraordinarily low incomes, by contemporary American standards or by the standards of the post-1945 world, of the 75 per cent of the population in the working classes, especially those outside the most skilled artisanal trades or those thoroughly protected by trade unions. Down to 1914, it was impossible under any set of circumstances for two-thirds of the adult male population to earn more than £100–£120 annually; for most of the nineteenth century the maximum (let alone the minimum) had been far lower. Although every one knows this, I do not believe that its implications are always realized by those who have participated in this debate. By 'Britain's industrial decline and failure' in the period between 1914 and 1939 is often tacitly meant, not merely a failure to retain its pre-1870 manufacturing dominance, or a failure to employ the new technology as in Germany or America, but a failure to evolve into a mass-based, consumer-oriented society, with the mass and near-universal availability of consumer durables, affordable by nearly everyone, which much of America had become before 1914 and certainly by 1939, of which the Model T Ford is probably the greatest symbol. But such an evolution in Britain was impossible, prior, in all likelihood, to the 1950s and certainly before the 1930s: the incomes of the great majority were simply too low. No matter how cheap a Model T Ford ever became virtually no British worker could afford to buy one. The absence in Britain of a mass domestic market for a modern consumer culture prior to the 1930s at the very earliest, and probably prior to the 1950s, was a potent influence on the direction the British economy was increasingly taking, with its ever-growing overseas investment and its perceived failure to modernize. British per capita real incomes per employed person were stagnant after about 1894, and may actually have declined. They were about £85–£90 compared with the equivalent American figure of £130 in 1900 and £160 in 1913.[7] Without the loosening effects of the First World War and the attendant rise of increased trade union power among skilled workers which followed, it is perhaps arguable that the kind of class-based society which Britain had become would not have seen its per capita incomes grow markedly for many decades to come.

But although Britain in 1914 was materially poorer than the United States, it is equally important to realize that it was in per capita terms a good deal richer than any European economy, and this is also a point well worth keeping in mind. Again and again, when European societies are compared, and on any European-wide scale, Britain comes off extremely well. Although German and French per capita incomes were growing rapidly they still lagged far behind the British figure of £85–90 per year; the French equivalent figure was about £70 in 1913 and the German figure about £65. Certainly to the ever-growing German and French Socialist parties and movements of the day, there remained an unacceptable degree of mass impoverishment and economic inequality, and certainly, too, France and Germany were, if anything, even further from a mass-based American-style consumer economy than was Britain. Indeed, it is not fanciful to speculate that, given the pervasive and rigid class-based nature of all pre-1914 European societies, the same levelling-off of per capita incomes would have occurred there as well a few decades hence, and no breakthrough into an affluent society would have been possible there prior to a fundamental restructuring of Europe's economies and social classes.

By any fair and comprehensive test of British economic performance, its decline by 1914 can easily be exaggerated. While it had lost its lead in steel and chemicals, and while it was very slow to move into the electric age, in other areas it had hardly declined in even a relative sense, let alone an absolute sense. In *Table 1* a few European comparisons have been presented, which, while generally well known to economic historians, should be kept carefully in mind when talking about Britain's economic decline. The overall impression created by these figures is that down to 1914 Britain's decline from its mid-Victorian supremacy was only relative and probably inevitable given the scale of competition and the various and varied factor endowments of each country, the disadvantages and peculiarities of Britain noted above, and, most importantly, which were consistent with each major country pursuing its comparative advantage. Where Britain maintained a comparative advantage down to 1914, for instance, in merchant shipping and raw cotton consumption, it still maintained a substantial lead. In merchant shipping its lead appeared to grow rather than shrink from the mid-Victorian period. Germany's growing industrial supremacy among European nations was one which manifested itself surprisingly patchily down to 1914, and only in several aspects of heavy industry, albeit those which most revolved around the use of novel technological techniques. Although British capitalism obviously had no room for complacency at the outbreak of the First World War, it is simply hyperbolic, even nonsensical, to talk of any general entrepreneurial collapse. Indeed, given the fact that in 1850 Britain had *no* international competitors in most industrial spheres, while in 1913 she had *six* or *seven* powerful competitors, including America the behemoth, as well as Germany, France, Italy, Russia, even Austria-Hungary in some areas, and possibly Japan, the remarkable and striking feature of Britain's economic performance was just how satisfactory it was, and it seems extraordinary to me that anyone could think that it wasn't.

This impression is fortified by several further considerations which are not directly conveyed by these figures. In the first place, the areas where Britain was performing most excellently of all – banking, merchant banking, and commerce – are only partially highlighted in the table. Very customarily, indeed, accounts of Britain's alleged entrepreneurial decline limit their indictment to heavy industry, all but ignoring the City of London and other commercial *entrepots* which were at the time (and not before) enjoying their absolute zenith of influence. Secondly, if there was an entrepreneurial decline to be explained, and if it was due to cultural factors, it requires some skill in my view to explain its surprising patchiness. If growth and prosperity were limited to purely commercial and financial pursuits, perhaps one might say that Englishmen were allergic to heavy industry, but Britain was surprisingly strong everywhere, even in the most classic manufacturing industry, cotton, as well as one of the newest, automobile production. Britain was comparatively slow to adopt electricity and technological methods of production compared with Germany and America, but this was only relative in the overall context of an economy which appears acutely ill only with the benefit of historical hindsight, a viewpoint which

Table 1: Selected comparative economic statistics, 1870–1938 (from B.R.Mitchell, ed., *European Historical Statistics*)

1　*Output of Coal* ('000 metric tons)

	1850	1870	1913	1928	1933	1938
UK	50,200	112,203	292,042	241,283	210,436	230,636
France	4,434	13,330	40,844	52,440	47,981	47,562
Germany	6,900	34,003	277,342	317,136	236,424	381,171
Italy	34 (1861)	59	701	832	718	2,353
Russia	300 (1860)	690	36,050	35,510	76,333	133,363

2　*Output of Steel* ('000 metric tons)

	1850 N/A	1870	1913	1928	1933	1938
UK		334	7,787	8,657	7,138	10,565
France		84	4,687	9,479	6,577	6,137
Germany		126	17,609	14,517	7,617	22,656
Italy		N/A	934	1,960	1,771	2,323
Russia		9	4,918	4,251	6,889	18,057

3　*Merchant Ships Registered* ('000 tons)

	1850	1870	1913	1928	1933	1938
UK	3,658	5,691	12,120	12,259	11,170	10,702
France	688	1,072	1,582	2,122	2,023	1,664
Germany	512	939	3,320	1,935	2,201	2,490
Italy	654 (1862)	1,112	1,233	1,780	1,983	2,039
Russia	173 (1859)	260 (1872)	783	322	840	1,273

4　*Raw Cotton Consumption* ('000 metric tons)

	1850	1870	1913	1928	1933	1938
UK	267	489	988	689	534	503
France	59	94	271	315	349	288
Germany	26	112 (1871)	478	388	419	350
Italy	12 (1861)	15	202	233	220	159
Russia	20	46	424	208	379	893

Table 1 (*cont.*)

5 *Electric Energy* (giga watts)

	1900	1913	1928	1933	1938
UK	0.4	2.5	15.63	21.20	33.77
France	0.34	1.8	14.25	16.40	20.80
Germany	1.3	8.0	25.14	25.66	55.33
Italy	0.14	2.0	8.74	10.59	15.43
Russia	N/A	2.0	5.01	16.36	39.37

6 *Motor Vehicle Output* ('000s Commercial and Private)

	1913	1928	1933	1938
UK	N/A	212	287	445
France	45	223	189	227
Germany	18	123	105	338
Italy	N/A	58	42	71
Russia	N/A	1	49	211

has the very notable advantage of never being mistaken. The third point which must be made is that, with the benefit of hindsight, Britain's 'choice' of industries to specialize in by the laws of economic comparative advantage were in the main very unfortunate, especially manufacturing, and would be those which were disproportionately affected by the chronic economic ills of the inter-war period, especially, of course, colliery, shipbuilding and shipping, and cotton. These three industries alone and between them accounted for the bulk of the economic malaise of those twenty tragic years. Given the economic growth and development which occurred elsewhere, and the health of the British service sector, had international circumstances not so adversely affected these three industries, there might well have been both full employment and unprecedented economic growth.

It appears fairly clear then, that 1870–1913 or any date in between does not mark a turning-point in Britain's economic development. I would suggest that the climacteric dates are 1860, when Britain began to resume its traditional role as an *entrepot* and financier rather than evolve decisively into a genuinely industrial power, and then, most certainly, 1914–18 and 1939–45. What the two World Wars have in common is, first that they were entirely exogenous and the economic havoc they wrought was not due to any pre-existing or deep-seated failing of British entrepreneurship or any similar factor, and, secondly, that the harm they did to Britain's economy was immense and can easily be forgotten in the rush to condemn British culture or Britain's entrepreneurs. The First World War transformed a quite satisfactory situation into one which was unprecedentedly unsatisfactory; just when Britain appeared to get on top of the situation, finally by the mid-1930s responding well to the unprecedented economics disasters which had occurred, the immediate effect of the Second World War was to produce a second set of economic challenges even more far-reaching and deleterious in their implications for Britain's long-term economic position. Again, both of these events were exogenous and had little or nothing to do with the quality of its entrepreneurs, its cultural values, educational system, or any other internal social or societal factor.

There is also the important point to be made – and it is so easy to overlook today – that until the 1930s or even later no one – literally, not one person – measured national success in terms of growth rates or even the other economic measures we commonly employ for this purpose, but primarily in terms of land area, population, and resources under that power's effective control. By this measure, Britain, dominant over palm and pine, was a most formidable power indeed, and unquestionably a great super-power down to the Second World War and certainly through the First; it was Germany which had the massive, vulgar, and visible inferiority complex and permanent chip on its shoulders, not Britain.

Of the chief deleterious economic effects of the First World War much has been written; these included the disruption of international trade routes and demand, the liquidation of much of Britain's overseas investment and the transferral of some of the traditional role of the City of London to New York, gross overcapacity in Britain's traditional staples and labour-induced cost increases which made British products increasingly uncompetitive. Again, most if not all of these were exogenous and beyond the control or responsibility of British entrepreneurs or business leaders. It is their responses to these challenges and disruptions which, if anything, provides a test of their abilities. The profoundly disturbing effects of the First World War were, of course, not limited to the economic sphere but extended to nearly every area of life from the political to the social. To take one example of many, from 1920 onwards it appeared quite possible that Labour would come to power, as it did in a minority capacity in 1924 and 1929–31. From 1918 onwards, Labour was committed on paper to a thorough-going socialism and few could foresee its conservatism when in office. Was this not likely to affect the optimism of business men or their long-term plans for investment? Another often neglected factor was the horrifying demographic effects of the War: 700,000 Britons killed, nearly all aged between 18 and 40. One need not accept the myth of a 'lost generation' to see the profoundly disillusioning and traumatically depressing effects of this slaughter on their relatives and associates who survived. If sociological factors do indeed influence entrepreneurial performance in any way, it is here, at this time, that one might most surely expect to see its effects at work. If one had lost a son, two sons, a brother, two uncles, one-quarter of one's classmates and friends to a war whose aims increasingly appeared pointless and whose accomplishments indefinable, one might well come to believe that the game of life was not worth the candle; on the continent, surely, the rise of Fascism and Communism can be directly related to the trench experience and the profound despair of those who survived. Again, it is from a Europe-wide perspective that Britain's inter-war performance ought to be seen, and here, by any reasonable test, she surely emerges even more satisfactorily than before 1914, not least of all by the strength of her commitment to democracy and moderation and levels of support accorded to the political extremes.

Both from the statistics in *Table 1* and from other economic facts several points about British economic performance in the inter-war period seem clear: it was, especially compared with its economic rivals, a period of remarkably steady growth which missed the worst effects of downturn and depression evident in, say, Germany – study, for instance, Germany's steel output compared with Britain's. I cannot resist pointing out here that although any downturn in British output is often attributed to the poor quality of its entrepreneurs, when did anyone ever hear the decline, say, of German steel output from 14.5 million tons in 1928 to 7.6 million tons in 1933 attributed to its third-rate entrepreneurship? And where Britain declined, as in cotton production, everyone declined. Although the rise of totalitarian governments on the continent seemingly increased output there at a rate which dwarfed even Britain's highly creditable performance, the human cost of this growth was simply beyond calculation, while the published statistics of output in Fascist Italy, Nazi

Germany, and, especially, Stalinist Russia were very likely to have been deliberately padded and inflated for political propaganda purposes.

The major hallmark of Britain's economy during this period was its rock-like solidity. I would attribute this first and foremost to Britain's admirable clearing bank system, which probably shielded much of the British economy from disappearing down the drain during the Depression in a manner which very nearly happened in, say, the United States, whose Jacksonian, anti-monopolist banking laws, especially the bans on branch banking, were almost tailor-made to aggravate any substantial economic recession still further. When it is remembered that the 1930s saw the famous growth of semi-detached London and its high street, consumer-oriented ambience, it is not surprising that so many economic historians now view the 1930s in a favourable light. Contradicting this viewpoint, obviously, is the mass unemployment of the period, so heavy in the old staple industries and the old industrial areas in the north of Britain. It seems clear that a solution to this problem was beyond any British entrepreneurs and their response to this challenge did not represent an entrepreneurial failure. No amount of further investment, modernization, or managerial training by a shipbuilding firm could sell one additional ship when there were simply no customers for their ships; it was this failure of demand, rather than a failure of entrepreneurship, which was the hallmark of the first fifteen years at least of the inter-war period.

The effects of the Second World War on Britain were even more disastrous than the First. By no means the least of them included the unequal lend-lease and post-war foreign aid agreements with the United States wherein Britain surrendered many of her old foreign markets to America. But despite the undoubted costs of this war, the post-war period has also been notable, in my view, as being the first time in modern history when British entrepreneurship may legitimately be charged with gross incompetence. In particular, the failure of Britain to capitalize on the strong position she enjoyed as a manufacturing nation in the ten or fifteen years following 1945 when most of Europe and Japan were first in total ruin and then rebuilding, and which now seems virtually inexplicable, must in part be due to entrepreneurial failure, much more so than in the previous period since 1870. Yet even here there are many mitigating circumstances. In the first place, the social composition of Britain's entrepreneurs, especially the management of industrial firms (as opposed to banking firms) has increasingly been open to outsiders promoted for their ability, like, say, Lord Keaton or Lord Stokes. Certainly there appear to be fewer heads of major industrial concerns whose dual claim to promotion was lineage or an old school tie than forty years before. Secondly, against even the apparent failure of British entrepreneurship in the post-war period must be set the arguable gains for British society which occurred after 1945: the Welfare State paid for in large part by levels of direct taxation absolutely unprecedented in peacetime, genuine full employment for the first time in history until the 1970s, and, uninterrupted even by the recession and industrial decline of the past ten years, an increasingly affluent society. Despite unprecedentedly high rates of unemployment in the first half of the 1980s, statistics of the ownership of consumerable durables, to take one index, are at record highs and at levels closely resembling all other Western societies, including the United States. Home ownership, as is probably well known, has risen from 25 per cent of the population in 1945 to over 60 per cent today, a percentage which, when the disproportionately elderly population of Britain is taken into account, is actually as high or higher than the equivalent percentage in America or even Australia. Living standards, in my view, are at least as significant a test of economic performance as growth rates, and by that test, Britain has performed as well as or better than any of her rivals.

Finally, the recent and unprecedentedly terrible economic malaise in Britain must again clearly be seen in its West European perspective: unemployment rates in socialist France and in the home of the former Economic Miracle, West Germany, are nearly as high – in the case of countries like Belgium and Italy, actually higher – and are clearly due to a common cause, the shift of much manufacturing industry throughout the globe to the rim of East Asia, a shift which has affected the entire Western world, including the 'rust bowl' of America and Western outposts like Australia. Without this shift, it is arguable that there might well still be full employment in Britain.

If this description of the evolution of the British economy here is correct, it seems apparent that Britain's economic failure has been greatly exaggerated, especially prior to 1945, while the role of entrepreneurial decline in this wider failure is certainly overstated. It is easy enough to link together Britain's economic decline (assuming it has occurred) with whatever aspects of British culture one cares to highlight, and assume that there is a causal connection between the two in a *post hoc ergo propter hoc* manner. But is there? Such explanations have, of course, been around for decades; everyone has heard them and was weaned on them, and they were just as common twenty or twenty-five years ago when Anthony Sampson brought out the first edition of his *Anatomy of Britain* and Mr Wilson was to transform Britain through the 'white heat of technological revolution' as they are today. As the normal indices of British economic decline have proceeded in their seemingly remorseless way, such explanations have become even more frequent and more comprehensive; they reached their zenith, it is safe to say, in Professor Wiener's excellent book, which encapsulates the argument and makes the case for British culture as a cause of British economic decline probably as fully as the case can be made.

As noted before, there are in my view good reasons to accept part of the cultural thesis, but many more reasons to reject it as invalid. In writing this section, I have deliberately not re-read any reviews of Professor Wiener's book or any part of the debate which may have emerged from its publication, and in the not unlikely event that these points have been generally anticipated, it should be said that they nevertheless strike me as most important to the discussion.

Is British culture anti-capitalist and anti-business? Perhaps, indeed, it is, but the absolutely central point must be made that every cultural system in the world is anti-capitalist and anti-business. Indeed, it is probably no exaggeration to say that all of Western high culture in its ideological substance over the past 150 years has *consisted of* attacks upon capitalism, and the liberalism with which it is strongly associated, from the perspective of the extreme right, the extreme left, or from a generalized anti-urban, anti-technological standpoint. On any comparative basis – and here we come once again to this central matter of comparison – British culture has been markedly less strident in its condemnation of capitalism than virtually any other Western culture, probably because doctrinaire and self-conscious ideology of any standpoint has been so much rarer and less extreme than in most other countries. There is absolutely nothing in British culture, for instance, to set beside the cosmic anti-bourgeois sarcasm and distilled hatred and loathing of a Brecht or any other Marxist writer on the left or a Nietzsche or any other proponent of proto-fascist 'cultural despair' on the right so common in Germany. Even in the United States, the homeland of capitalism rampant, the writers and intellectuals who lived contemporaneously with America's industrialization, like Emerson, Thoreau, and Melville, notably ignored it; many of their successors from Henry Adams through Hemingway and T.S.Eliot, left America to escape it; those who remained behind regularly attacked it, from left-wing writers like Theodore Dreiser and Upton Sinclair to right-wing anti-urbanist writers like William Faulkner; not one, or hardly any one, embraced it, although most personally profited mightily from the American reading public's apparent taste for self-flagellation. If the milk and water equivalents of Brecht, Nietzsche, and Henry Adams who are seen as comprising the British equivalent of this tradition, from Matthew Arnold to Dean Inge, so essentially affected British entrepreneurship, how is it that American and German culture failed to be so affected? I know little of Japanese culture, but what little I do know suggests that it was and is even more ostensibly radically anti-capitalist than its Western equivalents.

Patently, too, the notion that British culture was pervasively anti-capitalist ignores those cultural and quasi-cultural figures who are not anti-capitalist – more numerous, in all likelihood, than in most Western countries – who explicitly defended capitalism from Adam Smith, Macaulay, and, obviously, Samuel Smiles and his many imitators, to philosophers like Herbert Spencer. At least as importantly, it ignores the arguably more significant tradition which emphasized rationality and science as the primary desiderata of evolving society, a tradition which in my view animated such important intellectual movements as Utilitarianism and Fabianism; plainly, too, an emphasis on science, technology, and rationality was close to the centre of the ideology connoted by what we commonly term 'the Victorian middle classes'.

In any society or national history which is reasonably diverse and multifaceted, virtually any national ideological tradition can be constructed by historians for whom the temptations toward systematic exaggeration of its previous importance, when it seemingly explains the distinctive later outcomes of that national history, are often overwhelming and are made surprisingly often. Let us listen for a moment to the sage words of the American sociologist Peter F. Drucker, writing in 1943:

If the national character explanation is untenable the national-history explanations are meaningless. If the Germans instead of Nazism had developed a German form of Gandhi pacificism, we would now have many books showing the 'inevitability' of this development in the light of the Reformation, Luther, Kant, Beethoven or F.W.Forester; and there were a great many more devoted pacifists in the Germany of 1927 than there were devoted Nazis. If the English had ·developed a totalitarian philosophy, the pseudo-historians would have had a field day with Henry VIII, that great totalitarian Cromwell, Hobbes, Bentham, Carlyle, Spencer, and Bosanquet.[8]

How often, indeed, are 'national-history explanations', and the closely-allied 'national-character explanations' part of our common imagery of nations and national behaviour, and how frequently does this popular imagery change! A good case in point are the common and contrasting popular images of China and Japan: fifty years ago, Japan was a military aggressor and behemoth, China a gentle land of peaceful peasants; twenty or twenty-five years ago, in the United States at least, the wheel had swung fully 180°, with China under Mao now the fanatical aggressor bent on communizing Asia at all costs. Japan was renowned at the time only for having no army and producing and exporting cheap imitative junk which inevitably fell apart in the box before you got it home; once more, in the latter 1980s, the wheel may have swung if not the whole 180° round once again, at least quite a wide angle; who knows how these two countries will be popularly viewed in 2000 or 2050? I have no doubt that at every stage learned treatises were written on the inevitability of the then current Chinese and Japanese national characteristics, with their roots deep in the history of each nation.

However, argument aside, any historical thesis, no matter how debatable, may after all be true: all one needs to demonstrate this is evidence. In my view, the closer one carefully examines the evidence and the links in the argument, the more doubts one must have about the cogency of the thesis. Take, for example, the nexus or lack of nexus between the transmission of cultural values and entrepreneurial performance: just how was Britain's anti-business ethics transmitted into a haemorrhage of talent from business life and into a notably poor entrepreneurial per-formance? The major nexus which is so often postulated is, of course, the public school system, wherein the sons of successful middle-class businessmen absorbed the gentrified values of the older elite, pursued social status and the standing of the gentleman at the expense of their old entrepreneurial drive, and created the celebrated intergenerational haemorrhage of talent away from business life. Professor Wiener has given us an epitome of this process:

The public schools gradually relaxed their entrance barriers. Boys from commercial and industrial families, however, were admitted only if they disavowed their backgrounds and their class. However many businessmen's sons entered, few future businessmen emerged from these schools, and those who did were 'civilized'; that is, detached from the single-minded pursuit of production and profit.[9]

As plausible and frequently-encountered as this critique doubtless is, the best evidence now available is that it is only partially true at the very best. Before turning to my own evidence, I should note that the only source given as a citation in support of this statement in Professor Wiener's book is Bishop and Wilkinson's book on *Winchester and the Public School Elite*, 'passim'. On examining Bishop and Wilkinson's book however – a book I have frequently used and cited in my own research – I am regrettably unable to find a shred of evidence which supports the statement I have just quoted. The only relevant evidence on this matter in Bishop and Wilkinson is a comparison of the author's Chapter 4, Table 5 (pp. 104–8), which outlines the occupations of 8,187 fathers of Wykehamists educated between 1820 and 1922, with Chapter 2, Table 10 (pp. 64–9), which similarly outlines the occupations of the 7,105 Wykehamists educated in this period for whom occupational evidence could be traced in the Winchester Alumni Books. A comparison of these two tables reveals that 11.1 per cent of the Wykehamist's fathers were businessmen, while 16.4 per cent of the Wykehamists themselves were businessmen – in other words, precisely the opposite of the point made by Professor Wiener. (In fact, since only the Winchester Alumni Books have been used as a source by Bishop and Wilkinson, the actual total of both businessmen fathers and sons was likely to be somewhat higher, since many entries either give no information as to occupation or only limited information.) As it happens, I have recently conducted quite extensive research into just this matter with the aim of studying in a very detailed way the occupations, probate valuations, and much other information from samples of 60–100 entrants at eight leading public schools, entering in 1840, 1870 and 1895–1900, going beyond the school alumni books with comprehensive use made of birth, marriage, and death certificates, probate data, and the like. The results of this larger study are, seemingly, extremely similar to those of Bishop and Wilkinson.[10] Most public school-educated sons entered, broadly speaking, the same types of occupational fields as their fathers – the sons of professionals generally became professionals, the sons of businessmen became businessmen. Even when there was a drift away from business life in the second generation, it is nothing like the massive shift implied by Professor Wiener's remarks.

At Rugby, for example, businessmen accounted for 14.8 per cent of the fathers of my 1840 entrants, 31.5 per cent among the fathers of my 1870 sample, and 38.1 per cent among the fathers of my 1895–1900 sample. Sons – that is, the Rugby entrants themselves – who became businessmen as their chief (or exclusive) occupations accounted for, respectively, 10.9 per cent, 28.9 per cent, and 25.3 per cent of these cohorts, figures which are underestimates since they exclude Rugby men who became businessmen abroad – a further 4.3 per cent and 10.1 per cent among the 1870 and 1895–1900 samples. The most striking aspect of these figures is, of course, how small was the 'haemorrhage of talent' to land or the professions. Rugby was the northernmost of boarding-schools of the absolute first rank, and may have attracted disproportionately more sons of northern industrialists who were required to enter the family firm. At Dulwich College, however, the day school in South London almost exclusively for the sons of London professionals and businessmen, the picture was very similar. In the two samples in this study, entrants in 1870 and 1895–1900, businessmen comprised 49.2 per cent of known 1870 fathers and 35.4 per cent of entrants, although the later percentage rises by 10 per cent or so if entrants who migrated abroad and became businessmen there are included.[11] Dulwich's 1895–1900 cohort is, again, much the same: among fathers, 33.3 per cent were businessmen; among the entrants themselves, 28.9 per cent, a figure that probably rises above one-third if businessmen abroad are included. At Harrow, a *creme de la creme* school in the meaning of the act, it might be expected that there would be an endless array of military officers, colonial administrators, diplomats, and clubland idlers, cads, and bounders among its alumni. Although such men did exist, they were much less common than one might assume; the drop off between generations was, respectively: 1840: 22.0 per cent of fathers were businessmen, 13.7 per cent of entrants (excluding all entrants who emigrated); 1870, fathers: 37.9 per cent; entrants: 24.2 per cent; 1895–1900: fathers: 45.7 per cent were in business, compared with 30.0 per cent of sons, but again excluding 17 of 100 entrants in my sample who migrated abroad, many of whom were businessmen there – throughout the Empire or even in America. There is certainly little or nothing in the available evidence which permits us to say that the public school *ethos* led its products away from business life. Why is there such a widespread notion that it did? Among many other reasons, I strongly suspect that there is a pervasive demographic illusion involved, wherein the third, fourth, fifth, and sixth sons of businessmen, superfluous to the continuing needs of their family firms, often left the business sector for the professions; towards the later part of the nineteenth century, they may well have been compensated for by the superfluous sons of landowners and professionals who moved the other way.

In the more recent past and down to the present, given the decline, presumably to the vanishing point, of the older type of landed gentry, clubland *rentier* wastrel, and *pukka sahib* administrator of Empire, it is only to be expected that many more public school graduates would enter business life or professions closely related to business life. One study of *The English Public Schools* by James McConnell, published only in 1985, noted a survey of 2,035 old Etonians who left between 1967 and 1977 which showed that 450 were 'in accountancy, stock broking, insurance, or some form of banking', while over 100 other occupations were noted.[12] Observers of elite education in Britain have for some decades noted the profound changes, in the direction of modern-looking, technological and utilitarian training, which have recently occurred in the syllabi of the public schools. According to McConnell's recent survey, to take some fairly random examples, 'Marlborough: until 1983 Engineering attracted the biggest number of Marlboroughs going on to degree courses, but in that year Business Studies took the lead ... Turning to Cheltenham, when Cheltenham outgrew its strongly military identity and the ideal of the Empire became outmoded, no new inspiration was found. From 1932 until the late seventies [Cheltenham] steadily fell behind other Great Schools. The past six years have been a period of ... renewal and fresh direction ... A new thrust has been in Electronics ... the new Electronics lab is probably the most advanced in the UK'. At Rugby, 'in the last 30 years the number of students doing Science has risen from 10.6 per cent to 26 per cent', and so on at every major school.[13]

None of this will be news in any sense to Britain's left-wing sociologists and social historians of elites. As everyone will know, it is a stock-in-trade of their critique of British society and its economic development over the past century that Britain's elite economic positions such as the chairmanships of the major corporations, have been overwhelmingly dominated by a small, closed circle of men from well-to-do backgrounds educated at public school and Oxbridge. This common perception is seemingly supported by objective evidence. In Stanworth and Giddens' study of 495 leading company chairmen holding their position between 1900 and 1970, the percentage educated at what the authors term a public school rose from an already high 58 per cent among those born in 1840–59 to 74 per cent among those born in 1900–19. Among those born between 1840 and 1879 – in other words, holding office between about 1890 and 1945 – nearly two-thirds were educated at one of the eight Clarendon Schools and about 45 per cent at Eton and Harrow alone.[14] Even a brief comparative perusal of the entries in the *Dictionary of Business Biography* will make clear the striking change, from backgrounds of small family firm and apprenticeship, to backgrounds of public school and university, which has overtaken Britain's business leadership over the past century or so. Certainly public school education had few adverse effects upon these business leaders.

The second point to be made about the empirical evidence is this. Commonly the movement away from business life across the generations is depicted as the search for status, and, normally, the acquisition of status in Britain is seen, equally commonly, as entailing the purchase of land as an absolute prerequisite to achieving gentry status. Yet those recent historians who have studied the empirical evidence concerning the purchase of land on a large scale by businessmen, like the Stones and myself, have found, remarkably, no evidence whatever for the large-scale purchase of land by businessmen.[15] In 1884, at the time of the compilation of the official *Return of Owners of Land* by Parliament, much less than 20 per cent of all land by landowners with 3,000 or more acres was owned by post-1780 businessmen, and only a minority of very wealthy businessmen, even those leaving £500,000 or more, owned so much as 3,000 acres. Moreover, most of those who purchased very large landed estates, like the Rothschilds or Lord Overstone, were multi-millionaires who still retained vast investments in their business firms and securities. Even if these wealthy businessmen did purchase very small estates, or a country address and a gentry *mien*, the point is that the vast bulk of their assets remained in business investments or securities and were *not* transferred into the land, contrary to the widely-held myth. Indeed, Professor Stone has recently suggested that land purchase of this kind may well have been far more common on the continent than in Britain. Quite conceivably too, the percentage of all successful businessmen purchasing land in quantity declined markedly from the pre-industrial period. I find the behaviour of these wealthy businessmen quite inconsistent with the popular image of a status-seeking, ever more gentrified class.

Yet another point of dispute is the matter of profits and profitability. In the quotation from Professor Wiener given above, there was also the suggestion that second-generation businessmen were no longer dedicated 'to the single-minded pursuit of profit and production'. This is an interesting point; quite conceivably, second- and third-generation businessmen may as a rule have headed companies which were less profitable than those built up by the founder; but possibly they didn't. Against those whose profit rates declined must be set, presumably, all first-generation bankrupts and ne'er-do-wells, while it would be exceedingly difficult to attribute a decline in profitability to entrepreneurial inability alone, as opposed say, to the effects of untimely depressions or to changing market conditions. Most business millionaires, if this is any test, were actually the sons of moderately successful businessmen — fathers who improved upon the family fortune, like Lord Leverhulme, whose father was a moderately successful soap maker who left £75,000. It depends what one means by a public school, but a fair share of these were public school-educated, it would seem, although quite possibly there is an important negative connection here which I will discuss shortly.

Although it appears that the difficulties in compiling an overall index and the overall share of profits in company net output has prevented a broad historical index prior to the Second World War, there have been several detailed and reliable studies of the overall amount of business profits in the British economy in this century.[16] The overall amount of profits among firms where this could be measured varied directly with general economic conditions, peaking, during the inter-war period in the 1919 boom, in the late 1920s, and declining by roughly 40 per cent during the 1920–22 and 1930–33 depressions.[17] There is no evidence of any general, secular decline or any abandonment of profit-seeking by British entrepreneurs: quite the reverse. Indeed, the whole thrust of wage-cutting during the inter-war period (and before, obviously), was to increase profits. In the first post-Second World War years for which figures exist for the share of profits in company net output (profits and wages paid), for 1950–4, this stood, according to two Marxist economists, at 25.2 per cent, which hardly sounds like an abandonment of the profit motive.[18] Indeed, the point of this Marxist critique, and many others from a similar perspective, is that the extraordinarily high rates of profits in British industry were 'squeezed' by rising labour costs and international competitiveness from the 1960s on, which may have led directly to Britain's present unsatisfactory economic circumstances. This also happened in other Western countries, like America. The restoration of profitability by many Western governments during the 1980s, may, indeed, be the most important long-term contribution by monetarist governments to the long-term health of Western economies in the post-Keynesian period. A final point is that since 1850 profit-making may have been too easy rather than too hard for Britain's businesses: presumably, most critics of Britain's economic decline would have preferred that investors or entrepreneurs have deferred the making of super-profits in, say, Malayan rubber plantations or property development in order to invest in long-term growth areas involving initially vast commitments of technology and capital.

Does all this – everything I have said in this paper – mean that the cultural thesis would be rejected *in toto*? I do not believe this. It seems to me unarguable that there are distinct national cultures and that they heavily influence economic performance in demonstrable ways – the example given by Professor Wiener, of India, is probably a good one. I would like here briefly to point to three or four such specific areas.

First: although the public schools may well not have been responsible for a large-scale intergenerational movement of businessmen's sons away from business life, nevertheless, there is evidence from the probate records that the sons remaining in business (or transferring to it from other sectors) were in the main markedly poorer than their fathers. There are innumerable *caveats* to accepting this at face value, such as the facts that many of these sons, from the 1895/1900 public school cohorts, died in very recent decades, when levels of estate duty avoidance were much higher; that large numbers were killed in the World Wars; that families with many siblings would have had to divide their father's legacy into smaller portions, and so on. Nor is this conclusion, if true, in any way inconsistent with the fact that a minority of such sons were wealthier than their fathers and better entrepreneurs. Nevertheless, the *quality* of entrepreneurship, at least as judged by wealth accumulation, may have declined across the generations. Whether this was due to anything peculiarly British, or was or is common to all capitalist societies following the first generation of entrepreneurs, must in my view by examined objectively.

Secondly, some *types* of business life might well have been virtually immune to entrepreneurial failure of this kind: in particular of course, the City of London, the most upmarket, establishmentarian, gentrified realm of all – and the wealthiest – which nevertheless never 'failed' in the sense so frequently claimed of British industry, and whose dynasties have never withdrawn from business life. Why this is so would probably repay as much careful study by proponents of the cultural thesis as their obsession with Britain's industrial and manufacturing failure.

Thirdly, this: proponents of the cultural thesis frequently talk of the aim of British entrepreneurial activity as status attainment and gentrification, for example by the acquisition of landed estates. In my view this misrepresents the essential motivation of the modern British middle classes, which is not the attainment of status, but the attainment of *security* – two values which, though superficially resembling each other, are quite different. If the attainment of security rather than the attainment of status be seen as the overarching goal of much of the middle classes, including its businessmen, I believe that much which is seemingly puzzling and contradictory in the behaviour of the middle classes will become much clearer. Recent scholarship appears to provide evidence to the consistent attractiveness of *secure* stocks and securities as consistently the most attractive to the British investor from the mid-Victorian period at least;[19] the popularity of secure stocks and other investments was unquestionably reinforced by the increasing importance of trustee investment – for family trusts, probate income, charitable and educational institutions, and so on – that was especially important in a country with as much 'old money' as Britain.

Finally, the suggestion is that British culture has influenced the British economy. It should be equally clear that the British economy given *its* peculiarities, constraints, and evolution, has profoundly influenced British culture and cultural values. The stronger claim of causality runs this way rather than its reverse.[20]

NOTES

1. D. C. Coleman, 'Gentlemen and Players', *Economic History Review*, second series, XXVI (1973); D. H. Aldcroft, 'The Entrepreneur and the British Economy, 1840–1914', *Economic History Review*, second series, XVII (1964); David Ward, 'The Public Schools and Industry in Britain After 1870', *Journal of Contemporary History*, vol. 11 (1967) (Ward's article was the first to employ the phrase 'haemorrhage of talent' to apply to public school-educated sons of businessmen who were, allegedly, 'gentrified'); A. L. Levine, *Industrial Retardation in Britain, 1880–1914* (New York: Basic Books, 1967); William P. Kennedy, *Industrial Structure, Capital Markets, and the Origin of British Economic Decline* (Cambridge: CUP, 1987). Kennedy highlights 'weaknesses' in late Victorian capital markets which reinforced a failure of entrepreneurs to invest and modernize.
2. Correlli Barnett, *The Audit of War: The Illusion and Reality of Britain as a Great Nation* (London: Macmillan, 1986), p. 304. There were, similarly, many self-flagellating essays and collections of essays by British writers bemoaning Britain's decline. One of the earliest and most typical was a collection edited by Arthur Koestler, *Suicide of a Nation?* (London: Hutchinson, 1963), which included seventeen essays by commentators ranging from Malcolm Muggeridge to Austen Albu, M.P. The striking irony of such a collection – all the contributors were doing very well, thank you, as Britain 'suicided', came, generally, from the same establishment background as those who had misruled Britain for generations, and had unlimited access to the media and other instruments of opinion-making – seems self-evident now, if not at the time.
3. See, for instance, my essay 'The Victorian Middle Classes: Wealth, Occupation, and Geography', reprinted in W. D. Rubinstein, ed., *Elites and the Wealthy in Modern British History* (Brighton: Harvester, 1987), pp. 39–42.
4. P. L. Payne, 'Iron and Steel Manufacturers', in Derek H. Aldcroft (ed.), *The Development of British Industry and Foreign Competition 1875–1914* (London: 1968), p. 85.

5. B. R. Mitchell, *European Historical Statistics, 1750–1970* (London, 1975), pp. 399–401.
6. Payne, *op. cit.*, p. 77, n. 5, citing Ross J. Hoffman, *Great Britain and the German Trade Rivalry, 1875–1914* (New York, 1964), p. 26.
7. E. H. Phelps Brown and M. Browne, *A Century of Pay* (London, 1968), p. 178.
8. Peter F. Drucker, *The Future of Industrial Man: A Conservative Approach* (London, 1943), p. 8.
9. Martin J. Weiner, *English Culture and the Decline of the Industrial Spirit* (Harmondsworth: Penguin, 1985), p. 20.
10. This research will be detailed by me in two forthcoming books.
11. Dulwich had no 1840 cohort since the school was reorganized into its nineteenth century form in 1853.
12. James McConnell, *The English Public Schools* (London: Herbert, 1985), pp. 212–13. On the public schools, the most useful studies are Brian Gardner, *The Public Schools* (London: Hamish Hamilton, 1973); J. R. De S. Honey, *Tom Brown's Universe* (London: Millington, 1977); and Jonathon Gathorne-Hardy, *The Old School Tie* (New York: Viking, 1978). Gardner's book straightforwardly gives a capsule history of each school, its normal clientele, and famous alumni, aspects of the public schools often bewildering to those on the outside.
13. McConnell, *passim*.
14. Philip Stanworth and Anthony Giddens, 'An Economic Elite: A Demographic Profile of Company Chairmen', in Stanworth and Giddens, eds., *Elites and Power in British Society* (Cambridge: CUP, 1974), p. 90.
15. See Lawrence and Jean Fautier Stone, *An Open Elite?* and my 'New Men of Wealth and the Purchase of Land in Nineteenth Century Britain', in W. D. Rubinstein, ed., *op. cit.*, pp. 145–71.
16. P. E. Hart, *Studies of Profit, Business Savings and Investment in the United Kingdom, 1920–1962* (London, 1965); W. A. Thomas, *The Finance of British Industry, 1918–1976* (London: Methuen, 1978).
17. Hart, *ibid.*, p. 32.
18. Andrew Glyn and Bob Sutcliffe, *British Capitalism Workers, and the Profits Squeeze* (Harmondsworth: Penguin, 1972), p. 58.
19. See for instance, Kennedy, *op. cit.*
20. A number of other recent histories and studies might usefully be mentioned here. C. H. Lee's excellent *The British Economy Since 1700: A Macroeconomic Perspective* (Cambridge: CUP, 1986) usefully summarizes the most important recent interpretations of Britain's economic development, giving much more weight to its financial/commercial sector than in most such studies. There is an extensive, up-to-date bibliography. David Coates and John Hillard (eds.), *The Economic Decline of Modern Britain: The Debate Between Left and Right* (Brighton: Wheatsheaf, 1986), contains very useful extracts from leading

economists and commentators representing distinctive ideological viewpoints from Marxist to Friedmanite. There is an extract from Professor Wiener's book and the editors are very much aware of the debate examined here.

Harold James

The German Experience and the Myth of British Cultural Exceptionalism

The assertion that hostile cultural attitudes – or what recently has been termed the absence of an 'enterprise culture' – have led to a comparatively weaker British industrial performance, or even to 'deindustrialization' and 'industrial decline',[1] has recently attracted considerable support from historians: notably Correlli Barnett, Neil McKendrick, Tom Nairn and Martin Wiener. And as popularized by Sir Keith (now Lord) Joseph, this view became politically influential, and led directly to an attempted redesigning of British school and university systems.

Those alleged hostile cultural attitudes can be summarized as the cult of the gentleman, contempt for applied science and for technology, and hostility to business: in general the enshrinement of *ancien regime* values. If the historical critics are to be believed, Britain, far from leading the world's advance to industrialism, retained the values of the pre-modern era longer than any other industrial culture.

Correlli Barnett claimed in 1972 that from the late nineteenth century, 'the fire of creative purpose flickered low in the blackened grate of the British industrial regions', partly because 'the cult of the "practical man" led to a positive distrust of the application of intellectual study or scientific research to industrial problems'.[2] Martin Wiener writes: 'The end result of the nineteenth century transformation of Britain was indeed a peaceful accommodation, but one that entrenched pre-modern elements within the new society, and gave legitimacy to antimodern senti-ments.'[3] Tom Nairn says: 'Britain's social philosophy, embodied in an authoritative politico-cultural hegemony, sustains social relationships in a way that defuses invention.'[4] The view that nostalgia for an old way results in mutually reinforcing cults of the classically educated gentlemanly generalist on the one hand and the unintellectual handy practitioner on the other goes back at least to the middle of the nineteenth century, and appears in the correspondence of industrialists,[5] as well as in political tracts. In 1932 Harold Laski, warning of 'The dangers of Being a Gentleman', opined that 'the main defects of British enterprise have been exactly those most characteristic of the gentleman.'[6]

A thesis with such potentially wide-ranging policy implications deserves a rigorous scrutiny. The most fundamental of the sup-positions underlying this analysis is that there exists an identifi-able national culture which moulds belief within the confines of a particular political unit: or, as Neil McKendrick puts it, 'inherited assumptions, educational imprinting, subtle social indicators of preferred occupations, accepted modes of social ascent, profoundly affect the adoption of *distinctive national attitudes* to work and leisure, to risk taking and the search for security, to money and how to acquire it. Our *national culture* both reflects and arguably *determines* these values.'[7]

The problem of the anti-industrial culture thesis has consis-tently lain in the difficulty of actually demonstrating the precise nature of the links between national culture and economic decisions. Few economic historians examining entrepreneurial actions have been able to find substantive evidence of major irrationality. Donald McCloskey and Lars Sandberg have demonstrated the extent to which business decisions were a response to British factor endowment, and to the chronology of British industrialization.[8] The recent comparative history of German and British steel-making by Ulrich Wengenroth also attacks the received notion of entrepreneurial failure in Britain, and points out that in the late nineteenth century German steel makers were slow in making the transition from lower quality Thomas steel to the use of the Siemens-Martin process.[9]

There are certainly purely economic penalties borne by the early industrializer such as Britain: an infrastructure is estab-lished that makes new and more modern investment unattractive in a business calculation. In the most familiar example, a railway built with a light track bed, steep gradients and sharp bends, and which in consequence can only carry small waggons, is unlikely to be replaced by a more expensive system bearing bigger loads because of the 'lumpiness' characteristic of large investment projects. The cost of switching over from old to new is simply too great. In addition, the early industrializer will inevitably face faster growth in other economies as they embark on the long haul of 'catching up'. This happened to late nineteenth century Britain at the same time as the supply of labour moving out of agriculture began to dry up: or, in other words, as the factor endowments began to turn to Britain's disadvantage.

It appears that there is here a clash between two approaches: why on the one hand are economic historians so keen to assert the rationality of entrepreneurial decisions, and on the other cultural and political historians so eager to impugn them? The most obvious criticism of the economic historians is that they are prevented by their framework of neo-classical assumptions from supposing that decisions could be anything but rational: perhaps wrong, or based on misleading information, but certainly always profit-maximizing in the context of the knowledge available at the time to the decision makers. If a business decision is mistaken, it can only be shown to be so in the light of subsequently available information. The 'economists' find it impossible to see non-rational entrepreneurs; while simultaneously the 'culturists' find it impossible to demonstrate the connections between culture and the economy. Perhaps some cultural critics are only using the economic argument as a form of polemical ammunition to discredit a cultural system of which for other reasons they disapprove.

This essay uses a comparative approach in order to overcome this apparent dialogue of the deaf. It examines the German example as a case analogous to that of Britain; and in particular it attempts to show for what purposes in economic history cultural explanations can be used, and also to demonstrate the limits of that use.

How do we describe a 'national culture' in the first place? It is certainly not easily guessed at, measured, or quantified. Usually statements about national culture are only made in a comparative way: Germans are more militaristic than Frenchmen, Englishmen are less good lovers than Frenchmen etc. We are usually happy to leave analysis and statements of this sort to the popular press. In economic life, through most of the twentieth century British experience is usually held up against an American (US) yardstick; at the end of the nineteenth century, the comparison was more usually made with the German Empire.

The first great panic about British inferiority reached a preliminary highpoint with the publication of E.E.Williams's book *Made in Germany* in 1896. Williams described the new successes of German textiles, chemicals, printing, and musical instrument manufacture in alarmist terms: 'Roam the house over, and the fateful mark [giving nation of origin, as required by the 1887 Merchandise Marks Act – itself a statement of British fear of an invasion of foreign goods] will greet you at every turn, from the piano in your drawing room to the mug on the kitchen dresser, blazoned though it be with the legend *A Present from Margate.*' 'Moreover, German antagonism is systematic, universal, deadly, and may be considered as a thing of evil and a thing apart.' Germany owed her commercial successes to a sympathetic state, but above all to a vigorous national culture 'madly in love with Industrialism, and vigorous to pursue her love, with sufficient stimulus.' Britain, conversely, had become locked into blind obedience to the dictate of conventional practice. All the charges made by Barnett and Wiener are already present here. 'It is all very well to run an old-established business; but you must diligently and continuously be striving to bring its methods up to date. And this is what English manufacturers fail to recognise.'[10]

In Williams's work and in subsequent, twentieth century, accounts, the secret of the German triumph becomes repetitively familiar. It lies deep in national character: in the extensive support of commercial endeavour from Germany's consular service, German capacity to work hard, a willingness to make adjustments to customers' tastes, and above all in a 'love affair' with industrialism.

How can assertions of this kind be examined critically? Traditionally, three areas have preoccupied historians searching for the cultural roots of national economic decline: general social values as reflected in and transmitted by imaginative literature; cultural values as instilled through education; and finally the behaviour of businessmen and would-be businessmen themselves as a response to a cultural ambience.

I

Literary evidence has played a central part in the arguments of the vast majority of recent exponents of a thesis of culturally induced decline. Creative writing sometimes reflects social attitudes, but also often moulds the way reality is perceived by others. Nairn complains that 'literature can too easily be dismissed as a witness of the social condition', and claims that 'in modern Britain it actually has been quite important in justifying the old ways of the state to man.' English literature has been, according to this view, engaged in a systematic luddism – or at best a pastoral nostalgia for the romance of a lost world – when it tries to show how modern life is fundamentally 'alien to the English temperament'. It sets up an unsympathetic vision of the future, in which through technology 'Englishmen are reduced to the conditions of Morlocks or proles'.[11]

The initially attractive area of literary analysis is, however, fraught with difficulties. First of all, it is in practice extremely hard to gauge what effects an imaginative product has on real life. Even if a strong anti-business culture exists, it is quite conceivable that businessmen might shrug it off. Are entrepreneurs supposed to be so morally and psychically enfeebled that they depend on massive public acclaim for their actions? They are scarcely likely ever to find it. Are would-be entrepreneurs deterred by unsympathetic fictions? It is unlikely that literary stereotypes about businessmen will have a pernicious effect on career choices. From Charles Lever's *Davenport Dunn: A Man of Our Day* (1857–9) through Anthony Trollope's Augustus Melmotte and Ferdinand Lopez to Caryl Churchill's gruesome cast from LIFFE (London International Financial Futures Exchange) in *Serious Money* (1987), literary pictures of financiers have been almost uniformly exceedingly unattractive, but the City has never found recruitment hard. In addition, the world is full of examples of the odd or even perverse mixture of business activity and anti-business resentment. Many of the early supporters of revolutionary socialist movements in late nineteenth century Russia had a background in enterprise. In a striking scene in Rainer Fassbinder's clearly anti-business film of 1979, 'The Marriage of Maria Braun', the heroine explains the links between her social origins and family existence and her activity as an amoral managerial type in the *Wirtschaftswunder*:

'Because I'm a master of deception. A capitalist tool by day, and by night an agent of the proletarian masses. The Mata Hari of the *Wirtschaftswunder*.'[12] We can read Günter Grass or Heinrich Böll on our way to well-paid business positions: in general, an anti-business culture may actually be a safety-valve in an atmosphere of heady economic success.

Moreover, describing the tone of a literature of a whole country is inevitably highly subjective. Often such description is carried out in a rather casual fashion, and can easily be countered simply by the use of other examples. Jay Winter has rightly complained of the 'somewhat cavalier' treatment of literary evidence by Wiener.[13] Charles Dickens notoriously portrays grasping and wicked industrialists – the Dombeys, Bounderbys, Merdles – but it has also been pointed out that he presents highly sympathetic portraits of charitable and Christian men – the iron-master Rouncewell in *Bleak House* or the merchant Nicholas Nickleby or the Cheeryble brothers. If it is true that the fundamental attitude of most writers is 'ambivalence'[14] towards business, it is hard to enlist them as evidence of an inherently luddite culture.

A more subtle interpretation suggests that the large-scale demonization of entrepreneurs might have a positive effect on recruitment to business life: the main contribution of literature in this case would be in creating larger than life but above all socially prominent types. Such is Neil McKendrick's verdict; he complains that the British problem is not outright hostility to the businessman but the literary consignment of enterprise to insignificance and obscurity. 'Whereas in Germany and the United States the businessman is still the focus of serious literary debate because he is still seen as a central and important member of society, the fact that he has faded from the English literary scene need not betoken acceptance so much as the fact that he is no longer regarded as needing attack. ... In the England of economic decline the silence is deafening, the neglect almost total.'[15]

In fact no one writing on English industrial decline has yet attempted any systematic comparison of British and German literary attitudes. Modern German culture is, however, widely recognized as being largely anti-modern, pessimistic, and specifically anti-industrial. Such verdicts on German literature as have been reached sound surprisingly similar to those applied on the other side of the North Sea. Novelists went through a cycle of first ignoring business; then, in the 1840s and 50s concentrating on the ills of industrialism while a small minority welcomed the advent of a new bourgeois type; and then in high literature returning to a disapproving and hostile silence. Only in a more popular and less 'literary' genre did some writers take to a depiction and an extollation of the kind of industrial destiny – the solitary entrepreneur struggling upwards from a lowly background – whose time, if it had ever existed, had passed by the beginning of this century.

Twentieth century literature in Germany has had – as Gertrud Milkereit has pointed out – relatively few businessmen heroes and relatively few striking anti-heroes. 'German literature', she says, 'has nothing of equal standing to be put alongside the works of Balzac, Flaubert and Zola, or those of Sinclair Lewis, Upton Sinclair, and Graham Greene. In novels, the nineteenth century ignored the process of the industrial revolution and entrepreneurial activity.'[16] Those novelists that examined industry generally presented a 'reactionary socialism' – an attack on modern existence as sordid and debased. Bullivant and Ridley reach the following verdict: 'Instead of attempting to analyse the economic forces of the age, they [German writers] preferred to brand factory owners as over-life size examples of moral corruption and to make them responsible for the evils of the age. Instead of giving new shape to traditional values, they allowed these values to become removed from existing reality, and to become at the same time sentimental and ideological.'[17] And when business figures are presented as heroes they become highly romanticized depictions of early industrial revolution figures, and not of the actual types in professional management and cartellized and trustified industry.[18]

The first literary depiction of a factory in German literature occurs in Karl Immermann's *Die Epigonen* (1836), a work whose title indicates its theme: the problem of living in a world from which genius has departed, the world after Goethe or Schiller, or after Napoleon and Scharnhorst. The conclusion of the book offers an optimistic solution: the evolution of a new type of man through a merging of bourgeois and aristocrat. Two different societies confront one another. On the one hand is an aristocratic household, exhausted by generations of indebtedness and dissolute living. On the other hand is the new world of the self-made man, the hero of the book whose life re-enacts the progress of Goethe's Wilhelm Meister. One of the characters concludes:

'We are moving into a new epoch where men will be bourgeois/ citizens [the German word for the two, *Bürger*, is identical], just as once under the influence of Christianity men lived in expectation of the future. This [new bourgeois age] is the holy inspiring will of the world spirit in the guise of the political movements of our time.'[19] In this world, however, the agglomeration of miscellaneous factories owned by the hero's (never named) uncle represent not the future but the past: there are too many plants for one man to control, and the combine breaks apart on the uncle's death, leaving small family units to prevail once more. Immermann actually had a real model for the manufacturing uncle: Johann Gottfried Nathusius, an entrepreneur in the Magdeburg area who had made a fortune speculating in the assignat currency of the French Revolution, and who at the height of his prosperity owned thirty-three factories and printed his own paper money.

Immermann's generally positive picture of a rather unusual businessman was soon superseded by rather grimmer depictions of the new commercial and industrial age. In the 1840s there developed a critical school, parallel to the 'Condition of England' novels of Disraeli (*Sybil*) and Elizabeth Gaskell (*Mary Barton*). In Germany, the moral degeneracy of factory life excited particular and lubricious attention: Ernst Adolf Willkomm's *Weisse Sclaven oder die Leiden des Volkes* ('White Slaves: Or the Suffering of the People', 1845) described factory immiseration and looked hopefully towards concerted proletarian action as the way of liberation. Workers are degraded and sexually exploited. *Weisse Sclaven* raises one central problem about the relationship of literature and business conditions. There can be no doubt that the novel is a forecast and a fiction: it represents not an account of current conditions, but a vision of what Germany might become if she followed the more industrialized Western countries, Britain, Belgium and France. In Britain, in September 1830, Richard Oastler had already started an emotional campaign against the 'child slavery' of the Bradford textile mills. Willkomm purports to describe an upper-class textile manufacture in Upper Lusatia, but in reality in the 1840s there were there no large spinning works employing a thousand workers and also no aristocratic entrepreneurs. Willkomm never provides any detailed description of actual machinery. Instead he is setting out a 'black and white picture with the goal of producing a distinct ideology through emotional and agitational means'.[20]

The negative depiction of factories reached a preliminary high point with Johannes Scherr's novel *Michel* of 1858, where the term 'white slaves' is once again liberally deployed, and in which a factory owner claims that some of his colleagues are forcing their female workers to have sex and then refusing to pay the wages for the time the unfortunate girls spent not actually working. How far such intentionally propagandist works actually influenced their readers' opinions may be doubted. By the middle of the century, a contrasting sentiment was at least as strong in middle-class circles: that Germany needed business and a successful modern industry. Otherwise, as the economist Bruno Hildebrand pointed out in 1848, Germans would become more like the potato blight stricken Irish, and not like the more prosperous Britons or the French.[21]

In the period after the political revolutions of 1848 and the hunger crises of mid-century there followed a remarkable period of bourgeois self-confidence. Undoubtedly its most popular and influential literary product was Gustav Freytag's *Soll und Haben* ('Debit and Credit') of 1855. Freytag's long novel fits well into the tradition of the German *Bildungsroman*, the novel of maturation and development. Freytag's orphaned hero, Anton Wohlfahrt ('Anthony Prosperity'), takes a job in a large merchant house, resists temptations to give himself out as an aristocrat, reorganizes his employer's business in Russian Poland after a Polish insurrection, and helps a nobleman threatened by bankruptcy to establish the correct principles for running an estate in Poland. Eventually he marries his former employer's sister, and goes back into commerce. One of the consistent themes of the work is Wohlfahrt's resistance of the lures of the aristocratic way of life: he eventually sees that the beautiful and energetic but spiritually limited aristocratic girl he formerly admired is not as desirable as the clever bourgeoise and her associations with commercial enterprise. As he grows older and wiser, Wohlfahrt becomes more bourgeois. The other theme is the distinction between honest and dishonest trade – a treatment to which Freytag gives a strongly anti-semitic element. The decent trading business of Wohlfahrt's employer T.O.Schröter stands in contrast to the money-lending business of the Jewish merchant Hirsch Ehrenthal, and in even greater opposition to the unsavoury methods of Ehrenthal's employee Veitel Itzig, a Jew who conspires to defraud both his employer and the aristocratic father of Wohlfahrt's original belle dame.

The firm of Schröter has its own distinct bourgeois pride – Freytag even says its 'own poetry'. Sabine, Anton's eventual wife, tells her brother the merchant that he should not fear her falling in love with an aristocrat: 'Do not forget that I am your sister. I am the child of bourgeois and he [her aristocratic admirer] will never belong to us. I am as proud as you.' Schröter offers a similarly upright view of what is proper to the bourgeois, and how the old families have thrown away their chance:

Believe me, a large number of these gentlemen who suffer from all their old family memories cannot be helped. .... Many of our old established families are destined to decline, and it will be no misfortune for the state when they decline. Their family resources make them arrogant without justification, limit their mental horizon, confuse their judgment. ... Where the active force comes to an end in a family or an individual, there wealth should come to an end also, money should freely roll into the hand of him who knows better how to use it. And the family that exhausts itself in enjoyment should sink back onto the ground level of the life of the people, and make room for freshly emerging forces.[22]

The combination Freytag offered in *Soll und Haben* - bourgeois (though not necessarily industrial) self-assertion linked with a commentary on the decline of old rural and aristocratic wealth – provided a formula for a great deal of later nineteenth century German writing.[23] Novels on the erosion of the aristocracy are two a Pfennig: the most interesting and thorough in setting out the economic and managerial problems of aristocratic farming being Wilhelm Polenz's *Der Grabenhäger* (1893), and the most valuable from a literary viewpoint the quiet melancholia of Theodor Fontane's elegiac last novel *Der Stechlin* (published posthumously in 1899).

Fontane is also highly skilful in his depiction of the upstart qualities of the new classes: probably most tellingly in the story of the parvenue *Frau Jenny Treibel* (1893), a small shopkeeper's daughter married to a big Berlin manufacturer, who steps in to prevent the mismatch of her son with the clever and fascinating daughter of a Professor who had been her own youthful admirer.

Very few works of fiction deal with manufacturers in their workplace. In Fontane's novel, we have no glimpses into Kommerzienrat Treibel's business venture. The exceptions are rare: among positive accounts of industry, the liberal writer

Friedrich Spielhagen's *Hammer und Amboss* ('Hammer and Anvil', 1869) stands more or less on its own. The work is set back in the 1830s and 1840s, and takes up many of Immermann's themes. Like Immermann's novel, it is concerned with the reconciliation of apparent opposites. Its conclusion – that man should be neither the hammer nor the anvil but both – is already adumbrated in the title. The hero Georg Hartwig rejects the safe prestigious careers proposed to him by his father: he refuses to become an academic or a civil servant, and instead runs away to join a smuggler. Captured and imprisoned, he comes to see the attraction of business as a way of improving the life of others; and eventually combines the manufacture of railway machinery with the amelioration of workers' conditions.

Spielhagen's novels – like Freytag's *Soll und Haben* – rely in their construction on a foil of the bad businessman, the dishonest merchant, the speculator. In *Hammer und Amboss* the fundamentally honest Hartwig is contrasted with Streber (= 'Striver'), a man who wants to speculate on the stock exchange, but not to invest in factories, and whose eventual ruin is richly deserved. Spielhagen also provided in *Sturmflut* ('The Storm Flood', 1877) a fictionalized account of the stock exchange crash (the so-called *Gründerkrach*) of 1873. In this novel, a wise Prussian official of the old school explains: 'a people cannot dance around the Golden Calf and sacrifice to Moloch for ever: it either sinks under the floodstorm of its sins, or it clings to the rescuing rock of true, manly, bourgeois virtue.'[24] Spielhagen's plot concerns a railway speculation in which overpriced stock for a commercially useless project is to be floated on the bourse, and made respectable by the use of gullible aristocratic names: it is an exact depiction of the real-life scandal of the railway adventurer Baron Bethel Strousberg. At the climax of the novel, a banquet in the house of the speculator Philipp Schmidt (at which the police later try to arrest the host), one of the positive figures calls for a toast to Eduard Lasker, the German liberal parliamentarian who on 7 February 1873 in a speech to the Prussian Landtag had unmasked the Strousberg affair.

Indeed the sentiments of Spielhagen's fictional Prussian President and of Lasker (and of Spielhagen himself) are very close. Lasker had said: 'Whoever is legitimately active in commerce or in any other form of business, and contributes more than the average to our national wealth, should receive a larger profit.

But now the difference between legitimate and illegitimate profit, between legitimate and fraudulent firms has become so blurred that all over the country entrepreneurs of whatever sort are called by the same names and are thought of in the same way. This represents one of the worst symptoms of the serious damage done.'[25] After 1873, denunciation of speculative manias, and of materialism in general, became a commonplace: and Lasker and Spielhagen had led the way.

The Spielhagen example is revealing: in depicting bourse speculation, the novelist had a contemporary model in real life, and a literary genre into which he might fit the work (and speculation novels were also immensely popular in England at the time). In depicting his businessmen – Hartwig or Schmidt's father Ernst Schmidt (a large-scale stonemason) in *Sturmflut* – Spielhagen found no clearly available model for a positive picture of German business life; and the result is schematic characterization and absence of any amount of technical detail. In dealing with business, authors maintained a substantial distance from real life.

After Spielhagen, industrialists appear usually as caricature villains. The most famous is Heinrich Mann's relentlessly scheming and wicked paper manufacturer Diederich Hessling of *Der Untertan* (usually translated 'The Man of Straw'; also 'His Imperial Majesty's Loyal Subject', substantially complete before the First World War, but only published in 1918) and the sequel to *Der Untertan*, *Die Armen* ('The Poor') of 1917. Hessling engages in every conceivable act of betrayal: of his mistress, of the German army, of his wife, of the decent old liberal establishment in the little town of Netzig, of his fellow conservatives, and of his employees. But in *Der Untertan*, there are no ordinary workers – Hessling's initial enemy and then co-conspirator is the union organizer Napoleon Fischer who is elected as a socialist Reichstag deputy with Hessling's (indirect) support. *Die Armen*, which seeks to demonstrate Hessling's villainy by telling the stories of workers in his plant, is one of Mann's least successful novels: both the good and the bad characters are no more than flat unidimensional cut-out figures. Other businessmen appear as minor characters in a grander scheme in which the enemy is materialism or a whole economic system, but not the vices of individual men: the oppressors, for instance, in Hans Fallada's depression novel *Kleiner Mann was nun?* ('Little Man, What Next?', 1932) are wholly invisible: it is an impersonal moloch that destroys the small salesman protagonist Pinneberg.

Fallada's one novel which has an entrepreneur hero is *Ein Mann will nach oben: Die Frauen und der Träumer* ('A Man wants to Rise', published posthumously in 1953): a depiction of the triumph of progressive individualism in the mould of Freytag's *Soll und Haben* or indeed of Dickens's *David Copperfield*. The story examines the struggle of a series of good women for the affections of Karl Siebrecht, a rugged individualist who time after time rejects external help: and in the end calls his transportation firm Siebrecht, Niemand & Co. (Siebrecht and Nobody Else Inc.). But *Ein Mann will nach oben* is much less well read or known than *Little Man What Next* or Fallada's peasant novel *Bauern, Bonzen und Bomben*.

Alfred Döblin, the author of *Berlin Alexanderplatz*, also wrote a business novel, which also proved to be one of his least commercially successful novels (*Wadzaks Kampf mit der Dampfturbine*, 'Wadzaks Struggle with the Steam Turbine', written 1915, published 1918). It examines the business collapse and subsequent psychic disintegration of a small engineering manufacturer, who eventually complains that technology has become immoral in the modern world: but 'Technology cannot be undertaken without morality, especially not technology'.[26]

The Weimar Republic did produce two of the most remarkable German literary depictions of business life: by Robert Musil in his powerful *Mann ohne Eigenschaften* ('Man without Qualities'), where the industrialist Arnheim is a demonically fictionalized portrait of Walther Rathenau, the heir to Germany's second largest electrical firm AEG: secondly, Erik Reger's *Union der festen Hand* ('Union of the Steady Hand'), a *roman a cléf* of Germany's powerful iron and steel industry of Rhine-Ruhr produced by a journalist who had been a Krupp employee. The principal factory depicted, Risch-Zander, is based on the Essen Krupp works; like Gustav Krupp von Bohlen und Halbach, the owner Freiherr von Zander is an aristocrat who married an industrial heiress. Schellhas father and son are August and Fritz Thyssen, the inflation speculator Ottokar Wirtz is Hugo Stinnes, Felgenhauer the coal and steel industrialist Emil Kirdorf etc. etc. It cannot be said that any of the businessmen, with the possible exception of Freiherr von Zander, are sympathetic. Wirtz typifies for Reger the modern business ethic: he is the 'characteristic entrepreneur of the epoch of high capitalism, who was born in the midst of his trade and whose enterprises grew out of a desire for risk and commercial adventure. He did not create, but bought, bought, bought, indiscriminately, profitable and unprofitable items alike.'[27]

The novel, however, lampoons white collar workers, bankers, economics graduates, trade unionists, socialists, communists, and Nazis as well. It takes up some of the nineteenth century stereotypes – the sexually exploitative managers and foremen of 'White Slaves' – but unlike the traditional anti-business novels there is no hint of a positive picture of the world lost as a consequence of modernity. Its concern – like that of most other Weimar works – is with the exposition and uncovering of a gigantic system.

Post-1945 literature retains many of the characteristic attitudes of Weimar writing: there are businessmen in Heinrich Böll's and Günter Grass's works, but they stand on the sidelines. The novels criticize a society, not individuals particularly: in this way they embody that 'antitechnological humanism and pre-capitalist fantasy [which] appear to be endemic in all capitalist states'.[28] The enemy is the acquisitive 'performance society' (*Leistungsgesellschaft*); and the heroics belong to those who like Leni and her son Lev in Böll's *Gruppenbild mit Dame* ('Group Portrait with a Lady', 1971) refuse to perform and undertake what Böll describes with the comic-bureaucratic abbreviated language of modern German bureaucracy as *Lvw.* (or *Leistungsverweigerung*, refusal to perform). Society is a monolith which requires attack and opposition by those Böll believes to be truly moral. Some of Böll's businessmen indeed appear attractive in their ability to challenge the world – as does Leni's father in the *Gruppenbild*.

In others words, the observation that 'in the Germany of the economic miracle Brecht and Grass and Böll have savagely criticized those in charge of industry' is scarcely true.[29] Like British writers, Germans have ignored business and concentrated their polemic on other targets – politics, the church, the popular press. In addition, they now have the inviting target of the hypocrisy of Germans faced with their Nazi past – and some German commentators see the scholarly and literary wrestling with the legacy of Nazism to be functionally equivalent to the guilty rejection in British cultural life of the vices of early industrial exploitation.[30]

A literature which on the whole ignores manufacturers, and which when it pillories the business world looks at financial and housing speculators rather than at industrialists: this is probably the best way of describing both British and German responses. There are indeed surprising parallels. The attacks generally link aristocratic corruption (rather than solid bourgeois probity) with financial speculation. It is instructive to compare Spielhagen's *Sturmflut* with Anthony Trollope's roughly contemporaneous and bitterly critical *The Way We Live Now* – published in 1875, but composed from 1873 and dealing with the same wave of European and North Atlantic bourse mania for railway stock.[31] Trollope wrote immediately under the impact of events on the European continent – the Austrian and German stock exchange collapses – as well as south and central American schemes such as the Honduras Interoceanic Railway. His 'Merchant Prince' Augustus Melmotte put forward a scheme for a South Central Pacific and Mexican Railway, and raised money for himself and some of his aristocratic backers by selling off stock at prices stimulated by artificial transactions – like Strousberg or Spielhagen's fictional Philipp Schmidt. The climax and turning point of Trollope's novel is a dinner and ball for a thousand guests to show 'how an English merchant lives' – at which in practice Melmotte's web starts to unravel. It is exactly the same dramatic turning point, in other words, as in the *Sturmflut*. Melmotte has in addition clear links with the European continent: he was associated with a fraudulent Franco-Austrian assurance company, and had once been imprisoned for fraud in Hamburg.

That there should be so many analogies and similarities between German and British fictional attitudes to business is scarcely surprising – at least it should not be so. Not only was the process of industrialization in the nineteenth century one in which ideas and people moved across Europe: the banking dynasties Rothschild, Baring, Schröder came to England, as did manufacturers such as Mond or Allhusen in chemicals. The spread of industrialization to the continent often meant the peregrination of Englishmen, Welshmen, Scots and Irishmen: Cockerill in Belgium, Mulvany, Biram or Foster in Germany. The founder of the Berlin woollen industry was an Englishman; and of leading Ruhr entrepreneurs in the nineteenth century a significant minority (8 per cent) were foreign.[32]

But in addition, and more importantly for perceptions of contemporary society, the genres of fiction leapt across national frontiers. The striking parallels between Trollope and Spielhagen's novel of two years later is only one example of the wholesale transference of literary types. In particular, it is not surprising that the 'ambivalent' attitude towards business of Charles Dickens appears in Germany, since Dickens held a powerful attraction over German readers. The critic Julius Schmidt reported with astonishment that even in the revolutionary turmoil of 1848–9 the German public was less interested in politics than in Dickensian fiction: 'There was overall more disputing over Dora and Agnes than about Radowitz and Manteuffel'. Dickens offered to Germans a view of life in a more advanced country, and as it might emerge in Germany if industrialism continued. The frustrated novelist Berthold Auerbach complained: 'Dickens had the luck to be an Englishman. And what are we? We are eternally provincials. We have no centre that everyone knows, we have no national types ... What have Freytag or I done? Only depicted provincial life.'[33] The similarities of Freytag's most famous novel to Dickens's *David Copperfield* have been pointed out over and over again, by observers from Rudolph Borchardt to Ellis Gummer. Uriah Heep corresponds to Veitel Itzig; Steerforth to Fink; Rosa Dartle to Rosalie Ehrenthal; and the struggle between two good and virtuous ladies for the affections of the hero have been transferred from Dora and Agnes in Dickens to Lenore and Sabine in *Soll und Haben*.

An equally powerful case can be made that German non-fictional critical perceptions of the industrialization process stemmed not from observation of actual conditions at home but from a fear that West European miseries would eventually be transferred there. The two most important contributions to the discussion of the 'condition of Germany' in the 1840s were in fact Lorenz von Stein's *Socialism and Communism in the France of Today* (published 1842 in Leipzig) and Friedrich Engels's *Condition of the Working Class in England* (also published in Leipzig, in 1845). In short, British and German cultural responses were so similar not simply because they emerged from cultures fundamentally alike and drawing on common European roots, and not simply because they represented reactions to a general process of industrialization and urbanization, but also because of the direct transfer of perceptions.

II

Different educational systems, and attitudes to technology induced by education, are more obvious candidates when it comes to explaining differences between late nineteenth century British and German performances. This indeed, rather than the more nebulous concept of 'cultural' differences, remained the preferred explanation of Victorian Britons for the rapid rise of Germany as their industrial rival. The Darwinian T.H.Huxley thought that Germany had won because she 'had put her strength' in science. E.E.Williams endorsed this opinion, and added that the German superiority lay in the deliberate application of science to practical ends. 'The Technical Education to be obtained in Germany is thorough, and thoroughly scientific; *but it is meant for application.* Active use, rather than abstract mental improvement, is the main object kept in view; so it produces, not "superior" shopkeepers and "soulful" governesses, but artisans and engineers of the best class, men who know the why and the wherefore of their work, and do it well.'[34] By contrast English public schools and Oxbridge offered an education too general, too ill-directed when it came to practical purposes, at best suited to the development of the all-rounder rather than the more useful specialist.

Before the mid-nineteenth century there was in Britain a complete hostility to any practical or technical orientation in universities, and scientists such as Thomas Graham at University College London boasted their intention of avoiding 'the temptations of technical chemistry'. Only later did the new civic universities do something to correct the balance: Manchester, Liverpool, Leeds and Birmingham. In Birmingham, Joseph Chamberlain announced: 'We desire to systematize and develop the special training which is required by men in business and those who either as principals or as managers and foremen will be called upon to conduct the great industrial undertakings.'[35] From the 1880s, even London turned to industrial science and in particular to chemistry: but it took several generations before British universities began to catch up with the German academy.

The German educational advantages did not arise as the result of a persistent cultural orientation towards science, but developed in the particular historical circumstances of the late eighteenth and early nineteenth centuries: during the era of the French Revolution and of the Napoleonic occupation of Germany. After that came periods when German education underwent profound crises: Germans by no means constantly cheered the chemist or eulogized the engineer, and Germans also accused their universities of offering too general and too ill-directed a training.

The German state did indeed initially pay more attention to education, and such cherishing produced technical and economic results. Eighteenth century states already demonstrated an active interest. State concern in this field began as an interest in revenue raising and, ultimately, military advantage. Frederick the Great sent mining engineers to England to learn the latest techniques and apply them in the royal Prussian mines. In the eighteenth century mining academies were set up in Berlin, Freiberg and Clausthal.

The most celebrated state institution is the Technische Hochschule, established initially on the model of the Paris Ecole Polytechnique of 1794. An engineering school in Karlsruhe was in 1825 united with a building school, and the resulting Polytechnik became a major centre of scientific enquiry – in large part due to the efforts of the Austrian Ferdinand Redtenbacher, who played a major role in importing the most modern French engineering techniques. The goal of the Technische Hochschule, according to the Baden Minister Nebenius, who was instrumental in promoting it, lay in the formation of 'higher productive classes': in other words the schools began as a product of that hope for universal improvement characteristic of the era of the French Revolution. Engineering did indeed in practice offer a successful route to social improvement, and it remained one of the principal channels of mobility.

Nevertheless, in the later nineteenth century German engineers regularly complained that they lacked status, and that the Technische Hochschule did not have the same standing as a university. Often these institutions were deprecatingly called 'bourgeois universities'. The complaint was precisely that engineering had become too associated with the figure of the parvenu. Many of Germany's most remarkable engineers had come from a background of relatively humble family and then commercial or technical school: C.Hoppe, L.Schwartzkopff, H.Gruson, and most famously of all E.Rathenau. One of the major goals of the Association of German Engineers (the Verein Deutscher Ingenieure, founded in 1856) was to escape from the stereotype of breakneck social climbing, to raise the social standing of the engineer, and to attain real bourgeois respectability.

Only in 1899 was a Technische Hochschule allowed to award doctorates, and thus gain formal equivalence with universities. But the sense of inferiority remained. In 1907, the engineer Friedrich Dessauer complained about the lowly status of his profession in the business world. Echoing the frequent British complaint about the relative relegation of practical knowledge, he lamented 'the subordination of technical activity to business generalists'. Such an argument was frequently voiced in the years before the First World War.[36]

At a lower level, social discrimination against science and technology seemed even clearer. The more practical secondary schools (Realschulen) were universally agreed to be inferior academically to the predominantly classical and literary Gymnasien; and even the invention of a new in-between category of Realgymnasium (in Prussia in 1882) did not increase considerably the standing of its pupils. From 1820 in Prussia each administrative district had its own commercial school, or 'Gewerbeschule', but they operated at such a low intellectual level that the rather more prestigious Commercial Institute in Berlin (Central-Gewerbeinstitut) actually preferred to admit elementary school pupils.[37]

However, later nineteenth century German business did owe a great deal to the strengths of German academic science, and to the research conducted not only in Technische Hochschulen, but in full universities, and not by the graduates of Realschulen but by the products of the Gymnasien. It was in the chemical, optical and electrical trades that the most perfect application of scientific advance for economic benefit took place. This 'secret marriage' between business and university proved an unqualified success. In 1895 in his rectoral address at Strassburg university, Rudolf Fittig boasted that 'in the extension of knowledge of chemical processes over the last fifty years our small Fatherland has taken a greater share than the rest of the world put together.'[38]

Justus Liebig, an academic scientist with laboratories at the University of Giessen, applied his chemical knowledge to produce plant fertilizers. He actually moved into business in order to make the products he had discovered, founding the Bayerische Aktiengesellschaft für Chemie und landwirtschaftliche chemische Fabrikate. There is no doubt that Liebig saw his activity as having not just scientific but also political and national significance. His own teacher, Karl Wilhelm Gottlob Kastner, had written in the immediate aftermath of the national political humiliation of 1815: 'Thus it is German to undertake science. Chemistry should serve the nation, just as conversely it is the mission of the nation and the state to promote chemistry.' Liebig himself saw how the application of chemical knowledge would raise agricultural productivity and thus reduce rural poverty, avoiding the revolutionary ferment that might otherwise rock the state. In 1844 he explained: 'Without a knowledge of chemistry the statesman will not appreciate the real life in the state in its organic development and perfection.'[39]

The chemist Emil Erlenmeyer founded his own factory even before he had finished his second doctorate (the so-called Habilitation). He experimented in lubricants, leather, food dyes, children's rusks and baking powder, and went on to be an academic adviser to the founders of BASF (the Baden Aniline and Soda Factory). August Kelkulé von Stradwitz developed through studying the benzene molecule a whole new science of inorganic chemistry. By 1890 there were twice as many academic scientists in Germany as in Britain, and they often worked directly with business. In the chemical industry, the number of employed rose from 47,000 in 1865 to 81,000 in 1880 and 290,000 on the eve of the First World War.[40] In dyestuffs in particular, the harnessing of academic science led to a virtual German world monopoly before the First World War. Although the crucial discovery for the commercial manufacture of aniline dyestuffs was that of a British chemist, William Perkin in 1856, by 1890 Germany produced six times as much dye as Britain, and by 1913 twenty-five times.[41]

Germany's businessmen quickly recognized the importance of academic scientific development. The founder of the electrical firm, Werner von Siemens, for instance sent his son Wilhelm to study physics at the University of Leipzig. He also set the pace in the foundation of a natural science research institute (Physikalisch-Technische Reichsanstalt, 1887), explaining that 'research in the natural sciences always forms the secure basis of technical development, and the industry of a country will never gain a leading position internationally and maintain it if the country does not at the same time stay in the lead in making advances in the natural sciences. Achieving this is the most effective way of promoting the industry'.[42]

To a substantial extent, however, this German triumph was not the result of the *deliberate* application of science to business problems. The expansion of German universities at the outset of the nineteenth century had begun with the humanistic reforms associated with the brief tenure of Wilhelm von Humboldt as Prussian Education Minister, and with his creations – the new university in Berlin and the Gymnasien. Humboldt's education ideal emphasized knowledge for the sake of knowledge – and not for any other purpose. It resembled closely the classical principles of the Victorian educational reformers in Britain. John Stuart Mill's Inaugural as Rector of St Andrew's took Humboldt's line in advocating the educational ideal of the civilized generalist: 'Universities are not intended to teach the knowledge required to fit men for a specific livelihood. Their object is not to make skilful lawyers and physicians or engineers, but capable and cultivated human beings'.[43] Exactly this approach was widely credited with having generated Germany's scientific superiority. The famous physicist and physiologist Hermann von Helmholtz wrote in this way about German advances:

Whilst in the investigation of inorganic nature the different nations of Europe progressed pretty evenly, the recent development of physiology and medicine belongs pre-eminently to Germany. The questions regarding the principle of life are closely allied to psychological and ethical questions. To start with, here also that untiring industry is required which applies itself to pure science for purely ideal purposes, without immediate prospects of practical usefulness. And indeed we may glory in the fact that in this German scholars have always distinguished themselves by their enthusiastic and self-renouncing diligence, which labours for inner satisfaction and not for outer success.[44]

The difference was simply that Germany concentrated her efforts on universities and not on 'public schools'. Germany achieved later a staggering supremacy not because she was looking for applicable results but because her scientists experimented widely without any end in mind, and then discovered that they could apply their new information. Already from the middle of the 1830s, long before economic historians find any traces of an industrial revolution or of a 'take-off into modern growth', Germans made more discoveries in the fields of energy, electricity, magnetism and optical research than did Frenchmen or Englishmen put together.

By the end of the nineteenth century, clouds began to appear on the German scientific horizon. Perhaps German science had been too successful for its own good, or had developed too much of an institutional momentum that would take it away from industry. From the beginning of the 1880s, the new and dynamic chemical industry criticized German chemical education for not providing enough general education in chemical principles, for being too remote from practical concerns, and for not instituting a common nation-wide examination system that might allow an easier guide to what chemistry graduates had really been taught at college. Like many British university scientists, German professors felt a temptation to retreat into a world of 'purer' research. At the same time, the statistician Wilhelm Lexis concluded that his survey of student numbers (in 1889) showed a 'dangerous excess of chemists' in relation to the number of positions available for them. While the initially harmonious marriage of business and university science was showing signs of strain, the Technische Hochschule failed to do its job: the chemist Carl Duisberg, who conducted a survey of industrial chemists in the 1890s, found that only 17 per cent had been trained in a Technische Hochschule.[45]

By the 1900s, the universities and the Technische Hochschulen had moved, like the rest of German society, into a fin-de-siècle crisis of confidence. German classicism now seemed a heavy burden. Even the young Kaiser Wilhelm II complained: 'We want to educate young national Germans, not young Greeks and Romans.' The great classical scholar Ulrich von Wilamowitz-Moellendorff paid a graceful tribute to the past successes of German academe: but these were victories that lay in the past. Expansion of Germany's universities had been part of her 'rise to world power, not only in the political realm but also through the undeniable achievements of German labour of hand and mind.' On the other hand, the universities were now blind to their own traditions, and were failing in their mission. They had come to ignore the true 'heroes in the peaceful struggle of modern life' – industrialists such as August Borsig or Alfred Krupp – and instead elevated an irresponsible and outdated aristocratic-feudal-military ideal: a model for social behaviour at least as hostile to commerce as the English gentlemanly code.[46]

The scientific community began to air its discontents. Industrial chemists complained of low pay: the first post as an industrial chemist was generally remunerated at 200 Marks annually (compared with a schoolteacher who might receive 300 M). And in the decade after the Technische Hochschulen were at last allowed to award doctorates, student numbers fell: a fall usually attributed to a general cultural disillusionment with science. 'This', one historian writes, 'would correspond with the extra-ordinary widespread impulses critical of contemporary civilization, which were partly responsible for the simultaneous great rise in the number of students in philology and history.'[47]

After the First World War, the same complaints continued: low pay, an excessive number of graduates, poor prospects and high unemployment levels for those with scientific and technical training. 3,000 engineers with diplomas and 10,000 less trained so-called 'graduate' engineers were looking for jobs in the 1920s.[48] The state's response both during the economic crisis at the end of the decade (during the world depression), and later, under the National Socialist dictatorship, was to cut student numbers in technical and scientific subjects drastically. The number of all university students also fell: measured as a proportion of the age group 18–25, university students were 1.15 per cent in 1932–3, and only 0.72 per cent by 1937–8. But the Technische Hochschule attendances plummeted even more dramatically than the general university population: here the number of students fell by half from the winter semester 1932–3 to the winter semester 1937–8.[49] The removal of Jewish professors and the simultaneous acute politicization of parts of science reduced the intellectual standing of the subject and also its attraction for potential students. By 1940 it had become clear that a generation of scientists had been lost; and in the immediate term that the new shortage damaged Germany's mobilization for war.

The recovery in prestige of technically trained personnel and the increasing numbers of students after the Second World War open a much happier chapter. In large part these developments represent a reaction to the scarcity caused by education policies in the Third Reich and to the opportunities created during the economic expansion of the 1950s *Wirtschaftswunder*.

The high post-war standing of the practical scientist and of the engineer derives from the volatile history of the past half century. It is probably not a reflection of long-term cultural preferences for engineering – as many British observers of Germany have supposed. Two management sociologists write that German salary relativities (with higher remuneration for engineers) are 'quite consistent with the proposition that the status of engineers is higher in Germany'. The important report of the committee under Sir Montague Finniston, 'Inquiry into the Engineering Profession', surmised that 'it is clear that, unlike their contemporaries in other industrial countries, engineers in Britain lack the special social standing which attracts young men to aspire to an engineering career … We formed the impression that engineering is regarded [in Germany] as an attractive career both in status and in tangible terms.'[50] This kind of argument reflects a certain naïvety. Pay is a reflection of a complex network of considerations: supply, demand, historical patterns of remuneration. In many cases (the most obvious are perhaps clergymen or university teachers) high social regard has meant that the available supply increases to such an extent as to drive down pay levels. The relatively high status of German engineers in the late nineteenth century corresponded to pay levels rather lower than those of teachers, and after the Second World War this pattern has been reversed. The reason lies in that shortage of skilled engineers arising from the legacy of the Third Reich's education policies, and in the increase in demand for engineers during the economic boom. The resulting high levels of remuneration were then built into the structure of German social expectations.

As the demand increased and as the conditions of work for engineers improved, the number of would-be entrants to the profession also rose. The number of students at the Technische Hochschulen increased continually after the War – though as a proportion of the total student population it fell. (See Table 1.)

Table 1: Percentage of West German university students at Technische Hochschulen (or Technische Universitäten):

	(winter semester)
1950/1	21.1
1955/6	24.3
1960/1	22.3
1965/6	20.4
1970/1	16.8
1976/7	15.9
1980/1	15.7

Source: calculated from *Statistisches Jahrbuch der Bundesrepublik Deutschland*, various issues.

In the late 1970s, German engineering graduates represented 2.3 per cent of their age group (as compared with 1.7 per cent in the UK or 1.6 per cent in the USA).[51]

The rise after the Second World War was characteristic of all European countries. The German figures can be put alongside those for Britain, where a general expansion of universities also accompanied a greater sensitivity to the needs of scientific education in modern society, the creation of new and more technically oriented universities, and expanding numbers studying applied sciences. (See Table 2.)

Table 2: Percentage of full-time British students in Applied Science:

1938/9	10.6
1949/50	12.8
1957/8	14.5
1966/7	20.6

Source: Sanderson, *Universities*, p. 352, p. 365.

The story of German technical education told here takes issue with the conventional interpretation as set out by Wiener that 'revivified public schools and ancient universities' 'set England apart from its emerging rivals, for in neither the United States nor Germany did the educational system encourage a comparable retreat from business and industry'.[52] Germany in the nineteenth century benefited economically as much from classical and humanistic educational principles as from a self-conscious and planned orientation to science. The classical model at first appeared successful. Then, between 1900 and 1945 Germany converged with the British pattern: the educational system was in crisis and increasingly distanced from industrial needs. That crisis was in Germany part of a larger social, economic and political deadlock: which led via anti-modern *ressentiments* to a destructive political system, a lost war, and a political reorganization. This then allowed after 1945 a more positive attitude to business in the educational system by way of a new reaction to what had gone before. Britain, which was not forced to undergo such a profound transformation, may have missed out on the radical shift in attitudes after the war, and out of the climate of reconstruction which encouraged social mobility and once again made the engineering profession highly lucrative and attractive.[53] But Britain too shared in the general European scientific and technological boom.

III

One of the clichés of the picture of an anti-business culture is that entrepreneurs were induced to defect from their proper vocation: they moved 'from shirt-sleeves to shirt-sleeves' or 'from clogs to clogs' in three generations. Corrupted by their desire for land and traditionally legitimated social status requiring conspicuous consumption, the sons of businessmen relapse into conventionality and complacency. The entrepreneurial candle flickers. For Germany, the literary monuments to this transition are particularly impressive. Thomas Mann in his great novel, *Buddenbrooks* (1901), depicts the 'decline of a family' and its turning away from business, and towards a world of ideal values. Erik Reger's fictional industrialist Felgenhauer explains entrepreneurial decline across generations: 'It is a peculiar phenomenon, that the riches of a parent limit the intellectual development of the offspring.'[54]

A German–British comparison once again shows more similarities than dissimilarities. Research on how business elites are recruited and on how wealth and status are passed from generation to generation – by Harold Perkin, Charlotte Erickson, Peter Payne, William Rubinstein or Roy Church for Britain and by Hartmut Kaelble, Toni Pierenkemper, Ottfried Daschker, Wilhelm Huschke and Hansjoachim Henning for Germany – yield comparable and rather similar pictures.[55] The result of more rigorous and quantified studies has been to show that the recruitment of businessmen – and indeed the whole pattern of social mobility during and after the industrial revolution – proceeded in Europe and North America much more homogeneously than those looking for national differences would like to admit.[56] During the early period of industrialization there were relatively few self-made men, and a great proportion of businessmen were sons of businessmen. Only in the twentieth century, in the aftermath of the 'managerial revolution' and the growth of professionalized and bureaucratized business structures, did recruitment become slightly more open. This massive and international research on social mobility has, surprisingly, been utterly ignored by the adherents of the thesis of culturally induced British decline.

The proportion of business leaders coming from a family tradition in the mid-nineteenth century appears remarkably similar across national frontiers: 60 per cent in the steel industry in Britain in 1865 (Erickson), 50 per cent in the hosiery industry in Britain in 1844 (Erickson), 62.5 per cent of all business leaders in Britain 1880–99 (Perkin), 66 per cent in the USA 1831–60

(Bendix and Howton), 54 per cent in Germany 1800–70 (Kaelble and others).[57]

Such figures at least seem to challenge any theories which seek to demonstrate a British peculiarity in entrepreneurial behaviour. The sense that manufacturing and commerce are ungentlemanly should affect the behaviour of businessmen, and especially of their children. If it were true that business was so unpopular that the children of successful entrepreneurs went via Oxbridge into the professions, we should expect a lower than average British figure. (Donald Coleman has acutely pointed out that if such a drainage did indeed occur, it might even have been economically beneficial, since the defection of business children might leave the way open to more brilliant outsiders: 'if successful businessmen, before and during the industrial revolution, had not been so anxious to attain a life of rural gentility might there not have ensued a much more rigid, inflexible, and unadventurous course of business enterprise than in fact there was?'[58]) But there was no such British peculiarity.

To an astonishing extent, then, business in Europe and North America ran in the family. Among Lancashire cotton manufacturers, families such as the Birleys, Fieldens or Parks went through many generations: 'the masters who led industry and society in Lancashire between 1830 and 1860 were already a substantially hereditary, increasingly well-educated body, supplemented less by self-made men than by the sons of the prosperous middle classes of rural and urban society'. Towns such as Ashton and Preston had a homegeneous wealthy mill-owning elite, whose members ('cotton lords' or 'millocrats') were proud of their hereditary position. William Gladstone noted that nepotism, far from being an exclusively aristocratic vice, characterized all classes of society.[59]

The pioneering role played by cotton in Britain in generating a new group with its own values was taken in Germany by iron and coal, which experienced a remarkable surge of production in the mid-nineteenth century. Henning's work covers the industrial region of Westphalia, the centre of major iron and steel and brewing industries.[60] Big businessmen can be relatively easily isolated in the state of Prussia by identifying those with the honorific title Kommerzienrat (Commercial Councillor). From 1865 the government applied a pecuniary eligibility test in granting these titles: a freely available capital of 750,000 M (£37,000), which after 1892 became a million Marks or £49,000. In the period covered by Henning's analysis (1860–1909) Westphalian business was overwhelmingly self-recruiting. Eighty per cent of businessmen stood in a family tradition. First sons generally followed their fathers into trade, while it was second sons who went on the professional path.

This well established pattern changed only slightly over time. Henning notes that after the dramatic stock exchange crash and business recession of 1873 (the *Gründerkrach*) for a brief while self-confidence ebbed: and some first sons at this time even took the more secure professional career of the civil servant. After 1890 the size of business units increased, and owner entrepreneurs gave way to professional managers. A substantial group of managers came, however, from a background of owner-entrepreneurs: the dynasties of Mummendorff, Meininghaus or Delius. Within the managerial elites, new dynasties began to emerge as well: Dresler, Baare, Brügermann, Springorum or later, in the Rhineland, Reusch.

The longevity of some German steel dynasties is nothing short of amazing: the venerable Krupps, who began with Friedrich Krupp (1787–1826) looked recent compared with the Hoeschs. From 1637 the Hoesch family had been engaged in metal industry in the Eifel; at the beginning of the nineteenth century Eberhard Hoesch introduced English puddling techniques; the Eisen- und Stahlwerk Hoesch AG was still essentially a family firm in the inter-war period.[61]

Other examples of how the conduct of industry remained in the nineteenth century a family concern are the South German engineering dynasty of Buz of MAN, or the beer-brewing clans of Breys and Pschorrs in Munich. In highly modern industries the same family proclivities prevailed: notably in the electro-technical industry. The Siemens family exercised a substantial control of their firm into the twentieth century. Indeed the notion of family lay at the centre of the firm's strategic calculations. The original firm was founded in 1847 by Werner Siemens, and by the 1850s it worked together with branches run by brothers in London and St Petersburg. Werner (later ennobled and von) Siemens insisted on the family basis for his plans. In 1887 he wrote in a letter: 'From my early youth, I was enthusiastic about founding a worldwide business à la Fugger, which would give power and reputation not only to me but also to my descendants, and which would provide the means to raise also my brothers and sisters and other near relatives on to higher standards of life.'[62]

Banking had its own dynastic structure, and its own regional traditions. Some houses were already associated with industrial development in the eighteenth century, such as Süsskind or Schaezler in Augsburg. Others, notably the great Berlin merchant houses (which were usually Jewish) restricted themselves to a more narrowly defined banking business: such was the house of Mendelssohn, descended from Joseph, who in 1795 as a young man set up his own bank.[63]

These dynasties formed self-enclosed and narrow patrician elites. The richest Berlin families realized themselves to be an isolated 'aristocracy of money' (*Geldaristokratie*).[64] Commentators frequently noted how such a group imitated the aristocracy in creating their own code, without much contact with the real aristocracy. Intermarriage, for instance, was rare, even for the Berlin oligarchies – much rarer, at any rate, than in the fictional depictions where the Jewish bankers' daughter became a well-known stereotype whose dowry was needed to rescue impoverished noble houses. To a lesser extent than in Britain or the USA German businessmen came from a rural large land-owning background:[65] in this sense the German elite was more self-contained, and more consciously bourgeois.

Neither in Britain, according to Lawrence and Jeanne Stone,[66] nor in Germany did industrialists match up to the stereotype of moving out of business and into landed idleness once some measure of business success had been achieved. Where land purchases did occur, there often was a quite rational purpose connected with the immediate goal of business activity: the ownership of land or of an entail (*Fideikommiss*) represented the best way of assuring the continuity of family property and with this the dedication of the family to its original business task, and not to an apeing of the nobility. Such a technique, for instance, was used by the largest Bavarian engineer, Theodor von Cramer-Klett in 1877 to preserve all his diverse properties as a single enterprise.[67] A substantial amount of bourgeois purchase of land in the nineteenth century can thus be interpreted as an attempt to cement the bourgeois dynasty, and as demonstrations of how business had become a family affair.

Here was a 'new social elite', which could only 'achieve and retain significance if it assumed the same forms as the previous power elite, but at the same time distinctly preserving its social independence' in a 'socially exclusive position between the social groups'.[68] Such commercial 'aristocracies' took over quite successfully in the life of the Rhineland, or Berlin, or Munich; and had always been socially pre-eminent in the Hanseatic cities of the north. There are parallels to the role of, for instance, the Coats cotton dynasty in Glasgow, or the Earles of Liverpool.

Family businesses continue to play a major role in German economic life. A highly critical commentator noted that in 1969, of the 150 largest German firms, 60 were in the hands of a family or a single entrepreneur. Most of these were old-established names: in 1969, Siemens occupied place 3 in the rank order, the Thyssens 4, the Flicks (Daimler-Benz) 5. Only a very few of these large family firms were the creation of a 'new' entrepreneur (and those that were generally lay in retailing, not in production: Gustav Schickedanz's Quelle and Helmut Horten's firm are department stores, Werner Otto a mail order business).[69] Though the development of the previously rather sluggish stock market has encouraged sell-offs and take-overs, and by 1989 many of these 1969 family firms have ceased to be family controlled, the longevity of family traditions of doing business in Germany is still remarkable.

Was clannishness and the family firm dysfunctional? Such a case has frequently been made for England and France: small businesses, fearful of losing their independence, avoided borrowing from banks and thus frequently consciously limited their expansion. In consequence, they eked out a humble existence on the margin. Their ability to exit from and then to re-enter the market prevented other firms investing in significant and costly improvements, and thus placed a burden on the whole economy. In Britain, the industrial structure, and in particular the family firm, thus prevented the adoption of new techniques: such as ring-spinning in the case of cotton. 'Vested interests in the old structures,' conclude Elbaum and Lazonick, 'proved to be formidable obstacles to the transition from competitive to corporative modes of organization'. In this picture, the institutional legacy of firm size plays the part of villain in the British economic process. Reduced to its simplest level, this case claims that businessmen so liked their own culture that they were intent on staying within it, even at a price to themselves and to society in general.[70]

In Germany there are instances in which family considerations restricted growth: Siemens's failure in the 1880s to take up the challenge thrown down by the newer AEG; or Krupp's unwillingness to join the steel trust Vereinigte Stahlwerke in the 1920s. In the end, however, most family firms adapted successfully. Siemens's family control actually facilitated the establishment of a new and very flexible and advanced decentralized control system in the 1900s.[71] When the firm could or would not adapt, it sold out – as did Cramer-Klett in 1920, or Flick, who owned Daimler-Benz until 1986. In most instances, the advantages of a long-term strategic calculation that sprang from the family view outweighed those disadvantages associated with a wish to retain independence.

When looking at the emergence of the German (or English or Scottish) commercial and industrial dynasties, and the creation of what might be called commercial pseudo-aristocracies, we find that the national unit is not an appropriate unit for historical analysis of this sort. For Britain, Rubinstein and many others have pointed out the social chasm that existed between the City and the manufacturing centres of the Midlands, the North, and Scotland. Anthony Howe describes a quite discrete business elite forming in South Lancashire. Joseph Chamberlain's Birmingham or Sir William Bower Forwood's Liverpool had an assertively proud and self-consciously mercantile culture which ignored the metropolis and Oxbridge (Forwood's father for instance told him not to go to Cambridge since a 'university training would spoil me for a business career').[72] The Rhineland entrepreneurs had their own separate and highly prestigious social life and institutions: the Düsseldorf Industrieklub, or the professional interest associations such as the League of German Steel Industrialists and the Society for the Preservation of the Interests of Rhineland-Westphalia. But the men who lived in this world did not feel a need to mingle with the agrarian aristocracy of Germany east of the River Elbe. Though some Rhineland businessmen played a substantial role in national politics already from the 1870s, and some London bankers stayed in close touch with Whitehall, on the whole the local and provincial business notables limited their influence to their trade and their locality. In their own cities and provinces they formed an elite of such high distinction and status that there was neither a need nor a wish to escape from it.

The managerial revolution after the turn of the century and the numerical expansion of the business elite in the twentieth century made German recruitment a more open process: as was the case in Britain or France or the USA. By the mid-1960s only 21 per cent (Zapf) or 36 per cent (Pross and Boetticher) of leading businessmen were from a business family (Zapf's figures refer to board members from the fifty largest firms, Pross and Boetticher's to board members, directors and those immediately below the directorial level in thirteen large companies).[73] The business elite still came, however, from a largely upper class background.[74]

Comparative analysis of the social origins of entrepreneurs deflates many myths: in particular it undermines the Schumpeterian picture of the heroic entrepreneur rising from a lowly social position by dint of a forceful personality and innovative ideas. Doubtless such Schumpeterian figures existed, but they were exceptional. It also shows how business leaders emerge out of quite specific local and regional environments long dedicated to the culture of business, and not out of a generalized 'national culture'. Such environments are not restricted to one political unit, but appear quite widely across northern and western Europe and in North America.

IV

The comparison of literary attitudes to business, of educational structures, and of business careers suggests considerable similarities in the patterns of British and German development rather than marked differences. Perhaps looking at national cultural differences cannot help historians concerned with characterizing the beliefs and conventions of commercial and industrial communities. Instead they should look on the one hand at smaller units: regions or cities, Glasgow and Manchester and Berlin and the Ruhr rather than Britain and Germany. On the other hand, certain features are present over wide areas, and we should examine European and Atlantic patterns. Industrialization and the reactions to it were international phenomena, not ones limited to a particular national sphere. The 'industrial revolution' was not limited to one country, and elements common to European culture and to the political structure of the European state system facilitated its rapid spread.

Whatever it was on which the new industrialism rested, it was rarely widespread social approval. If we take evidence such as that presented in this essay, it should be clear that business activity, and profit seeking, were rarely viewed from the outside with approbation. It would be surprising if they were, and if the spectacular enrichment of individuals and families did not provoke widespread resentment, or feelings that the system operated unfairly. Such sentiments made anti-capitalism an attractive option to political actors – and as democracy was extended one that would catch votes. The political impulse to attack business, to carry out a new version of the venerable medieval and early modern practice of states in 'making the financiers disgorge', is counterbalanced in recent centuries by an opposite impulse. States saw in business activity a resource that increased their military and diplomatic power. The fact that there were many states in the European system – rather than, say, one single empire – limited the extent to which individual governments could mistreat their subjects. Ill-handled businessmen and persecuted bourgeois could simply pack up their bags and leave: if they had no political 'voice' they could still affect events by their capacity to 'exit' from the state (to use Albert Hirschman's terminology).[75] Such exit would weaken the political system that had engaged on the course of sympathetic response to anti-capitalist sentiment.

In the light of considerations such as these, it should be evident that it is misleading to attribute relatively small differences in growth rates to national cultural attitudes: over the period 1870–1913, for instance, Britain grew less quickly than did Germany, but the difference on Angus Maddison's calculation is less than 1 per cent. In the late twentieth century, as an explanation of slower growth Martin Wiener's book *English Culture and the Decline of the Industrial Spirit* was out of date as soon as it was published in 1981. If we take as a guide to economic performance data on annual growth of total factor productivity (TFP), until circa 1980 the data does indeed look depressing. For 1961–73 the British figure is 2.1% (Germany 2.8%); and for 1973–79 0.3% and 1.8% respectively. That there was a malaise in Britain in the 1970s was, and is, scarcely doubted by any observer: and the 'cultural induced decline' school seemed at the time to offer a powerful explanation of the British sickness. But for the 1980s, British TFP growth is above that of Germany (1.0% as against 0.8%);[76] and diagnoses of economic problems of the later 1980s set the issue more as a general European and North American one in the face of East Asian competition.

'Eurosclerosis' has replaced the 'British sickness' as a fashionable theme for commentators.

The cultural attitudes that induced growth were always, and still are, common European properties; what differed can be better accounted for in strictly economic terms: different sizes of market, or endowments of factors (labour, capital, land), or different impacts of government policy. To use the cultural explanation is to take an instrument that is capable of generating explanations for very large-scale phenomena (such as the emergence of industrialization in Europe), but is less readily applicable to smaller scale differences in performance. Such accounts as those of Barnett or Wiener run the danger of using explanatory sledgehammers to crack rather modest nuts.

NOTES

I should like to thank Knut Borchardt, Diane Kunz and Peter Mandler for their helpful suggestions and comments on this paper.

1. For these terms, see the recent book by S. Newton and D. Porter, *Modernization frustrated: The Politics of Industrial Decline since 1900* (London: Unwin Hyman, 1988).
2. C. Barnett, *The Collapse of British Power* (London: Sutton, 1972), p. 90, 94.
3. M. J. Wiener, *English Culture and the Decline of the Industrial Spirit 1850–1980* (Cambridge: CUP, 1981), p. 7.
4. T. Nairn, 'The Future of Britain's Crises: A political Analysis', in (ed.) I. Kramnick, *Is Britain Dying? Perspectives on the Current Crisis* (Ithaca, New York, 1979), p. 236; also P. Anderson, 'The Figures of Descent', *New Left Review*, 161, (1987).
5. See the letter of George Courtauld of 1856 quoted in D. C. Coleman, 'Gentlemen and Players', *Economic History Review*, 2nd series, XXVI (1973), p. 107: 'I have had some little experience now, and my feeling is very strongly that, for the great majority of young men in our position in life, a college course is not fit preparation for business life.'
6. H. J. Laski, *The Danger of Being a Gentleman and Other Essays* (New York, 1940), p. 24.
7. (My emphasis) N. McKendrick, ' "Gentlemen and Players" Revisited: the gentlemanly ideal, the business ideal and the professional ideal in English literary culture', in N. McKendrick and R. B. Outhwaite, *Business Life and Public Policy: Essays in Honour of D. C. Coleman* (Cambridge: CUP, 1986), p. 98.
8. D. N. McCloskey, *Economic Maturity and Entrepreneurial Decline: British Iron and Steel 1870–1913* (Cambridge, Mass.; Harvard UP, 1973); L. Sandberg, *Lancashire in Decline* (Columbus; Ohio State UP, 1974).

9. U. Wengenroth, *Unternehmensstrategien und technischer Fortschritt: Die deutsche und die britische Stahlindustrie 1865–1895* (Göttingen, Zürich, 1986).
10. E. E. Williams, *Made in Germany*, quotes from p. 11, p. 69, p. 163.
11. Nairn, 'Britain's Crises', pp. 237–8. J. B. Priestley quoted in Wiener, *English Culture*, p. 166.
12. J. Rheuban (ed.), *The Marriage of Maria Braun. Rainer Werner Fassbinder Director* (New Brunswick: New Jersey, 1986), p. 110.
13. J. Winter, 'Bernard Shaw, Berthold Brecht and the businessman in literature', in McKendrick and Outhwaite (eds.), *Business Life*, p. 187.
14. See McKendrick, '"Gentlemen and Players" Revisited', p. 113.
15. McKendrick, '"Gentlemen and Players" Revisited', pp. 126–7.
16. G. Milkereit, *Das Unternehmerbild im zeitkritischen Roman des Vormärz* (Cologne, 1970), p. 5.
17. K. Bullivant and H. Ridley, *Industrie und deutsche Literatur 1830–1914* (Munich, 1976), p. 57.
18. This is the point made for the Wilhelmine era and for the inter-war years by H.-W. Niemann, *Das Bild des industriellen Unternehmers in Deutschen Romanen der Jahre 1890 bis 1945*, (Berlin, 1982).
19. H. Mayne (ed.), *Immermanns Werke*, Leipzig and Vienna, Vol. 3, *Die Epigonen*, p. 257.
20. G. Milkereit, *Das Unternehmerbild*, p. 28.
21. B. Hildebrand (ed. H. Gehrig), *Die Nationalökonomie der Gegenwart und Zukunft*, (Jena, 1922), p. 187.
22. G. Freytag, *Soll und Haben* (Leipzig, 1891), quotations from p. 377, p. 150, pp. 560–1. For an analysis, see P. Jackson, *Bürgerliche Arbeit und Romanwirklichkeit: Studien zur Berufsproblematik in Romane des deutschen Realismus* (Frankfurt, 1981).
23. See E. K. Bramsted, *Aristocracy and the Middle Classes in Germany: Social Types in German Literature 1830–1900*, (Chicago: UCP, 1964) (first published 1937).
24. Spielhagen, *Sturmflut* (1877), Vol. II, p. 157.
25. Lasker in *Verhandlungen des Preussischen Landtages, Haus der Abgeordneten*, 1872/3 II, 2, 945.
26. Alfred Döblin, *Wadzaks Kampf mit der Dampfturbine* (Olten and Freiburg, 1982), p. 172.
27. Erik Reger, *Union der festen Hand: Roman einer Entwicklung* (Berlin, 1931), pp. 100–1.
28. Nairn, 'Britain's Crises', p. 245.
29. McKendrick, '"Gentlemen and Players" Revisited', pp. 126–7.
30. K. Borchardt, review of D. C. Coleman, *History and the Economic Past*, in *Vierteljahrschrift für Sozial- und Wirtschaftsgeschichte* 75 (1988), p. 276.
31. For English stereotypes about financial speculation, see J. R. Reed, *Victorian Conventions* (Columbus, Ohio, 1975), pp. 172–92, and S. R. Letwin, *The Gentleman in Trollope: Individuality and Moral Conduct* (London: Macmillan, 1982), pp. 247–69.
32. O. Wiedfeldt, *Statistische Studien zur Entwicklungsgeschichte der*

Berliner Industrie von 1720 bis 1890 (Berlin, 1898), p. 79; L. Baar, *Die Berliner Industrie in der industriellen Revolution* (Berlin [East], 1966), p. 141; T. Pierenkemper, 'Entrepreneurs in Heavy Industry: Upper Silesia and the Westphalian Ruhr Region 1852–1913', *Business History Review*, LIII, 1975, p. 71.

33. E. N. Gummer, *Dickens's Works in Germany 1837–1937* (Oxford, 1940), p. 45, p. 57.

34. P. W. Musgrave, *Technical Change, the Labour Force and Education* (Oxford: OUP, 1967), p. 50; Williams, *Made in Germany*, pp. 151–2; also M. Sanderson, *Education, Economic Change and Society in England 1780–1870* (London: Macmillan, 1983). Most recently, J.Wrigley, 'Technical Education and Industry in the Nineteenth Century', in B. Elbaum and W. Lazonick (eds.), *The Decline of the British Economy* (Oxford: OUP, 1986), pp. 162–88.

35. M. Sanderson, *The Universities and British Industry 1850–1970* (London, 1972), p. 3, p. 82.

36. K.-H. Ludwig, *Technik und Ingenieure im Dritten Reich* (Düsseldorf, 1974), p. 24, p. 45.

37. F. Schnabel, *Deutsche Geschichte im Neunzehnten Jahrhundert III: Erfahrungswissenschaften und Technik*, p. 317.

38. L. Burchardt, 'Die Ausbildung des Chemikers im Kaiserreich', *Zeitschrift für Unternehmensgeschichte* 23, 1978, p. 32; E. Schmauderer (ed.), *Der Chemiker im Wandel der Zeiten: Skizzen zur geschichtlichen Entwicklung des Berufsbildes* (Weinheim/Bergstrasse, 1973), p. 259.

39. Schmauderer, *Der Chemiker*, p. 262, p. 264.

40. Burchardt, 'Ausbildung des Chemikers', p. 33.

41. Wrigley, 'Technical Education', p. 170; also H. W. Richardson, 'Chemicals' in D. H. Aldcroft (ed.), *The Development of British Industry and Foreign Competition 1875–1914: Studies in Industrial Enterprise* (London, 1968), pp. 110–11.

42. S. v. Weiher, H. Goetzeler, *The Siemens Company: Its Historical Role in the Process of Electrical Engineering* (Berlin, 1977), p. 44.

43. Sanderson, *Universities*, p. 5.

44. J. T. Merz, *A History of European Thought in the Nineteenth Century* (Edinburgh and London, 1907) (3rd edition), pp. 210–11.

45. Burchardt, 'Ausbildung des Chemikers', pp. 35–9; K. Jarausch, *Students, Society and Politics in Imperial Germany: The Rise of Academic Illiberalism* (Princeton: PUP, 1982), p. 57.

46. Jarausch, *Students, Society and Politics*, p. 49, p. 185.

47. Schmauderer, *Der Chemiker*, p. 302; Burchardt, 'Ausbildung des Chemikers', p. 35. On the rise of pessimism and anti-modernism, the classic text is F. Stern, *The Politics of Cultural Despair: A Study in the Rise of Germanic Ideology* (Berkeley: University of California Press, 1961).

48. Ludwig, *Technik und Ingenieure*, p. 24.

49. Ludwig, *Technik und Ingenieure*, pp. 273–5, p. 291.

50. S. Hutton and P. Lawrence, *German Engineers: The Anatomy of a Profession* (Oxford: OUP, 1981).

51. P. Lawrence, *Managers and Management in West Germany* (London: Croom Helm, 1980), p. 164.
52. Wiener, *English Culture*, p. 24.
53. See the case argued by C. Barnett, *The Audit of War: The Illusion and Reality of Britain as a Great Nation* (London: Macmillan, 1986).
54. Reger, *Union*, p. 226.
55. H. Perkin, 'The Recruitment of Elites in British Society since 1800', *Journal of Social History*, 12, 1978, pp. 222–34; C. Erickson, *British Industrialists: Steel and Hosiery 1850–1950* (Cambridge: CUP, 1959); P. Payne, 'The Emergence of the Large-scale Company in Great Britain 1870–1914', *Economic History Review*, 2nd Ser. XX, (1967), pp. 519–42; W. D. Rubinstein, *Men of Property: The Very Wealthy in Britain since the Industrial Revolution* (London: Croom Helm, 1981); R. Church, *The History of the British Coal Industry III: 1830–1913: Victorian Pre-eminence* (Oxford: OUP, 1986); H. Kaelble, *Berliner Unternehmer während der frühen Industrialisierung*, Berlin (New York, 1972); T. Pierenkemper, *Die westfälischen Schwerindustriellen 1852–1913* (Göttingen, 1979); O. Daschke, *Das Textilgewerbe in Hessen-Kassel vom 16. bis 19. Jahrhundert* (Marburg, 1968); W. Huschke, *Forschungen über die Herkunft der thüringschen Unternehmerschaft des 19. Jahrhunderts* (Würzburg, 1974); H. Henning, 'Soziale Verflechtungen der Unternehmer in Westfalen 1860–1914', in *Zeitschrift für Unternehmensgeschichte*, pp. 23, 1978, 1–30. For the USA, R. Bendix and F. W. Howton, 'Social Mobility and the American Business Elite', in S. M. Lipset and R. Bendix (eds.), *Social Mobility in Industrial Society* (Berkeley: University of California Press, 1959), pp. 114–43.
56. See esp. H. Kaelble, *Social Mobility in the 19th and 20th Centuries: Europe and America in Comparative Perspective* (Leamington Spa: Berg Publrs., Heidelberg, Dover N. H., 1985).
57. See table in Kaelble, *Social Mobility*, pp. 109–10.
58. Coleman, '"Gentlemen and Players"', p. 111.
59. A. Howe, *The Cotton Masters 1830–1860* (Oxford: OUP, 1984), p. 89; Gladstone quoted in O. Anderson, *A Liberal State at War* (London, 1967), p. 120.
60. H. Henning, 'Soziale Verflechtungen'.
61. See *Rheinisch-Westphälische Wirtschafts-Biographien* II (1937), pp. 277–8.
62. J. Kocka, 'Family and Bureaucracy in German Industrial Management 1850–1914: Siemens in Comparative Perspective', *Business History Review*, XLV, 1971, pp. 137–8.
63. On the Berlin Jewish banking elite, see W. E. Mosse, *Jews in the German Economy: The German-Jewish Economic Elite 1820–1935* (Oxford: OUP, 1987).
64. See H. Kaelble, *Berliner Unternehmer*.
65. Kaelble, *Social Mobility*, pp. 99–100.
66. L. Stone and J. C. F. Stone, *An Open Elite? England 1540–1880* (Oxford: OUP, 1986), p. 283: 'The real story of the English elite

is not the symbiosis of land and business, but of land and the professions, just as in the rest of Europe.'

67. J. Biensfeldt, *Freiherr Dr von Cramer-Klett, erblicher Reichsrat der Krone Bayern: Sein Leben und sein Werk: Ein Beitrag zur bayerischen Wirtschaftsgeschichte des 19. Jahrhunderts*, Leipzig/Erlangen n.d. Also W. Zorn, *Handels-und Industriegeschichte Bayerisch-Schwabens 1648–1870: Wirtschafts-, Sozial- und Kulturgeschichte des schwäbischen Unternehmertums* (Augsburg 1961).

68. Quotations from Henning, 'Soziale Verflechtungen', p. 15, p. 19, p. 30.

69. M. Jungblut, *Die Reichen und die Superreichen in Deutschland* (Hamburg, 1971), pp. 128–34.

70. See D. S. Landes, 'French entrepreneurship and industrial growth in the nineteenth century', *Journal of Economic History*, 9 (1949), pp. 45–61. Also D. S. Landes, *The Unbound Prometheus: Technological Change and Industrial Development in Western Europe from 1750 to the Present* (Cambridge: CUP, 1969), p.349. For the example of dysfunctional family firms in the British coal industry, see B. Supple, *The History of the British Coal Industry IV: 1913–1946: The Political Economy of Decline* (Oxford: OUP, 1987), esp. Ch. IX. On Britain, L. Hannah, *The Rise of the Corporate Economy: The British Experience* (London: Methuen, 1983); W. Lazonick, 'Industrial Organization and Technological Change: The Decline of the British Cotton Industry', *Business History Review* 57, 1983, pp. 195–236; B. Elbaum and W. Lazonick, 'An Institutional Perspective on British Decline', in Elbaum and Lazonick, *Decline*, p. 5.

71. See Kocka, 'Family and Bureaucracy'.

72. Howe, *Cotton Masters*, p. 311: 'However, far from being the "self-made men" of Smilesian mythology, the textile elite were by 1830 already a strongly hereditary group.' P. J. Waller, *Democracy and Sectarianism: A Political and Social History of Liverpool 1868–1939* (Liverpool: Liverpool UP, 1981), p. 275.

73. H. Kaelble, *Historical Research on Social Mobility: Western Europe and the USA in the 19th and 20th Centuries* (London: Croom Helm, 1981), p. 89.

74. See for instance the survey by D. Hall, H. C. de Bettignie and G. Amado Fischgrund in *European Business* 1969 quoted in Lawrence, *Managers and Management*, p. 57.

75. A. O. Hirschman, *Exit, Voice and Loyalty* (Cambridge, Mass., 1970). See also the arguments expounded in E. L. Jones, *The European Miracle: Environments, Economics and Geopolitics in the History of Europe and Asia*, 2nd ed. (Cambridge: CUP, 1987).

76. OECD, *Economic Outlook*, 42, December 1987, p. 41. On growth rates, A. Maddison, *Phases of Capitalist Development* (Oxford: OUP, 1982), p. 45.

Bruce Collins

American Enterprise and the British Comparison

As the preceding chapters make plain, cultural explanations of British decline have raised far more doubts than they have gained academic endorsement. Historians find them vague; economists dismiss them. Searching through the record of the past century or so leads to three possible avenues of more fruitful inquiry: changes in factor endowment, policy choices, and institutional constraints. If one looks at the British mix of the factors of production – in men, money and materials – then relative decline especially since 1945 could be attributed to a failure to raise or invest enough capital, or to the absence of any opportunity in Britain, compared certainly with Germany or Japan, to gain from a shift in the labour force from agriculture to industry and services. Britain had long before made that transition in employment and thereby reaped productivity gains. In some ways, too, the historically low price of many raw materials in the 1950s and 1960s eased the problems of those countries starting up with a poor mix of natural resources. The rise of various synthetics and the decline of steel also reduced the importance of possessing some traditionally vital raw materials. It is not accidental that the most painful of transitions in the post-war British economy came in the reduction of the large labour-forces in coal and steel.

Yet if changing patterns of factor endowment might help to explain, say, France's and Japan's relative advance since the

1940s, they do not necessarily help to explain Britain's relative decline. Nor do they explain why many Americans fear that their economy is beginning to follow a British route to the second division of world economic powers. Here the role of policy choices becomes prominent. For Britain it has been said that the failure to introduce protective tariffs before the First World War weakened British industry against American and German competition. Others might argue that expenditures on the armed services, on empire in the 1950s, on sustaining a world role in the 1960s frittered away government revenues that might have been more fruitfully applied to non-military technological research and to education. Yet others might point to a failure of central industrial planning or to mistaken exchange-rate policies as contributing to Britain's slide in the league-table of industrial nations. So, too, in recent years the policy choices of American governments have been much criticized on very similar specifics – the lack of tariff protection against Japanese consumer goods; the distorting effect of sustaining a world military and political role; the lack of any federal government strategy for industrial growth or civilian technological innovation. Added to these in the 1970s and 1980s was the monetarist critique that the commitment of increasingly large federal spending to welfare and social security, and then the existence of a substantial federal budget deficit, distorted market forces and dragged down the economy's rate of growth.

One problem in assessing the impact of policy choices is that the policies can be self-cancelling. Country A may pursue an inappropriate exchange-rate policy over the short-run only to be followed by a spell of years when competing country B gets its intervention in money markets and interest-rate policy 'wrong'. Similarly, the monetarist critique of American and British social welfare spending is usually answered by an indication that, say, Germany and Sweden devote comparable levels of their government spending to such matters. Moreover, statistical studies over the long-run typically fail to detect one particular wrong turning that led to relative decline. It is like asking whether the battle of Stalingrad and the Normandy landings defeated Nazi Germany, or whether the whole character of Hitler's military system and political ambitions led to ultimate disaster.

For this reason, economic historians and economists have increasingly inclined to an institutional explanation of economic performance. By institutional, they mean the whole mix of corporate structure, codes and regulations shaping market activities, and the ways both government and non-government bodies adapt to or promote economic change. Professor R.C.O.Matthews, in his presidential address of 1986 to the Royal Economic Society, criticized British neo-classical economists of the first half of the twentieth century for concentrating on the behaviour of economic man within 'a given institutional structure.' Yet he emphasized the formidable difficulties of measuring the impact of institutional change, once one allows for the complexity of institutions and the people in them. Peter Payne's chapter concludes that the study of the firm yields little evidence of systematic managerial incompetence; yet the larger institutional context may have inhibited growth. Professor N.F.R.Crafts, after surveying the historical literature, points out that 'institutional difficulties associated with education, research and development and restrictive practices ... show up prominently in international productivity comparisons as reasons for poor British performance.' Careful statistical studies of Britain's productivity highlight weaknesses in management and technical education and the diffusion of skills in the work-force.[1] It could be argued that such defects partly reflect cultural assumptions and attitudes and that economic historians' suspicions of any cultural explanation of decline may postulate too sharp a division between beliefs and institutions. But the important conclusion is that British failures in economic performance have been linked to defects in managerial and technical skills and to organizational arrangements within manufacturing industry. And the focus on institutional shortcomings may offer some chance for economists, economic historians, and social, intellectual and political historians – all with their own perspectives and blind-spots – to meet occasionally on common ground.

Given this interest in institutional factors, the following chapter explores various aspects of the American enterprise system to suggest ways in which institutional arrangements, influenced by political ideology and cultural assumptions, differed from those prevailing in Britain and may have contributed to more sustained economic growth than Britain has achieved. There is a danger in employing the term 'enterprise culture' because it is invoked in particularly loaded ways by the government headed by Mrs Thatcher.[2] British academics find the term vague and offensive, and feel it absurd that businessmen need to be puffed so profusely in public. This response has its ironies for British academics bewail the low status they are accorded in the 1980s and speak of a growing exodus of university professors to more lucrative posts and a more supportive atmosphere in the USA; the climate of opinion and acknowledgement of status do, then, bear upon their morale and performance, while they deny that such 'vague' factors earlier depressed businessmen's effectiveness.

The preceding chapters make it clear that a specifically cultural explanation of relative economic performance is fraught with conceptual, comparative and definitional difficulties. One can, however, build upon that debate rather than simply close it. The American experience shows that institutional arrangements, themselves shaped by political and cultural values, have indeed fostered American productivity and even resilience in the face of recent competitive challenges. But before exploring the enterprise system, it is necessary to see whether America has faced the same long-term decline in productivity and competitiveness as Britain has suffered since 1945. The view advanced here is that Britain has suffered a measurable relative decline, certainly since 1945, and that British economic performance is related to various broadly institutional rigidities or shortcomings, and that one may grasp those more readily by considering some prominent facets of the American system of enterprise.

I

Comparative decline enjoyed a certain vogue during the 1980s. A work commemorating the 75th birthday of the Harvard Business School's founding ruminated:

Starkly put, the question is whether the United States is in the early stages of a decline similar to the United Kingdom's which, over the last century, led ultimately to a reduction in its political and military role and more recently to a loss of capacity to achieve a rising standard of living.[3]

The years of American inflation, recession, uncertainty and overseas challenge after 1973 provoked various soul-searchings about industrial decline. There were almost as many explanations of relative decline and its reversibility as there were commentators on the subject. Milton Friedman wanted to halt government interference and to reshape the system of values and morals in which Americans worked.[4] More centrist interpretations argued that modest policy adjustments could re-fuel American exporting strength and shift the terms of trade.[5] A third broad response urged more sweeping federal government activism – be it in incomes and investment policy (as W.W. Rostow contended) or in comprehensive economic planning (as the Harvard Business School study recommended).[6] Marxian vultures had hovered over the staggering American economic giant of the mid-1970s eagerly anticipating its exhaustion, collapse, and decay.[7] Assessing such interpretations and determining whether America's economy is indeed declining along British lines should preface any consideration of America's enterprise system.

Milton Friedman certainly sees Americans losing their enterprise values. Entrepreneurial energy which infused nineteenth-century growth has been sapped by government bureaucracies which, apart from being incapable of developing economies, have misdirected tax revenues into wasteful defence and social welfare spending. Since 1945, according to Friedman, Britain pursued equality through redistribution. British bureaucracies became entrenched, immune in their personal pay and pensions and in their public importance to the corrosive financial and unemployment effects of inflation; trade unions became over-powerful; businessmen succeeded only by manipulating the law and government; productivity and efficiency fell and with them economic growth also lagged; a brain drain of talented professionals was the outward and visible sign of this failure. For Friedman, America followed a similar path leading to a profound crisis of values, politics and national will. Martin Wiener's emphasis on cultural assumptions found an echo in Friedman's claim that America's intellectual elite had, since the New Deal, deplored or denigrated business practices and concentrated on wealth distribution instead of wealth creation.[8]

The idea that America was following Britain's sorry example did not attract wide support. Numerous economic studies produced in the 1980s dismissed the British analogy as inappropriate. Robert Lawrence argued in 1984 that the performance of US manufacturing output during the crises of 1973–82 followed historical precedents of cyclical behaviour. Recovery would follow and America's relative share of manufacturing output among the developed countries would be sustained if government deficits were bridled and the exchange rate improved. W.W. Rostow, who did draw close comparisons with Britain, saw the decline as temporary, part of very long-run cycles of economic development, and reversible for both Britain and America. Edward F. Denison, one of the most thorough scholars in analysing economic growth, found no single cause of decline in the mid-1970s. He conceded that there may have been a convergence of developments leading to a slowing of the rate of technological innovation. But falling growth rates affected all leading industrial countries. High inflation, government regulation, rising energy prices, steep taxes, and changing attitudes may have contributed to reduce output. Denison, whose earlier work had emphasized the importance of education and of applying new knowledge to technology, did not detect any fall in research and development during the mid-1970s, and, implicitly, did not see the problems of that decade presaging the American economy's slide into senility. Other economists asserted that America had no fundamental competitive disadvantages with Western Europe. Its problems lay in meeting challenges from the newly industrialized countries of East Asia.[9]

Avoiding decline led some economists to more sweeping recommendations. Going beyond issues of deficits, exchange rates or tariff and non-tariff barriers to US exports, Rostow argued for the formulation of a consensus national plan by the President and involving Congress, business, and unions in a concerted effort to ensure growth without inflation. The ingredients were familiar from Britain in the 1960s: an incomes policy, with wage increases tied to productivity gains; a government investment bank to resuscitate older industries; a public works programme to improve and extend infrastructure; and a policy to ensure oil self-sufficiency. The rhetoric ballooned to match these soaring prescriptions; a 'sense of community – of communal commitment and communal purpose – which frames and tempers and enriches our free competitive institutions is the strand in our history and culture we shall have to nurture and on which we shall have to build to transit successfully the generation ahead.' The concluding paragraph unsurprisingly reminds us of the impending presidential election of 1984 and its vital importance.[10] Scott and Lodge touted vague but impressive ideas about comprehensive holistic planning, perhaps modelled on Japanese bodies such as MITI.[11] American analysts did not depict any equivalent to the British establishment's deadening influence upon entrepreneurship, but they suggested relationships between culture and values, widely defined, and industrial efficiency. Kevin Phillips, a leading conservative political analyst, argued for a comprehensive federal government strategy aimed at re-generating America's international competitiveness, a strategy that would require top level bureaucratic control. The strategy would encompass stiffening trade laws, revising anti-trust laws, providing tax incentives to foster international competitiveness, encouraging new industrial relations approaches to productivity and re-training, promoting technological research and techno-logical higher education.[12] Prescriptions for revival ran the gamut from re-awakened individualism and market opportunity to cen-trally orchestrated collaboration, collectivism and consensus.

As with Britain, so with America, the measurement or defini-tion of decline depends very much on the points between which one measures changes over time. During the early 1980s, follow-ing the oil price rises and recessions of the years 1973–82, it was more understandable to express despair than it was by the late 1980s. On the other hand, America's avoidance of prolonged high unemployment has been purchased at the price of far larger federal deficits than those predicted or thought acceptable earlier in that decade. Given the plethora of available statistics, the complexity of economic explanations, and the array of possible bench-mark dates, it is hazardous to attempt a dogmatic defini-tion of where the American economy was in the 1980s and of where it might be proceeding. Definitions turn out to be more complex than they seem at first sight; what might appear to be a significant trend from one time-series can change its shape dramatically or subtly if the time-series is altered. To take two examples: if one examines output per paid hour according to US Bureau of Labor Statistics, there was an average rise per year of 2.2 per cent in the years 1975–79 but a rise of only 1.4 per cent in the years 1976–79; the difference is important if one is assessing 'decline' from the average of 2.5 per cent annual growth in the period 1968–72. Again, actual officially reported figures are sometimes revised over the years, by amounts which make for considerable variations in precise international comparisons.[13] In looking at fine measures such as output per worker, one has to allow for considerable short-term fluctuations and statistical imprecision. Admitting such difficulties and the gross simplification involved, one might consider a few trends.

America has obviously declined from its position of world industrial pre-eminence which it enjoyed in the 1950s, just as

Britain slid from a similarly commanding position one hundred years earlier. But America's economic towering pre-eminence in the early 1950s obviously resulted from very specific circumstances, notably the destruction of manufacturing capacity in Germany and, to a degree, in the USSR, France and Italy, as well as the run-down in the quality of British manufacturing plant. If one took American GNP in 1950 to represent 100 per cent, then the GNP of the UK, France, West Germany, Japan and Italy (in descending order of size) *together* came to only 61 per cent.[14] This overwhelmingly dominant position followed from the Second World War; it was not the equivalent to mid-nineteenth century Britain's slowly and gradually accumulated industrial might and Britain's being first in many industrial fields.

If, however, we look at the internal structure of the American economy and at its relative performance in the last three decades, the image of decline becomes muddied. Manufacturing as a share of real GNP has scarcely shifted at all since 1950; from 24.5 per cent in 1950 to 23.3 per cent in 1960, to 24.0 per cent in 1970 and 23.7 per cent in 1980 and 22.9 per cent in 1982. This constant share disguised a massive increase in productivity and thus a slump in manufacturing employment as a proportion of a vastly expanded labour force. Manufacturing accounted for some 35.9 per cent of the national labour force in 1950, only 27.3 per cent in 1970, and 22.4 per cent by 1980. This fall, however, occurred from an all-time relative peak reached by the manufacturing sector in 1950, one matched as a percentage of the total work-force only in the 1920s; there was no decline from a long-lasting golden age of very high manufacturing employment at the beginning of the twentieth century. The post-war increase in productivity, partly driven by industry's need to cope with America's relatively high wages, meant that in 1980 American manufacturing production for each employed worker-year was 16 per cent higher than that in Japan and higher still than that in Germany.[15] Edward Denison notes:

Economists can point out that output per man or per hour is much lower in Japan than in America; that productivity growth has slowed down in Japan as well as America; that the breadth of Japanese competition this year (1982) has less to do with productivity than an undervalued yen, and that the depth of the onslaught in the automobile market results partly from the high relative wage of American automobile workers. Businessmen may accept these points but they nonetheless stress the urgency of improving productivity and product quality and their determination to do so.

Denison adds that this determination may not be related to any clear grasp as to what Japanese practices are superior or transferable to the USA.[16]

Even Professor Feinstein, who sees a convergence of industrial countries' performances over the long-run, notes a significant American holding operation in overall output. Using purchasing power parities, he shows that the American GDP per capita in 1984 was substantially higher than Germany's, over a quarter higher than Japan's and over one-third higher than Britain's. Again using purchasing power parities as of 1984, he also found that GDP per hour worked in the economy expressed in an index based on US$ showed a continuing American lead (*Table 1*), though one which he regarded as less dramatic than much writing might suggest to have been the case. By most measures, American

Table 1: Index of GDP per hour worked, 1984
(UK = 100) Derived from figures at US$ purchasing power parities

USA	124	Germany	112
France	121	Italy	101
Sweden	120	UK	100
		Japan	69

productivity failed to keep pace with most other industrial countries after 1945, but that failure did not produce a relative economic decline comparable to Britain's since the 1890s.[17] The most obvious reasons for this are varied.

America had little opportunity – as did, say, Japan and France – to achieve productivity gains by shifting workers out of agriculture and into industry during the 1950s and 1960s. Instead, productivity rose with continuing technological development whose contribution in that respect after 1945 was relatively greater than it had been before the Second World War. America also possessed a more highly educated and more mobile labour force than did Britain; reinforcing this mobility, high levels of immigration into America helped ensure that geographical inertia did not lock industries and work-forces into fixed locations as tended to happen in much of the UK. The continuing pace of technological development and productivity gains meant that

America could counteract the effect of other countries' catching-up. American companies remained adept at translating innovations derived from pure research into manufactured products. A prominent comparative economic historian concludes, 'the lead of the United States still remains an enormous one and in micro-electronics and biotechnology it appears to be growing rather than diminishing. During the early 1980s, once again, the United States emerged as the most dynamic country of the world in introducing basic innovations'.[18]

The strength of American manufacturing performance against British weakness is well illustrated by *Table 2*.[19] American

Table 2: Average annual percentage growth rates in manufacturing, 1960–80

	1960–70	1970–80
Japan	11.0	6.4
France	6.6	3.6
USA	5.3	2.9
Germany	5.4	2.1
UK	3.3	0.1

growth rates compared very well with Germany's, easily outpaced Britain's, and looked even better when one remembers that the Americans had a vast manufacturing base in 1960 whereas the fast-growing Japanese and French did not. Less reassuring, of course, is the prospect that Japan may sustain those high rates of the 1960s and 1970s. And other East Asian competitors – South Korea, Taiwan, Hong Kong, and Singapore – have been growing extremely fast. America's car producers, for instance suffered greatly from Japanese competition during the 1970s. But US car output increased by an annual average of 2.5 per cent for the period 1974–83, an increase small by Japanese standards but infinitely superior to the average annual decline of over 5 per cent for most of the European Community in those years.[20]

American decline in the 1970s and 1980s may be qualified by considerations other than the resilience of national productivity. First, industrial nations' prosperity depended on an exceptionally long spell of low basic commodity prices during the 1950s and 1960s. This ended abruptly in 1971–73 as grain prices and then oil prices erupted. The change in the trend of basic commodity prices hit all industrial countries.[21] Secondly, the rapid diffusion of technologies whose spread could not always be accurately predicted during the 1960s led to the global quest for comparative advantage. To say America lost and Japan gained, is to simplify a complex process of world-wide competition and specialization. New manufacturers emerged to challenge the Japanese in turn, with Japan becoming, for example, a net importer of textiles for the first time ever in 1979. On its side, the USA in 1981 retained the international edge in aircraft, non-electrical machinery, vehicle parts, office equipment, construction equipment, certain categories of chemicals, precision instruments, and plastics, in that order of importance to America's export trade. If many products yielded an American deficit in imports over exports, this reflected increasing global specialization. Thirdly, the Japanese miracle may itself be increasingly vulnerable. Japan, like America, will feel the burden of pollution controls in its heavy industries weighing more heavily than do South Korea or Taiwan.[22] Its own work-force may feel increasingly discontented at its long hours and high internal costs of housing and consumer goods. The political consensus which outsiders so glibly assume might be transferable to more politically mature countries looks less familial and firm in 1990 than it did a few years ago. It is always easier to project a consensus when one party rules for more than a generation, as the Liberal Democrats have done since 1955. But the Socialists are more restive than they have been for some time. Finally, the invidious and superficial comparison outsiders make between the Japanese ability to bring government officials and businessmen together in their industrial planning, trade and investment apparatus – the MITI or Ministry for International Trade and Industry – looks somewhat less impressive in the light of the Recruit scandal, in which ministers were heavily bribed by a major company. Ironically, many American economists and political scientists who hold the MITI model up for American emulation would deplore the close, and financially corrupting, association of officials, politicians and leading businessmen which is the more sordid reality behind the benign façade of Japanese industrial 'consensus'. In that sense, American political culture would not tolerate Japanese corporatism.

Continued growth in American manufacturing output during the 1960s and 1970s kept the American economy large. The

OECD, for instance, established a composite index for Gross Domestic Product originating in industry for 1985 and based it upon the exchange rates prevailing in that year and upon national weighting patterns. Taking the full OECD membership of the world's twenty leading economies together, the USA accounted for 42.7 per cent of all those countries' industrial production, Japan for 18.0 per cent, and the UK for 5.5 per cent. Even if Germany, France, Italy and the UK were lumped together – and their combined populations roughly matched that of the USA – they would account for 24.8 per cent of OECD industrial production, against America's 42.7 per cent. If the comparison is extended from industrial production to GDP, the same difference of scale prevails. Between 1980 and 1988 Japan's GDP grew much faster than did America's. But, expressed in constant terms and allowing for a constant exchange rate, the American economy still dwarfs Japan's and exceeds in size that of Japan and the four principal European economies of Germany, France, Italy and the UK combined (*Table 3*).[23] The difficulties

Table 3: GDP at 1985 prices and at 1985 exchange rates $ bills

	1980	1985	1988 (provisional figures)
USA	3,445.7	3,967.5	4,394.7
Japan	1,094.5	1,326.0	1,496.8
Germany	587.0	621.8	672.3
France	485.6	522.5	564.0
UK	412.8	452.5	504.0
Italy	392.8	427.2	469.9

of sustaining high growth rates for so vast and so well developed an economy are too easily ignored by commentators. But the figures point to considerable American success in holding on to a powerful economic lead.

It would seem obvious that America has *not* suffered from a case of British disease. Of course there are those who insist that reports of Britain's industrial death have been much exaggerated. One argument goes that Britain has improved immensely in moral and social terms since 1945 : better health, welfare and education, more tolerant in interpersonal relations and improved opportunity.[24] But everywhere in Western Europe – and in the US as well as during the 1960s – increased social services have depended on prosperity. America's Great Society programme arrived, following tax cuts in 1964, upon a tide of burgeoning federal revenues.

A second caveat entered is that while Britain's relative position among industrial nations has slipped, the country enjoyed during the period 1945–73 (much derided in the 1980s as decades of intellectually, morally and financially flabby Keynesianism) rates of economic growth unsurpassed in the nation's history. The trouble with that complacent contention is that all the non-communist countries of Northern and Western Europe attained rates of growth unprecedented in their own history; so did Australia, Canada, the USA; so did Japan. The average annual rate of growth of GDP per capita at constant prices was 40 per cent or more greater than Britain's percentage rate of growth from 1950 to 1973 in Japan, Germany, Austria, Italy, Finland, France, Belgium and the Netherlands; and, as has been said, those countries all enjoyed their historically fastest rates of growth.[25] The true extent of relative British decline may be illustrated by reference to GNP per capita. Taking American GNP per capita as 100, then the British achieved a level of 56, ahead of France, West Germany and Italy, in that order in 1950. By 1975, however, Britain's GDP (at 62) had been overtaken by France (at 79.5), West Germany (at 79.2), and Japan (at 65.1). Of course these figures showed that some Western European countries and Japan had begun to catch up on America's GNP. But given the extraordinary nature of America's position in 1950, that process had still failed to topple America from its pre-eminence and it showed Britain performing less well than her European competitors. Between the mid-1950s and the mid-1970s, productivity in Britain fell behind that in France, West Germany and Italy. Moreover, British productivity in manufacturing industry, already substantially weaker than that in the USA during the 1930s, became distinctly worse by the 1970s: an American industrial worker produced about three times the real output of a British manufacturing worker.[26]

A third argument is that Britain did not possess the resource base or the size to compete with America or, say, Imperial Germany of 1870–1918. Fair enough – but this explanation is more difficult to make concerning post-1945 West Germany, distinctly smaller in land area and in relative population than its imperial antecedent, and impossible to sustain when one turns to France and Italy, neither of which were industrial challengers to Britain before 1939 and both of which had large segments of peasant agriculture into the 1950s. There is a considerable difference between British decline and American resilience.

Explanations of American slippage from overwhelming industrial dominance to a position of a potentially vulnerable lead hinge on various factors: notably technological defects, defence spending, low savings, and inappropriate government policies. Let us begin with technology. One problem was that Western Europe and Japan caught up with American consumerism during the 1950s and beyond.[27]

Table 4: Comparative car ownership, 1953–1985

Total of all cars/1,000 population (+ estimated)

	1953	*1961*	*1971*	*1976*	*1985*
USA	288	345	427	510	540+
UK	57	116	225	253	320
France	47	135	261	300	450
West Germany	22	95	247	308	420
Italy	13	50	209	284	390
Japan	1	8	102	160	230

The figures for car ownership in relation to population given in *Table 4* show the enormous gap between America and Western Europe in the 1950s: they also show how the growth of car ownership in Britain failed to match that of Western European countries which started behind Britain in the 1950s. Most important, a country as highly developed as America by 1961 enjoyed far less scope for some types of manufacturing growth than did western Europe and Japan. So, too, Western Europe and Japan followed American leads in the diffusion of numerous innovations. One theory contends that technologically innovative countries may suffer temporary dips in relative economic performance when industrial rivals catch them up. But older established countries then renew their technologies and revive their competitive edge.[28]

An illustration of this process of adaptation might be drawn from the steel industry. In the 1950s and 1960s large-scale integrated steel works dominated the industry. Then a general fall in steel output occurred in all developed countries between 1973 and the early 1980s. American failure appeared acute even within this overall pattern of decline; America's share of world steel output plunged from 17 per cent of world production in 1976 to 11 per cent in 1985. Yet that drop partly reflected a collapse of particular demands; the end of the boom in highway construction during the 1950s, for instance. It resulted also from the introduction of substitutes for steel, notably aluminium and plastics. Thus whereas American car output advanced from 14.5 million in 1973 to 15.7 million in 1985, the car manufacturers consumed 23 million tons of steel in 1973 and only 13 million tons twelve years later; the amount of steel input per car fell by 48 per cent. At the same time, the integrated plants proved less productive and profitable than technologically more advanced mini-mills. Those new mills accounted for 16 per cent of the American steel market by the mid-1980s and illustrated the need and the capacity for adjustment away from those approaches which engendered or accompanied an early industrial lead.[29]

One area of technological vulnerability for both countries was in shortages of engineers. The number of qualified engineers in relation to population was low in Britain during the 1970s. And those possessed relatively low prestige. There are fears concerning an American shortfall as well.[30]

A slightly different explanation – indeed model – for slippage was offered in 1988 by Paul Kennedy's *The Decline and Fall of the Great Powers*. Kennedy argued that the USA, like its 'imperial' predecessors, has suffered from over-stretch. Just as Britain frittered away excessive resources in the 1950s to bolster a sagging world political and military role while Germany and Japan wasted far less capital, manpower and political will on such global activities, so America has sunk too much government spending and planning effort into 'imperial' pretensions.[31]

This is a very difficult claim to assess. Against it one could point to positive resource consumption by the military. One estimate suggests that about 7 per cent of steel output was absorbed by defence in 1983, a useful customer for a hard-hit industry. Employment in a volunteer, and fairly well paid, armed service is also useful; the services have provided skills training and job mobility for the poor and for racial minorities. It is more difficult to become exercised about the funnelling of talent into 'wasteful' or non-productive occupations; the army, navy and air force provide service sector jobs comparable to the majority of services in an advanced economy. More positive spin-offs flow from direct spending, especially in aircraft production where America maintains a technological and output lead.

The Department of Defense justifies its own spending on research partially on the grounds that it stimulates science and technology more generally. The first electronic (as distinct from electro-mechanical) computer was built in 1946 for the US Army Ballistic Research Laboratory to calculate shell trajectories and firing tables. Between 1946 and 52 various new government offices contracted research in science and engineering, created to do so mainly by the armed services. One spin-off from the Stanford Electronics Laboratory, financed mainly by military research and development, stimulated growth of what became silicon valley. The Applied Physics Laboratory, established in 1942 at Johns Hopkins University through funding from the US Navy, had grown by the late 1980s to become a division of the university employing 1,600 professional and 1,200 other staff with annual revenues and expenditures topping $300 million: a staff size and turnover well in excess of that of virtually any British universities. While there are academic, moral and political objections to such a heavy Department of Defense presence on US campuses, the military have contributed significantly to progress in radio navigation, microwaves, solid-state circuits, non-linear optics, information and coding theory, software and computers, and, especially, super-conductivity. A key initiative has been the Joint Services Electronics Program; about 1/6 of the Department's budget for basic research is devoted to electronics and computer science. These are areas, together with aircraft, where America retains a distinct global comparative advantage. The case for the distorting effect of relatively high defence spending raises complex analytical issues; but it is not a straightforward case of military spending necessarily dragging the economy downwards. There are palpable spin-off economic benefits of military research and development. It is not entirely clear how diverting monies from defence to, say, poverty relief or education would yield greater economic benefits.[32]

Moreover, the American economy did succeed in generating large numbers of new civilian jobs. One measure of civilian employment based on American definitions shows that the number of civilian jobs increased from 100 in 1965 to the following by 1980: USA 136.8, France 114.9, and Japan 110.2. The number of civilian jobs fell by 1980 in some key countries: Italy 95.4, UK 97.1, West Germany 95.4.[33] This scarcely suggests that a defence-based economy impeded job creation.

An even more dramatic difference between America and Japan lies in the lower rate of American saving and investment. Again, the wider social and cultural context of this phenomenon needs to be considered. Japanese savings in the 1950s and 1960s at least partly reflected lower consumer expectations and opportunities. They also reflected the country's lower level of welfare provision; the Japanese system encouraged greater reliance on family support for old-age and sickness pensions. The USA provided a far wider range of social security and other benefits from 1965 onwards and Congress proceeded to index-link entitlements (an important shift in nomenclature) under Richard Nixon's presidency. Professor Bruce R. Scott of the Harvard Business School concluded, 'There is little evidence that industrial policy has bloomed successfully in the climate of any welfare state.' Friedman argued that heavy taxes on high incomes, together with high inflation, induced by excessive government spending, deterred long-range investment and savings. If taxes were cut and inflation were curbed, savings would rise.[34] Parts of the Friedmanite programme shaped federal policy during the early years of Ronald Reagan's presidency, in 1981–83. But one essential element – slashing federal spending – did not come into play. Policy changes helped improve savings rates, but not by much. Gross savings in the private sector rose from an average of 17.4 per cent of annual GDP in 1969–73 to 18.8 per cent and 18.7 per cent in 1974–78 and 1979–83 respectively and yet further to 19.6 per cent in 1984. A sharp increase in American real interest rates (interest rates after allowance for inflation) contributed to this rise after 1981. Even so, this savings rate only reached the levels obtaining in Britain and Germany; indeed 1984 saw Americans achieving for the first time in twenty years the private sector savings rate that Germany had long attained. Moreover, high government deficits meant that American gross savings overall, taking private and public sectors together, fell well short of German and British levels in 1979–83 and in 1984.[35]

The Friedmans claim that excessive government spending on social welfare serves to fuel inflation and to distort patterns of work, motivation and investment by subsidizing non-work, and raising, through heavy taxation, the costs borne by businesses. That combination of factors struck many critics as part of the

British disease during the 1970s. Robert Bacon and Walter Eltis argued that 'the structure of the economy will be undermined after a time in any democracy where non-market spending is increased at a faster rate than the one the population wishes to finance.' America did not face this problem of an excessive expansion of non-productive, or non-market employment on a national scale. But the incidence of local taxation, and local initiative in providing welfare, created in some eastern cities – most notably New York City in the mid-1970s – 'a series of mini-Britains with growing numbers of public workers and fewer producers to support them.' One American response to that was the shift of new investment and new industry to lower tax areas, with the consequent boom in the 1970s and 1980s of the Sunbelt cities.[36]

Debate also rages over specific government policies. An obvious response to what many regard as unfair Japanese competition – unfair because not accompanied by any reciprocal ease of American entry into Japan's markets – is to demand tariff protection or a more aggressive approach in erecting trade barriers.[37] There is an interesting parallel in Professor Rubinstein's suggestion in this volume that a key turning-point for Britain was the failure to protect her industries in the period of rampant protectionism before the First World War. Britain clung in the 1900s to an approach to political economy that had served her interests extremely well during her era of industrial and commercial dominance in the mid-nineteenth century. So, too, the USA became a proponent of trade liberalization when it squared with her own interests in the decades immediately after 1945. In addition to self-interest, an historical interpretation of economic events shaped US commitment to freer trade and global markets. That was the belief that the great depression had been exacerbated by the highly protective Smoot-Hawley tariff of 1930. These legacies of thought and practice led administrations in Washington during the 1970s and 1980s to persuade competitors to lower their restrictions – often carefully disguised – on American imports rather than to resort to stiff American protectionism.[38]

Another policy issue upon which economists argue (and claim to be central to understanding America's slippage in the pecking order of economic powers) is the exchange rate. In the 1960s Britain suffered from an over-valued £; the process of devaluation in an era before floating exchange rates became politically traumatic. In the 1980s, even after floating exchange rates have become accepted practice, reserve banks' support positions on their national currencies and on interest rates mean that there is still no fully free market. Moreover, the federal government deficit and its effect in driving up interest rates meant that the $ was over-valued, especially against the yen, for much of the 1980s. That fact made exporting more difficult and importing easier than it might have been. But some economists brush this issue aside; an over-valued currency may be the price America pays for possessing a strong basic economy and for being strong politically, a refuge for mobile if not fleeing capital.[39]

It is easy to see from this brief sketch that American economists differ widely as to the reasons behind and therefore the remedies for their country's relative slippage from the world's economic giant to the world's leading single economic super-power. There are arguments for more widely diffused technological innovation, for reductions in defence spending, for efforts to stimulate savings, for adjustments in trade regulations, exchange rates and other technical measures besides. But if one goes beyond these specific proposals, then there seems little historical rationale for claims that central planning is feasible in the USA. Rostow presses for a mammoth incomes, investment and infrastructure policy. Scott and Lodge look beyond even the Japanese MITI model to comprehensive economic planning. Even if one dismisses, as politically loaded, the obvious objections that the centrally planned economies of the world of the 1960s and 1970s proved to be lamentably inefficient and that what experts believe to be current technological panaceas may quickly be superseded, one still confronts the incontrovertible political facts of American history: the country's strength has been its pluralist politics and it has hardly ever adopted or implemented anything resembling a national plan. Finally there is an air of modishness about some of the models offered to policy-makers for American emulation. In the early 1970s Professor Lodge was calling for a new national ideology. One alternative example he held up for closer scrutiny was Yugoslavia's practice of worker participation and co-operation management.[40] From the perspective of 1990, Yugoslavia, with its intense regional conflicts, fragile political traditions, failed industry, inflation rate of about 2,000 per cent per annum and desperate dependence on foreign tourism, scarcely vindicates central planning and participatory management. So, too, the MITI model that appears so effective to the distant admirer would raise intense cultural, legal and political problems in the USA where political collaboration with business is already objected to by many liberals and intellectuals. The close working relationship between government and industry that prevails in Japan would raise profound questions about America's anti-trust laws and the potential for corruption.

Overall, though, the American economy retains its position as world leader, pursued by others but not yet overtaken. By the late 1970s America's gross capital stock in manufacturing was growing as fast as Japan's and, although labour productivity in manufacturing did not grow at Japan's rate, American productivity as measured in relation to worker-hours led the world.[41] Moreover, even in the depression of the early 1980s America did not suffer from the *long-term* unemployment that plagued Western European countries; the erosion of skills, incentives and morale did not cut as deep as it did in Europe. America's world performance in particular products was best where heavy investments in R and D were most appropriate, again suggesting that long-term capacity to improve investment and productivity remained strong. Finally, although America's own share of world manufacturing exports fell from 17.5 per cent in 1966 to 13.9 per cent in 1983 (with ups and downs between those years), the share of world manufacturing exports accounted for by US multinationals remained at 17.7 per cent in both 1966 and 1983.[42] That is a vital dimension to the US economy which other countries are beginning to match in the late 1980s, as Japanese and British firms establish themselves firmly and fully in overseas countries as indigenous manufacturers.

At best, the comparison most frequently made is between Britain in the Edwardian age and America in the 1980s. Both countries were wedded to an ideal of free trade and globalism whereas both faced increasing, though by no means crippling, challenges to the competitiveness of their domestic industries.[43] One difference, however, is the source of the competitive challenge. America is not under threat from the Western European economies either singly or together. The threat comes from Japan, a country whose cultural, political, economic, and managerial order differs profoundly from that of the USA. But that conclusion raises the obvious corollary; if America retains such a powerful lead over Western Europeans, and certainly reveals no parallel to British decline, may one find the explanation for

American resilience in a set of cultural values more favourable
to enterprise than Britain's?

II

Trying to describe some salient characteristics of an enterprise
system raises enormous difficulties. The word enterprise may
refer to a commercial organization or business, or a habit of
mind or mode of behaviour. In common parlance and perception
these two usages may be contradictory, for a large corporation
may not innovate or initiate in an enterprising manner; indeed
one criticism levelled against the corporate economy is that it
has become too dinosaur-like, with its giant enterprises crushing
out enterprise. Yet, going back a stage in considering industrial
development, the emergence in America of a corporate economy
at the beginning of the twentieth century illuminated underlying
American cultural values as they affected law and politics. The
birth of modern American enterprises revealed much about the
American enterprise culture. And it is worth dwelling on distinctive particularities lest we lose sight of national differences in
the long sweeping convergences that flow from some brands of
comparative history.

Early twentieth-century Americans, of course, did not subscribe to one set of values. Agrarians remained powerful;
workers' groups proliferated; small businesses did not work
easily with emergent corporate conglomerates. The tensions
flowing from rapid change may be readily grasped. In 1860
employment in America divided extremely unevenly, 60 per cent
being in agriculture, and 20 per cent each being in goods producing and service producing sectors. By 1910 these three broad
divisions of work approached parity; services absorbed 36 per
cent of the work-force while agriculture and goods producing
took up 32 per cent each. The relative decline of agriculture
naturally worried agrarians yet the even spread of employment
between the sectors meant that no single interest predominated.
Over the next fifty years, goods producing held on to its share
of employment but services approached 60 per cent, where agriculture had been a century earlier, while agriculture slumped
to under 10 per cent of the work-force.[44]

This transition occurred in two important psychological con-
texts. One was the fact that American farmers were essentially

small businessmen whose antipathy to big corporations stemmed largely from anxieties about scale and about their vulnerability as small producers to pricing arrangements with increasingly large food processors and shippers. Americans developed an agrarian myth, but it concerned attitudes to work, the family, plain habits and self-sufficiency rather than the imagery of thatched cottages and rose gardens, the Beaufort Hunt and social exclusivity, and retreat and relaxation that shaped so many British responses to the 'countryside'. Sir John Harvey-Jones, a former chairman of ICI has commented, 'As a country and as a race we take particular pride in our past and indeed are derided for living too much in it. Most successful British people wish to buy houses in the country, and to attach themselves to the countryside in a way that almost appears to imitate the patterns of life of the gentry in the eighteenth and nineteenth centuries.'[45] Americans have a more gritty and less class-conscious rural idyll, evoking in their imitations of the hunter and the cowboy folk memories of individualism, opportunity, the frontier, and men being tested in their personal contests with that frontier. The last American elite which self-consciously (and not very accurately) promoted a chivalric, anachronistic ideal – the Southern planters – found itself humiliated in the Civil War (1861–65).

The other context of the long transition arose from its geographical fluidity. The British industrial revolution depended on coal and tended to be fixed geographically by industries' need to be located near coal deposits. Coal dominated as the America's leading source of energy only from around 1880 to the 1920s; water and wood led before and oil and natural gas have led since.[46] Although key segments of American industry have been locked into place by considerations of energy supply, in general American industry has enjoyed greater scope for locating widely, for moving from narrow sources of raw materials. Both the agrarian myth and the geographical spread of heavy industry gave less weight to tradition and 'fixed' communities than was the case in Britain.

The size, spaciousness and 'fluidity' of the American internal market fostered corporate concentration on the one hand and regulation by contract on the other.

The corporate re-organization of America occurred essentially through the merger movement of 1898–1902, when 136 consolidations were effected, and through a managerial revolution in the generation that followed. The merger movement had dramatic short-term consequences. Single companies specializing in such products as cans and seeding machines, snuff and corn products, asphalt and school furniture, gypsum and steam pumps achieved control of 70 per cent or more of their industries – Du Pont, Eastman Kodak, International Harvester and Otis Elevator were among 42 consolidated corporations reaching that level of market power. The reasons for these mergers were largely defensive. Fast-expanding, capital-intensive industries faced severe problems with falling prices during the depression following 1893. The Sherman anti-Trust Act of 1890, and judicial interpretations of it, prevented cartels among businesses designed to fix prices. The sheer costs of machinery and plant led companies to continue to sell even at a loss in order to sustain cash flow. By the end of the decade merger offered the only route to safeguarding market share, setting higher prices and denying entry to new firms; the latter would find it harder to compete with industrial giants controlling large volumes of output and sales.[47]

Not all these consolidations worked to the satisfaction of their creators. But they did open the way to the managerial revolution, the shift from captains of industry to co-ordinators of committees. British industry lagged thirty or more years behind the USA in the scale of managerial re-organization. By the 1920s American conglomerates separated out their functions into divisional and clear sub-divisional specialisms (such as production, distribution, sales, and marketing) and simultaneously established firm overall planning and control from increasingly formalized head-offices. The reasons for this lay in the sheer scale of the American domestic market, the size of the conglomerates tied together in 1898–1902, and the way in which those conglomerates engaged in vertical integration, reaching from raw materials production to final distribution of finished products. No British equivalent to the scale, frequency and reach of this merger movement occurred until after the Second World War. It has been said that 'British industry developed along the lines of a sort of family capitalism', with, for instance, no more than 13 of the 100 biggest British companies in 1950 organized into divisions. Nor did British manufacturers develop the same skills at marketing and distribution; most large British corporations involved in world markets sold to other producers not direct to customers.[48]

The consolidations of 1898–1902 partly emerged from the

federal courts' anti-trust stance. Following the Sherman Act's passage in 1890, the courts had to decide whether that measure would supplement and shape or instead supplant the common law. Judge John A. Riner contended in *United States v. Trans-Missouri Freight Association et al* (1892) that 'the public is not entitled to free and unrestricted competition, but ... to ... fair and healthy competition.' This view, declared in a federal circuit court, fell foul of the Supreme Court. A majority of that court's justices held during the years 1897–1911 that the Sherman Act did not distinguish between unreasonable and reasonable restraints of trade. Congress and the presidents of the early twentieth century jibbed at enforcing unrestricted competition; federal officials during the 1900s thus sought to regulate the methods of competition rather than slice large corporations' increasing shares of their respective markets. The courts eventually fell into line. In 1911 the Supreme Court decided that the Sherman Act forbade both unreasonable restraints of trade, such as unfair methods to impair competitors, and operations against the public interest in manipulating prices or in the marketing of goods. The Court further stressed that trying to enforce unrestricted competition might endanger or impinge upon trading, contractual and property rights. A rule of reason – associated with common law enactments preceding the Sherman Act – had therefore to be applied in deciding where the balance of public interest lay; some degree of combination or co-operation between corporations might well serve that interest. A single company could come to predominate in a market sector as long as it did not act unfairly towards other companies remaining in that sector.[49]

American judicial rulings in the period 1897–1911 restricted conglomerate enterprises in order to sustain the principles of competitive enterprise. This distinction lay at the heart of an enormous amount of confusion as to whether early twentieth-century reformers opposed or supported business values. Public protest typically centred on tensions between small and medium-sized firms and monopolistic or oligopolistic concentrations of market-share, tensions between entrepreneurs trying to enter sectors of industry and well established corporations, and tensions between farmers, together with small-town merchants, and large trans-shipping companies whose transport rates discriminated against the small operator. Political reactions to the sudden emergence of great industrial oligopolies offered various complex prescriptions for the proper ordering of relations between the federal government and the corporations. But a fundamental commitment to market capitalism, however regulated or supervised by the state, remained. As Martin Sklar has written, 'The overriding principle at common law in the United States was not unrestricted competition, but the natural liberty principle of freedom of contract: that is to say, the right to compete, not the compulsion to compete.' Sklar sees a liberal corporatist order emerging in 1912–14. That order arose from the need for stability. Secretary of War Henry L. Stimson told a Republican meeting in December, 1911, 'Nobody thinks that modern business can be run permanently by a series of explosions' set off by attacks upon corporations. While no party advocated repealing the Sherman Act, Stimson continued, 'Nobody believes that the American people intend to regulate permanently the delicate operations of their modern trade from the office of the District Attorney.'[50]

The American compromise between protecting competition and establishing federal regulation of business differed, according to Sklar, from European models – derived from the political left or from the political right – of the corporate state.[51] If federal government and courts interfered less with business after 1911 than they had done in the decade or so before then, they still regulated it from the dual assumptions that cartels and price-fixing were repugnant and that competitive entry into industry and commerce was essential to freedom. Given the size of America and of its markets, impersonal contracts took precedence over personal contacts in the conduct of business.

If the emergent corporate giants and the federal government's rapprochement with them differentiated America from European countries, then so too did the fate of anti-market, socialist doctrines and groups set America off from, say, Britain, France or Germany by the 1920s. One reason for the weakness of alternative anti-capitalist groupings flowed from the relative failure of American trade unionism. This partly followed from Supreme Court decisions. *Loewe v. Lawlor* (1908) extended ideas concerning the restriction of trade to unions by penalizing a union for boycotting a factory in order to establish a so-called monopoly over that factory's labour. This encouraged the National Association of Manufacturers to look to the Sherman Act as a protection against both union power and large corporations. Trade unions enrolled 7.8 per cent of non-farm workers in 1900 and 12.5 per cent in 1910 (going even higher in between). But federal court rulings hedged in union negotiating powers. Various judgements of the 1900s and 1910s held that unions were voluntary associations with a legal personality and no capacity to sue to ensure the up-holding of agreements; individual members could sue, but if they remained in employment were deemed to be according implicit acceptance to their conditions. The federal courts in *Hudson v. Cincinnati* (1913) argued that the unions' function was 'to induce employers to establish usages in respect to wages and working conditions which are fair, reasonable, and humane, leaving to its members each to determine for himself whether or not and for what length of time he will contract in reference to such usages.' Although British trade unions of the period similarly faced legal challenges, they were assisted in overcoming some such difficulties by the Liberal governments of 1905–15, especially in legislation passed in 1906 and 1913. Congress offered no such redress to American unions. Employers could impose yellow dog (or non-union membership) contracts upon their workers.[52]

The unions failed to embrace a wide membership. Total membership rose from 2.7 million to 5 million between 1916 and 1920 and then fell to a constant level of 3.5 to 3.6 million in the years 1923–30. Britain, with a very much smaller workforce, had 4.6 million unionists in 1916, 8.3 million in 1920 and then 4.8 million in 1929, when the American total stood at only 3.6 million.[53] This failure of unionization meant that American socialists had no equivalent power base of members, and their subscriptions or dues, to draw upon for political purposes.

Many other factors explained the American socialists' weakness. One was the existence of considerable ethnic tensions within the working class. In 1900 the census estimated that 38 per cent of the working population was foreign-born or of foreign-born parentage; yet no fewer than 56 per cent of those in manufacturing and mechanical pursuits came from such a background, 28 per cent from Germany and Ireland together. Urban working-class neighbourhoods constantly felt the tension between immigrants and native-born Americans and between different immigrant groups. Other factors may be illustrated from the example of Massachusetts, where the Socialist party secured 9 per cent of the state vote in 1902. This propitious foundation for a new party soon weakened. Some locally important unions eschewed socialism. Samuel Gompers in 1903 more generally accused socialists of being anti-union. The Roman Catholic church in the same year also attacked the party. In the key factory town of Brockton, Democrats and Republicans both promised pro-labour measures in a local election campaign and, in 1903, the Democrats thwarted a socialist challenge. Subsequent factionalism atrophied the party. Even when a major strike of textile workers in Lawrence broke out in 1912 the socialists won no credit for backing a struggle which gained higher wages rather than advanced political reform. More widely, the Industrial Workers of the World, who helped win that particular strike, had rejected the Socialist Party from their formation in 1905.[54]

Relations between unions and socialist groups were more distant and disrupted than was the relationship between unions and socialists which led to the establishment of the British Labour Party in the opening years of the twentieth century. Perhaps as a consequence of this tension, the socialists' greatest strength up to the mid-1910s lay west of the Mississippi where mining, lumbering, and tenant farming flourished. Often the party succeeded in local contests, attracting a widespread protest vote. Given such a base, the party not surprisingly failed when other parties adopted municipal reforms, when more and more businessmen backed city managers and city improvements, and when new city governments replaced ward elections with city-wide contests thereby preventing socialists from gaining individual seats in local elections. But between 1911–12 and 1917 the Socialist Party's strongholds shifted from Western small towns and minor cities to New York state and north-eastern industrial cities. At the same time the proportion of party members who were foreign-born shot up from 20 per cent in 1916 to 53 per cent in 1919. Under pressure from such members, the party shifted to the left, becoming increasingly absorbed in following events and leads from Moscow rather than concentrating on American conditions. That radicalizing reaction partly followed from war-time restrictions on the party's meetings, members and magazine mailings. The drift of post-war events fuelled the Red Scare of 1919 and the anti-Socialism of the subsequent decade.[55] In Britain, by contrast, the First World War drew the Labour Party into government, and the 1920s, while witnessing intense industrial problems and disputes, raised Labour for the first time to the status of a party of government.

The factionalism and political failure of organized American Socialism by the 1920s weakened the momentum of anti-business ideas. Of course, criticism of and antagonism towards big business flourished. But anti-business ideas did not secure the political base they captured in early twentieth century Britain. The judiciary may have impaired large enterprises' activities in the late nineteenth and early twentieth centuries, but it did so in the cause of freer enterprise. And the American judicial system, by giving primacy to contracts, helped to entrench corporatism.

Other reasons for the failure of Socialism help explain the legitimating success of pro-business attitudes. Not the least of these was the belief that the economic order worked. When Werner Sombart in 1906 asked the question, *Why is There No Socialism in America?*, his principal answer, based on a very careful weighing of comparative statistics, was that the American worker was better housed, better clothed and better fed than his German counterparts. 'All Socialist utopias come to nothing on roast beef and apple pie.' Admittedly, Sombart predicted that American conditions would worsen to the point of permitting Socialism to breed. But we find, a generation later, Antonio Gramsci arguing that Fordism went beyond the provision of reasonable working hours, conditions and wages to the control of workers' lives beyond the factory, including the imposition of Prohibition in an effort to boost productivity.[56] These conditions were celebrated and disseminated by management in such a way as to legitimate the corporate set-up. Whether or not this popular acceptance of industrial capitalism amounted to false consciousness depends on one's assessment of the capacity of any socialist utopia then or since to deliver higher living standards than those attained in the twentieth century USA.

The importance of managerial strategies implicit in Gramsci's doctrine of Fordism – as distinct from general living standards alone – is well illustrated by a case-study of the Chrysler motor company from the 1920s to the 1970s. Its author found that workers' attitudes and militant actions there resembled those of Austin Rover's workers at their Longbridge plant. In the British case, shop-steward militancy grew especially from 1965 to 1977, because management had devolved considerable bargaining power to shop-stewards in the 1950s, in an effort to ensure steady output. The very wide range of British car models and the subdivision of the industry into different unions fostered shop-steward power. Americans did not face the same penny-packaging of models and union groups. But Chrysler adopted an organizational structure that was too rigid and too central-ized. It did not allow, as did General Motors' more flexible struc-ture, divisional managers to test various policies to counter-act strong union organization and pressure. Better wages and con-ditions may be necessary but not sufficient explanations of the relative weakness of American unionism.[57]

On the other hand, high living standards helped sustain the idea of Americanism. Some commentators have claimed that a wide-ranging nationalistic sentiment took so prominent a part in American life that little emotional or ideological space remained for such doctrines as Socialism. Americanism included ideas of equality of esteem and democratic participation stretch-ing back in their origins to the mid-eighteenth century. Sombart quoted the leading British Americanist of his age, James Bryce, for the view in 1888 that 999 of every 1,000 Americans were optimistic in belief as well as in behaviour. Sombart concluded that American workers felt well satisfied with their economic position, proud of their Constitution, confident of their full pol-itical rights, and almost complacent in their boast 'civis America-nus sum.' 'In the external appearance of the American worker there is not the stigma of being the class apart that almost all European workers have about them.' Part of that psychological robustness arose from America's vast natural resources, especially those in land; space allowed for considerable physical mobility, so that in 1900 20.7 per cent of Americans born in their country lived outside the states where they had been born. As Sombart noted, 'the mere knowledge that he *could* become a free farmer at any time could not but make the American worker feel secure and content, a state of mind that is unknown to the European counterpart. One tolerates any oppressive situa-tion more easily if one lives under the illusion of being able to withdraw from it if really forced to.' Sombart's formulation exaggerated the point, for Europeans could emigrate to America and American workers often expressed feelings other than con-tentment. But workers' basic optimism about the future remained, often for their childrens' material improvement if not for their own. While attitudes and aspirations may be extremely difficult to evaluate as against real world factors, the leading American authority on comparative growth, Edward F. Denison, noted in 1968,

In the United States, the belief that individual advancement depends on individual performance has been much more prevalent; it contrasts with the traditional belief of European workers that advancement was possible only by raising the position of a whole occupational group, if not a whole class. This attitude has been modified in Europe as societies and economies have become more fluid. The United Kingdom may have changed less than the Continent.

One consequence was greater union resistance in Britain to adaptation, to 'surrendering' jobs when new technology was introduced.[58]

Material abundance, and widespread access to it, provided the central back-bone of Americanism in David Potter's *People of Plenty* (1954). And Seymour M. Lipset's *The First New Nation: The United States in Historical and Comparative Perspective* (1964) emphasized that materialism and ideas of formal equality in America created intense pressure to further individuals' own interests rather than those of any social group or 'community'. Political decentralization also helped to reinforce these norms of individualism. All these factors enfeebled home-grown socialism and obliged trade unions, where they existed, to concentrate on local bargaining. A generalized Americanism sat side-by-side with very compartmentalized politics; the two together worked against alternative ideologies, especially ones requiring a highly centralized polity.[59]

The culture of enterprise was sustained by the judiciary, by the momentum of economic success, by an over-arching belief in Americanism, and by the failure of Socialism. Although the story of the relationship between courts, government and big business was, and is, a highly complex one, it is worth stressing that American practice emphasized contractual rights, and that even when courts and Congress acted against corporations they did so in the cause of competition. So, too, although strong trade unions emerged, they shied away from co-operation with the early twentieth-century Socialist Party and concentrated more on tough wage bargaining than on ideology.[60] And they did not gain the breadth of support won by European unions. The failure of socialist alternatives revealed the strength of the individualistic, capitalist order. In a particularly polemical statement of a common enough supposition, former Secretary of the Treasury William E. Simon argued that, unlike any other nation, 'America was born a capitalist nation, was created a capitalist nation by the intent of its founders and the Constitution, and developed a culture and a civilization that were capitalist to the core.' From this it followed that 'an American who is hostile to individualism, to the work ethic, to free enterprise, who advocates an increasing government takeover of the economy or who advocates the coercive socialization of American life is in some profound sense advocating that America cease being American.'[61] One of the founders, James Madison, had indeed noted in the *Federalist*:

Is it not the glory of the people of America that whilst they have paid a decent regard to the opinions of former times and other nations, they have not suffered a blind veneration for antiquity, for custom, or for names, to overrule the suggestions of their own good sense, the knowledge of their own situation, and the lessons of their own experience?[62]

Of course, Americans differed and differ widely over definitions of individualism or capitalism. Nor can one ignore strong and lively radical ideas, movements and traditions against big business and against the ethos of free enterprise. But these undoubted ambiguities have to be set against the enduring resistance of American society and polity to intellectually coherent doctrines of collectivism, let alone socialism. The American reality may not be one of completely free markets or thoroughly open competition. But the prevailing attitudes and assumptions of a country whose electorate in 1988 regarded the word liberal as a distasteful ingredient in its political vocabulary could scarcely be held to sustain an anti-enterprise culture.

III

Culture more generally defined raises familiar ambiguities, which are well emphasized by Professor James's contribution to this volume. Journalists, philosophers, historians, literary critics and novelists in profusion deplored American industrialism in its most expansive phase in the period 1865–1929. Yet one needs to ask – even if the historian finds it difficult to answer – how far such attitudes permeated popular consciousness and shaped popular culture.

Antipathy to business affected American literature from its

beginnings. Business seemed unnatural to people raised on the agrarian myth. As Richard Hofstadter wrote, 'The United States was born in the country and has moved to the city.' Given such roots, 'The agrarian myth represents a kind of homage that Americans have paid to the fancied innocence of their origins.' The farmer confronted with hard times retreated from his position as (effectively) a rural businessman into 'the role of the injured little yeoman.'[63] The pervasiveness of the myth made manufacturing industry seem, at least in the late nineteenth century, a deviation from the American ideal. Even the celebrated rags to riches sagas of Horatio Alger were full of ambiguity. His novels concerned the transition of well brought-up and well educated middle-class country boys to urban life. Their success in cities did not follow from virtuous living, self-discipline and application to work, although they abided by those standards, but from sudden good fortune, the result of exemplary conduct handsomely rewarded but brought to light in entirely fortuitous circumstances. Alger's 135 novels were published between 1867 and his death in 1889 and sold a phenomenal 17 million copies; they offered detailed guidance to the adjustment to big city life and enjoyed enormous popularity in an age of mass exodus from countryside to town.[64] Corporate expansion in the twentieth century took Americans yet further from the rugged individualism into which they had been born. Reinforcing this sense of betrayal was the idea that mere money-making was straightforward and that businessmen were stupid; Sinclair Lewis's fictional character of Babbitt in the 1920s secured that stereotype. Worse still, since business allegedly had its origins in the Puritan work ethic, fictional or non-fictional lapses from restraint exposed businessmen to charges of hypocrisy for indulging in luxury, display and sexual license.[65]

Of course, no single image of *the* businessman emerged. From the 1880s, the financier provoked particular anger. Well-established New England plutocratic families often won kindlier treatment, since many of them distinguished themselves for their cultural and philanthropic interests. Novels dealing in some sustained manner with economic issues showed businessmen in various guises as respectable, reliable townsmen or super-human capitalists, adventurers and fixers or idlers and dilettantes, social climbers or settlement workers, cynical stock manipulators or reformers and idealists. But the great mogul of business became probably the most fully developed literary type. He offended by creating a social order that breached the codes of simple neigh-bourliness, small-town Republicanism and Protestant order; his doings exacerbated social divisions between worker and employers to the point of fuelling social unrest. Despite refine-ments and variations, the image was widespread and negative.[66] Frank Capra's films of the 1930s and Orson Welles' *Citizen Kane* reinforced literary stereotypes.

Yet despite such literary representations and despite intel-lectuals' distrust of what Hofstadter disparaged as the 'hollow optimism' of American businessmen, important qualifications may be offered to this cultural revulsion against industry and industrialists. The novels which can be trawled and cited for their animus against big business did not form or establish a distinctive genre; the essential line of plot in late nineteenth-and early twentieth-century popular literature was the eternal meeting of boy and girl.[67] It was not necessarily industry itself that was attacked; speculation, corrupt business influence upon politicians, and railway rebates were.

More important, industrial interests counter-attacked. Self-help literature enjoyed a venerable history in America as did the anti-business theme in fiction. By the mid-nineteenth century, self-help propaganda contained a strong radical edge; well-estab-lished plutocrats were down-graded at the expense of those who had battled their way up, preferably starting with manual labour. But self-help as the ideology of rising men of business yielded in the late nineteenth century to self-help rhetoric directed against egalitarianism. Writers in this tradition responded to populists', progressives' and socialists' denunciations of the 'malefactors of wealth' by asserting that unequal rewards flowed, and rightly flowed, to those who had successfully applied unequal effort to the fierce competitive world of business. Opportunity existed everywhere, but the talent to seize it and the tenacity to secure it were confined to the distinguished few. This argument, and the moral intensity that sustained it, survived the depression of the 1930s. The venerable formula that effort plus insight plus yet more effort equals eventual reward remains as current and powerful today as it did in the nineteenth century.[68]

Self-help clichés counteracted literary anti-business carica-tures. Richard Hofstadter's eloquent treatise, *Anti-Intellectu-alism in American Life* did not simply document the flow of anti-business feelings; it demonstrated the force of anti-intellec-tual reactions. The cult of know-how and material values prevailed in public ideology. Religion was homespun and organized churches typically acted in a businesslike way to purvey what often appeared to be secular therapy rather than Christian theology or precepts.[69] And the political context from which Hofstadter's book sprang – the McCarthyite hearings and the resulting impairment of left-wing speech and activity in Hollywood, the press, television, and the universities – showed a far greater intolerance of dissent from what was regarded as Americanism than any campaign of anti-communism in Britain ever approached. Despite the literary prevalence of anti-business attitudes, the basic idea of Americanism purveyed in the 1950s and 1960s was of a fundamentally capitalist, pro-business society, even if it might be debatable whether it leaned in liberal or conservative directions.

Sustaining corporate capitalism – the enterprise system – against anti-business literati went far deeper than self-help ephemera. At precisely the moment that mass industrial mergers occurred and corporate juggernauts rolled in the first decade of this century, a twofold legitimation process began. Both profoundly affected American popular culture. One was the injection of business studies into universities; the other was the theoretical elaboration and expansion of scientific and then personnel management.

The opening up of the universities started with the curriculum. At Harvard, for instance, Charles W. Eliot, an establishment Bostonian if ever there was one, used his long presidency to move the syllabus away from the classics; by 1894 undergraduates could secure a BA by taking the requisite number of courses in *any* subject, save for minimum requirements in English and a modern language. Ezra Cornell established a university in his own name to enable any person to pursue any study. When Leland Stanford gave $24 million to found a university to the memory of his deceased son (1891), he wanted something practical, with the first academic staff being appointed being in engineering and science. When Joseph Wharton contributed to the founding of the Wharton School of Finance and Economics at the University of Pennsylvania, he commemorated his family's long business links with Philadelphia; but he also hoped to provide a liberal education in finance and commerce for the wealthy young who needed, in his opinion, instruction neither too classical nor too vocational.[70]

The educational revolution stretched further than merely providing business schools. Many universities originated in the last third of the nineteenth century as land-grant colleges to assist farmers and equip labourers with suitable skills. Student enrolments climbed from 2,245 in 1882 to 135,000 in 1916; since this occurred while agricultural employment fell in relative importance, providing non-agricultural skills to the young clearly constituted an important part of these colleges' and universities' role. Another boost to higher education came after the Second World War when the federal government gave grants for tuition and books and a monthly living allowance for any veteran trying to secure a four-year college education. These GI benefits were extended to Korean War veterans in the mid-1950s.[71]

So vast a commitment to human capital formation impressed European observers of the 1960s – such as Michael Shanks and J.J.Servan-Schreiber – who were hoping to galvanize Europeans into emulating American technology and organizational flair. Arthur M.Schlesinger, Jr, a leading liberal Democratic historian, wrote a glowing foreword to Servan-Schreiber's *The American Challenge* (1968) in which he noted that the author 'traces American dynamism to the social mobility, the individual responsibility, the equalitarian thrust of American life, and, above all, to the determination to invest in human beings, especially through the promotion of education.' This phenomenon had deeper social roots. The emphasis in education up to the age of eighteen upon socialization and assimilation made social fluidity and mobility easier – both vertically through class and horizontally through space – in America than it was in Britain. This in turn was reinforced by the ideas of the early twentieth-century philosopher, John Dewey, claiming that the school should be a living environment and preparation for society, not a separate enclave. Basic educational assumptions differed markedly from those prevailing in Britain.[72]

To return to the specific; Wharton's foundation in 1881 set a precedent for university business schools. In 1898 a business school was founded at the University of Chicago, itself dating only from 1892 and dependent on massive injections of John D. Rockefeller's money to become viable. Business schools then proliferated in the first decade of the twentieth century, with the imprimatur of respectability being accorded when Harvard set one up in 1908. William Lawrence, scion of Boston's industrial elite, episcopal bishop, and fervent supporter of Harvard, helped promote the new business school out of 'loyalty to the business traditions of my family and a conviction that this was a real missionary enterprize for the welfare of the country.'[73] One must always distinguish, of course, between Harvard College, for undergraduates, and the university which incorporated specialist graduate schools, notably in Law and Business Administration, whose enrolments by the late twentieth century vastly outstripped the undergraduate population. This addition of professional graduate schools in the early twentieth century did not dispel the social exclusivity of Harvard College's undergraduate recruitment; of some 405 boys from Groton, the boarding school designed on English models, who applied to Harvard in the years 1906–32 only three were rejected.[74] But although the older style of gentlemanly education remained, a professional adjunct was added. Nothing equivalent in business education affected contemporary Cambridge or Oxford.

These developments occurred also when American universities' academic quality and international reputation were improving. It has been said that in 1890 only Harvard and Johns Hopkins attained international distinction among American universities, whereas by 1905, some 15–20 of them compared with the best European or British institutions. Subsequent expansion of business education was massive. By 1970 there were nearly as many business schools in America as there were university schools of education. In 1975 earned bachelor's degrees in business totalled 133,010, the third highest number by subject and not very far behind education's 167,015, the country's most heavily subscribed undergraduate degrees. By 1985 universities and colleges awarded 233,351 bachelor's degrees in business and management, nearly one-quarter of all bachelor's degrees awarded that year and far in excess of the 88,161 degrees in education, the next most popular subject.[75] These degree courses may not have been the most intellectually rigorous or refined in the country and their profusion showed a national concern to train corporate *apparachiks* rather than inspire inquiry, initiative and enterprise; the phenomenon satirized by Malcolm Bradbury in *Stepping Westward* where Benedict Arnold University promotes its Business Administration degree with the slogan, take a BA in BA from BA. On the other hand, a degree course in business typically includes a great deal of liberal arts and social science instruction within the curriculum.[76] Yet the sheer scale of this university and college involvement in business and management education and sheer number of young people so trained shows how pro-business sentiments permeated the popular culture; no remotely comparable degree programmes got underway in Britain until the 1970s and 1980s.

Business education went beyond the preparation of junior officers for the burgeoning corporate army; it instructed the elite. The most prestigious business schools – listed by one survey in 1976 as Stanford, Harvard, MIT, Chicago, Carnegie-Mellon, University of California (Berkeley), Pennsylvania, University of California (Los Angeles), Northwestern and Cornell – nearly all emerged at the country's leading universities and concentrated on postgraduate MBAs. By the mid-1970s, 19 per cent of the top three executives in each of *Fortune* magazine's sample of 500 leading companies had graduated from Harvard Business School.[77]

The comparison with Britain is instructive. Although some universities nodded in the direction of studying the world of business, their efforts palled beside those of the great American institutions. At the turn of the century Birmingham University led the way by setting up courses in commerce; but this yielded no dynamo for a new subject. Oxford and Cambridge made no provision for business or management studies at degree level until the 1970s and 1980s; and even then the impetus often came from outside donors pressing at the gates, as in the case of the founding of Templeton College, Oxford, by the Templeton family, specifically for management education. When the realization eventually built up that more management training at a fairly sophisticated level might be needed, the response took the customary form of an inquiry and report, by Lord Franks (1963), on national needs. Two business schools broadly modelled on Harvard followed, at London and Manchester, as recommended by Franks. Together they produced about 200 graduates a year by 1971, a minuscule supply. Interestingly enough, the first choice of careers for London Business School's graduates was the highly traditional one of merchant banking. During the 1970s only 30–40 of Britain's top management were graduates and a lower percentage of graduates with Firsts went into industry or commerce than the percentage of graduates with less good degree results. One leading scholar of comparative management concluded, 'Precisely because industrial management is not a prestigious career in Britain as it is elsewhere, less vigour, inventiveness, and risk taking is shown by British managers.' He argued that while British lower and middle management was often very competent, top management was typically traditional in thought and not as well educated as American or French top management.[78]

This does not mean that British universities, for instance, have been insensitive historically to the demands of science and technology. The British problem seems to have been four fold. First, those educated in the very best schools avoided the more technologically innovative universities. For example, boys from the fee-paying Manchester Grammar School in the early twentieth century did not rush for places at the University of Manchester (despite the fact that their local university diluted any applied or scientific image it might possess by being situated in Oxford Road). Secondly, the Victorians did not establish high-status technological higher education institutions, as did the nineteenth-century French, Germans, and Americans. This problem remains today, with the universities which were formerly colleges of advanced technology having little of the prestige enjoyed in America by MIT or Cal. Tech. Thirdly, British employers showed considerable sluggishness in employing and promoting the technically educated, a by-product perhaps of a more general managerial resistance to change. And, finally, non-academic technical training received relatively less attention than it did from certain German educationalists and government authorities.[79]

By contrast, American management has typically been more highly educated. In 1964 a survey of the top three officials in each of 593 of the largest American non-financial corporations showed that 90 per cent of them had attended college and that 17 per cent of them held degrees from Harvard, Yale or Princeton, while a further 14 per cent possessed degrees from MIT, Cornell, Stanford, Pennsylvania, Dartmouth and Columbia; men with very good educational backgrounds had entered industry a generation earlier. And an analysis of business leaders during the 1950s showed that, of those born in 1891–1920 only 18 per cent were entrepreneurs (founders of firms) as distinct from half being salaried managers and the rest being heirs to entrepreneurs; the latter two groups were twice as likely to have attended college than the entrepreneurs, a very clear majority of those two groups having done so.[80] This resulted from the generally high social esteem attached to business. The celebrated British-born commentator, Alistair Cooke, noted some thirty years ago that 'the oldest of European lamentations about America' was that it 'pays exaggerated respect to the arts and skills of business-men.' Cooke himself rejected the lamentation, concluding 'that on the whole the most straightforwardly intelligent men tend, in America, to go into business. Not the most intellectual – or the most brilliant, or the most individual, but the shrewd and intelligent boys who in another country might go into the civil service or university teaching or the law.' Cooke admitted to having shared the anti-business attitudes of one who read English at Cambridge in the 1930s and he chose the words just quoted 'as carefully as a cat picking the fish from the bones.' But from a wide experience of meeting such people Cooke regarded the first-rate American businessman as 'more precise, more imaginative, watchful, and intelligent about his trade than ninety per cent of the writers and academics who despise him.'[81] Such testimony may be dismissed as purely impressionistic; but it suggests common enough beliefs, which themselves influence entrepreneurial morale, self-esteem and perhaps performance.

Businessmen so praised by Cooke had not necessarily been trained academically in management. And it would be absurd to suggest that a single, coherent management ethos emerged in America. In fact, a considerable methodological gulf separated MIT and Chicago, with their enthusiasm for quantitative analysis, and Harvard, with its absorption in the case-study approach. Nor was the academic quality of the business education provided always high. Harvard has often found the contrast between its business school's rich financial endowment and its intellectual attainments to be acutely embarrassing.[82] But even allowing for those qualifications, the scale and quality of American business education, following from the respect for business values, far surpassed any comparable developments in Britain.

Founding business schools and formulating a management ideology accompanied each other. Treatises on business long predated the beginnings of formal business studies, but they proliferated in the early twentieth century; some 240 books on business management were published in America in the years 1900–10 alone. From all this writing emerged a concern for personnel management far in advance of British theory and formal practice. By 1900 many observers believed that very long hours of work and inadequate leisure harmed workers' health, morale, staying-power and efficiency. Frederick W. Taylor's ideas for more rigorously planned management assumed that improving workers' physical conditions would enhance productivity. Such concentration on workers' performance gave way from the 1920s to greater concern for management techniques and performance, the consequence of the enlargement of corporations and the replacement of founding captains of industry and capitalists of robber baron infamy by salaried managers. The evolving approach to personnel emerged in the influential ideas of Elton Mayo, who became a professor at Harvard. Whereas Taylor emphasized workers' individualism and the role of environment, Mayo stressed workers' camaraderie, their collective solidarity, their bowing to peer pressure. Management then had to become involved in counselling, in leadership through co-operation and persuasion; good physical conditions and good wages did not suffice. By the 1950s corporate leaders at least talked of moderating the profit motive in the interests of stimulating creativity. Joseph Scanlon argued that companies should open the work-place to debate, self-appraisal and suggestions for improvement. Benefits from cost-cutting proposals should be shared among employees. Orderliness in the work-place would be less important than collective attention to increasing productivity. In the manner of packaging ideas in simplistic form, fashionable writing in the 1950s contrasted the rival claims of so-called theory X, with its structured, authority-bred concept of management, and theory Y, which postulated that people enjoyed work and would exercise self-control, responsibility and creativity at work if sufficiently committed to company objectives. Management by objective gave way to theories of self-actualization, with the boss acting more as consultant than commander.[83]

The formal analysis of management was not ignored in early twentieth-century Britain, or Europe, but at each stage of corporate development American theory seems to have led. One reason for this was the simple fact that American corporations grew bigger quicker than did British corporations and concerned themselves with producing for large national markets. Elton Mayo's ideas about 'human relations' had little impact in Britain in the 1930s, and European changes in management styles and strategies have generally followed rather than inspired American models, given Americans' experience with very large corporations.[84]

This does not mean that one accepts Americans' theoretical writings at face value. It may be that American industrial relations have sometimes looked better than British ones because of the relative weakness of American shop stewards, or because of the earlier and steadier reduction in the relative size of the industrial work-force (beginning before the 1970s and 1980s) or because of the lack of vast nationalized industries, or because of weaker legal protection for trade unionism. Management theories are not always translated into practice. Indeed the message of contemporary management evangelists, such as Tom Peters, suggests in its echoing of these earlier invocations, that the personnel ideology of the 1950s has not permeated as deeply as its advocates may have wished or claimed. Morever, some exponents of new management ideals in the 1950s may not have reflected the assumptions of an enlightened culture; their arguments became invectives against the contemporary Marxist challenge.[85] And among historians David E. Noble has questioned the motives behind the drive for technological improvement and industrial mechanization. He argues that those responsible for technological change – especially in the air force – wanted quantitative approaches to problems and command and control over workers. Technological innovation flowed therefore not from a careful assessment of higher productivity and efficiency, but from American managers' anxiety complexes about workers' rights, about the bargaining power of workers in skilled subjects, and about the declining work ethic. The military especially, with their large budget and preoccupation with command and control, led the way in automation, with techniques developed for the Department of Defense being diffused into the private sector. In this view American management, far from being inspired by theory Y, desperately wanted to squeeze out the work-force. Industry fell under the spell of an ideology of technological progress.[86]

Against these qualifications, the effects of higher education and personnel management – and a long-standing American enthusiasm for technology – must be considered in relation tot the corporate restructuring of American industry that occurred at the very beginning of the twentieth-century. Two consequences followed from that restructuring, the emergency of managerial capitalism and the diffusion of research. Once very large corporations emerged around 1900, their growth became self-propelling, as managers increased in function and in power, taking over from industries' great founder entrepreneurs, and as such companies financed expansion from retained earnings. Managerial capitalism had emerged in America by the 1920s in response to the sheer size and complexity of American companies. Adding to those influences were the enormity of the domestic market and the challenge of running the far-flung transport networks necessary to its operation and the highly integrated American (as distinct from British) system of mass production and mass distribution. Alfred D. Chandler argues that a distinctive approach to vertical integration, controlling marketing and purchasing functions, was the main reason why American management developed faster than did British and European; a similar ascendancy of salaried management did not occur in Britain and Europe until after 1945. An obvious objection to this is that British firms depended on world markets and tackled more challenging marketing and distributing tasks than did American companies dealing almost entirely with a vast but domestic market. Here Chandler notes two differences. Outside food and brewing, most large British companies, he says, made goods for producers and not consumers; hence the lesser need for dynamic marketing strategies and, perhaps, the longer durability of informal, personal contacts in coming to agreements with large-scale customers. Secondly, founding families tended to retain control over their firms longer in Europe than in America; it is possible that this encouraged them to avoid massive expansion or consolidation and the accompanying need to hand power over increasingly to salaried managers.[87]

Whether or not there was a direct causal connection, it is worth stressing that an educated management promoted a high commitment to research and development. A symbolic, if exaggerated, example was the ascendancy in 1902 of the three MIT-educated du Pont cousins and the subsequent revitalization of the late eighteenth-century family company. Formal research in companies started in the late nineteenth century in order to meet direct competition. Standard Oil of Indiana opened a chemical laboratory in the 1880s to develop refining techniques and by 1912 had 120 research staff. Laboratories aided innovation and the creation of new markets; managers developed new markets through directed research. The research sector grew quickly. Whereas 10 per cent of new, American-trained physics PhDs went into industry in 1900, 29 per cent of a larger number of such scientists did so by 1920. Twenty years later 2,200 companies claimed to have laboratories, although the 45 largest laboratories employed over half the country's researchers, notably in electrical, chemical, pharmaceutical, car and oil industries.[88] In 1959, 74 per cent of American scientists and engineers were in industry, against 42 per cent of British scientists and engineers; and America had relatively more engineers than

Britain did in its total complement of such qualified personnel. By 1970 large-scale industry employed about 1.5 million workers in industrial research departments; in 1975 the USA still accounted for half the total expenditure devoted to industrial research and development by the eleven leading OECD countries; and in 1977 the USA employed 57.4 scientists and engineers per 10,000 people in the labour force, a proportion substantially ahead of Japan's 49.9, West Germany's 40.5 and Britain's slightly over 30.[89]

By the 1960s the leading R & D sectors – aerospace, electrical equipment and communications, and chemicals – absorbed the lion's share of researchers. This effort, with its emphasis on labour-saving technology, derived not simply from a desire to control the work-force, but from twin needs to contain high labour costs and to respond to what was perceived (though we can now say erroneously) as an intense challenge from the USSR manifested in the Russian launching in 1957 of the first space satellite, Sputnik. The number of American scientists and engineers engaged in full-time R & D nearly doubled in the years 1957–64, with much expansion coming through increased federal spending, especially on defence. At the same time, in 1957–61, over one million industrial production jobs were lost while output/man hour rose by 18 per cent. This automation occurred without bitter opposition from organized labour, somewhat surprisingly if Noble's emphasis on managerial control were so vital a factor in that process.[90] Moreover, there seemed to be an appreciation that automation would free workers from the most demeaning of jobs. Thus although the percentage of the labour force classified as blue collar workers fell only from 35.8 per cent in 1900 to 31.7 per cent in 1980, the percentage who were unskilled blue collar slumped from 12.5 per cent to 4.6 per cent. A big increase in skilled or semi-skilled workers occurred, including the important transport sector. The engine of much innovation was the individual company laboratory. The British industrial and economic journalist Michael Shanks argued in 1967 that R & D provided a central element in companies' self-images and structure: 'there tends to be a closer connexion in America than in Britain between the scientist and the boardroom, and a closer nexus between research and profitability.'[91] Shanks was no corporation-man, but an active supporter of the efforts by the Labour government of 1964–70 to modernize British industry.

The 1960s witnessed a good deal of European enthusiasm, and not from the political or economic establishment, for the introduction of American business methods. Servan-Schreiber in *The American Challenge* cited various forecasts prophesying that only the USA, Canada, Japan and Sweden had the technological and scientific sophistication to evolve into post-industrial societies by the early twenty-first century, societies run by cybernetics and geared to levels of technological innovation made possible only by an extremely highly educated work-force. In Germany, American officials and businessmen involved in postwar reconstruction deplored the German style of industrial concentration, cartels, and direct access to government ministers and bureaucrats, all giving rise to managed markets very remote from the American ideal. Americans pressed for de-cartelization (anti-trust preoccupations puzzled Germans greatly), for more vigorous competition, and for a less authoritarian 'Prussian' style of management. Germans studied American methods not just in standardization, through cutting the numbers of plants and models, but also in managerial models. Yet 'Prussian' approaches still won approval from the older generation of managers during the 1950s. The Harzburg Leadership Academy, for instance, opened in 1956 under Reinhard Hohn, a former Nazi Gruppenführer; by the early 1960s some 30,000 managers had attended courses there, designed by Hohn whose earlier writings had been on the führer principle. Gradually during the 1960s a younger generation of German industrialists adopted American management practices. But the transition to closer co-operation with trade unions was accompanied by often hysterical anti-unionism from business leaders. It came about after a period of industrial mergers, especially in the years 1968–75, export-led growth, and political changes culminating in the Co-determination Act of 1976.[92] That enactment owed more to the politics of the then ascendant Social Democratic party than to American management styles.

How much did these American approaches to management, or to enterprise, flow from a distinctive cultural background? Many foreign visitors certainly believed and believe that Americans more fully manifested the work ethic than Europeans did. After ten years in Boston, Francis Grund wrote in 1837:

There is, probably, no people on earth with whom business constitutes pleasure, and industry amusement, in an equal degree with the inhabitants of the United States of America ... . Business is the very soul of an American; he pursues it, not as a means of procuring for himself and his family the necessary comforts of life, but as the fountain of all human felicity. ...

This commitment to work was widely celebrated in mid-nineteenth century writings. A work ethic emerged not simply from Calvinist tenets, but also from secular sources. Work was viewed as a necessary part of the persistent struggle for life, as an essential antidote to sin (Henry Ward Beecher pontificated in 1844, 'The indolent mind is not empty but full of vermin'), as a creative, fulfilling act, and as a pre-requisite of worldly success. Some of these claims for the work ethic contradicted each other, notably the tension between work as a creative act and work as repression.[93] But although such claims were as vigorously promoted elsewhere – one notable example being Samuel Smiles's *Self-Help* (1859) – they attained unrivalled currency or support in the American North. Distinctive American characteristics included more open economic and social mobility. The massive availability of, and the lively market in, land diffused land ownership far more widely in America than in Britain and engendered a distinctive optimism about the prospects of self-improvement through acquiring small farms and trading up in farms and land-holdings. The mid-nineteenth century economy was dominated by small-scale farmers and market-town businessmen.

By the early twentieth century some of this optimism was harder to justify. Factory work swamped individualism; the McCormick reaper plant in Chicago, for instance, had 150 hands in 1850, 4,000 in 1900 and 15,000 in 1916; the Ford complex at Highland Park employed 33,000 people by 1916. Repetitive work done against the clock could scarcely be regarded as creative. Religious and medical leaders warned of the moral and health hazards of over-work and the spiritual and physical desirability of relaxation. Concern for consumerism led to the positive promotion of middle-class leisure. Liberal theology and the New Thought movement of the 1890s emphasized that the world was not as adversarial and combative as had earlier been asserted.[94]

Yet the work ethic remained resilient. Under attack from radical and socialist critics, great capitalists retorted, as J.P.Morgan did in 1915, 'the most of us work in this country.' One principal method of legitimation was the leading capitalists' heavy involvement in philanthropy, an involvement that long preceded the

early twentieth century but which burgeoned then. The businessmen engaged in massive giving distinguished between charity,
or donations to produce immediate relief, and philanthropy,
designed to enable people to function more effectively over the
long-term. The two princes of American philanthropy as the
twentieth century began, Andrew Carnegie and John D. Rockefeller, competed publicly in the race of giving. By 1913 Carnegie
had given $332 million and Rockefeller $175 million. The first
had established the Carnegie Corporation of New York in 1911
as his vehicle for further giving and had handed over the bulk
of his remaining fortune to it. One acerbic observer noted, 'Never
before in the history of plutocratic America had any one man
purchased by mere money so much social advertizing and flat-
tery. He would have given millions to Greece had she labelled
the Parthenon "Carnegopolis"'. His rival, who established the
Rockefeller Foundation in 1913, was far more discreet and
indeed had a stern, religious sense of purpose.[95]

Carnegie preached a heady message of self-improvement and
hard work. He was especially interested in providing free public
libraries and he and his foundations had built, by the time of
the millionaire's death in 1919, 2,811 free public libraries (over
two-thirds of them in the USA, most of the rest in the UK and
Canada) at a cost of $50.4 million. Carnegie initiated the library
project in a period when free libraries were extremely rare, and
carried it forward with a zeal born of a belief in practical, not
classical, education. Much of his other giving, which totalled
$350.7 million during his life-time, concerned education and
teaching. Carnegie's crusade for popular education arose from
his antagonism towards the over-mighty classics, his belief in
science, and his suspicion of the literary and elitist atmosphere
of Harvard, Yale and Columbia before they began to develop
professional graduate education. When he considered donating
large sums for education to his native Scotland, he wanted to
see American-style boards of trustees drawn from the world of
business oversee the Scottish universities' operations: 'Americans
do not trust their money to a lot of professors and principals
who are bound in set ways, and have a class feeling about them
which makes it impossible to make reforms.' Yet he was no
philistine in worshipping all things industrial. His first benefac-
tions were directed at making Pittsburgh pre-eminent in the arts
and sciences as well as in iron and steel.[96]

Despite such wider concerns, Carnegie vigorously promoted

a straightforward gospel of work and progress. Yet this doctrine has been regarded as increasingly anachronistic in the twentieth century as more diverse, and some would say more sophisticated, interpretations of human motivation have been set forward.

Freudianism, with its emphasis on the gratification of the libido, and behaviourism both undermined the credibility of the traditional work ethic, as have the hippie and drug cultures since the 1960s. Yet the American cult of work and self-improvement, and the high public status of the self-made man remained and have retained their vitality. There was no British equivalent to the enthusiasm and intensity of this American preoccupation with making oneself agreeable, efficient, and successful. When Dale Carnegie's *How to Win Friends and Influence People* appeared in 1936 it sold 5,000 copies a day for two years and had sold nine million copies world-wide by 1970. The benefits of success continued to be protected from estate duties and to be legitimated in public by individual entrepreneurs' establishment of charitable foundations, to disperse funds for education, research, Third World development and health-care. By 1981, charitable foundations had total assets of $41 billion; there were 34,000 foundations with assets over $1 million each and making average annual gifts of $100,000 or more. The very largest British trusts – Wolfson (established in 1955) and Leverhulme (1925) – would have been hard stretched consistently during the 1980s, depending upon the exchange rate, to have come within the fifteen most heavily endowed American foundations. Tax laws rewarded individual giving, and this further encouraged the cult of individual achievement. Wealth itself frequently appears far more fully as the key to public status in America than in Britain. Lewis H. Lapham's *Money and Class in America* is just the latest example of a genre in which money is depicted as the single most important symbol of status.[97]

There may be as much display, consumption and indulgence in leisure and pleasure found in America's supremely rich as are found among British plutocrats. And many successful British businessmen have involved themselves extensively in philanthropic activities. But there is surely a psychological difference between the American entrepreneur's self-glorification and the British process of gentrification: William Morris the great car manufacturer became Viscount Nuffield; James Mackay, the shipping and Far Eastern trading magnate, became Earl of Inchcape; William Lever, the soap mogul, became Viscount Leverhulme; Frederick Marquis, the retailer, became Earl of Woolton: the examples could be multiplied of the process whereby very successful businessmen – albeit through public and philanthropic service – seek a rather different identity in which to savour their arrival at the top.[98] Of course, there are many twentieth century instances of American businessmen seeking public office as a means of enhancing their personal prestige. And there are similarly numerous examples of the second and third generations of successful business families losing the entrepreneurial thrust and common touch of the founders. But upper-crust heirs in America have normally been compelled to shed their elitist habits and image if they were to gain wide public acceptance.

This does not mean that America's rich have not experienced gentrification. Perhaps the most readily cited example is the first industrial elite, the Boston Associates who developed the Waltham-Lowell complex of textile factories, and planned settlements, from the 1810s and 1820s onwards. By 1850 the Associates controlled 20 per cent of the nation's cotton spindle capacity. Most of the Associates' children chose careers other than textiles. Many of them went into the ministry or the law. Some of that generation felt guilty about their backsliding. Thomas Jefferson Coolidge, a banker, remembered mid-nineteenth-century Boston from a later vantage point: 'Everybody was at work trying to make money and money was becoming the only real avenue to power and success both socially and in regard to your fellow men.' By the early twentieth century social kudos attached itself more readily to clerics, writers, educationists, academics, architects, even astronomers. Those from the old elite engaged in business involved themselves heavily in local philanthropic and cultural activities. Disdain for commerce crept into the old elite's talk and thinking. Some retreated from business, law and politics because of personal failure to keep up in the increasingly competitive conditions of the late nineteenth and early twentieth centuries. Others found their family fortunes tied up in trusts; this, together with the relative shrinkage in Boston's capital base, meant that old families' involvement in late-nineteenth century mining, railway and other ventures had to be discontinued for want of fresh investment capital which New York's banks readily supplied. Finally, some family fortunes were reduced by the relative decline in cotton textile manufacturing from the 1860s to the 1920s.[99] But if the retreat from business occurred on all fronts, there were important contrasts with Britain.

First, the elite remained an urban one. It did not shift its locus of status and power to, say, western Massachusetts and sink a large slice of its wealth into landed estates. Secondly, individual Boston Brahmins led – though many others did not approve – considerable educational reform. Harvard did not follow Oxford and Cambridge in their attitudes towards the classics and towards business. Charles Francis Adams, Jr, endorsed the widespread view that Boston suffered too much from classical education: 'I want to see more university men trained up to take a hand in the rather rough game of American twentieth century life.' The two presidents of Harvard from 1869 to 1932 – Charles W. Eliot and Abbott Lawrence Lowell – were both from the Boston Associates industrial elite; the first broadened the curriculum, while the second supported the Business School.[100] Thirdly, this elite was a local Boston elite. This was a more general phenomenon. The compilation of social registers began in 1890 with the publication of those for New York and Boston. Nineteen others followed by the 1920s for major cities, although nine of these registers failed through lack of interest.[101] These volumes celebrated or tried to celebrate local urban elites quite different from the national British aristocracy and gentry, with their diverse rural roots in county society, their town-houses in London, their education at a small number of public schools and Oxford and Cambridge, their entré into the London social season, and their focus on the rituals of the Court. Down to the 1960s, the outstandingly successful entrepreneurs in gaining peerages also obtained hereditary places in the upper house of Parliament, something unthinkable in America.

The existence of a British establishment is a topic of much debate. What often impresses about it is the relative narrowness of its educational and social experience. Even in the 1980s the narrow educational base of Britain's traditional professional leaders shows how a national elite has endured, even if it has widened its spread of recruitment. In 1981 of the nine law lords (the rough equivalent of the American Supreme Court) eight had been at Oxford; the other had not attended university; and seven went to private schools, including two at Winchester. Of the eighteen top civil servants in 1981 (excluding the Foreign Office), fourteen graduated from Oxford and Cambridge, three from Edinburgh, and one had not been at university. The head of the Home Civil Service had been at Eton. Of the 22 Conservative Cabinet ministers in June 1982, 19 were Oxford or Cambridge graduates; only one had graduated elsewhere. The majority had been educated at private schools; including three at Eton and three at Winchester. The point is not that these leaders shared the same background of wealth or precise social status, but that they experienced in their formative years a fairly uniform and traditional process of socialization beyond the confines of the family.[102] There was no equivalent to that in the USA, and old families found it difficult to hold firmly to public office within their states. The US Senate in 1982 showed the localized and disparate origins of the American political elite. Of the 98 Senators (out of 100) who had attended college and university, the vast majority had been undergraduates in institutions essentially of local, state or regional significance as far as their undergraduate recruitment went. Those 98 senators had attended no fewer than 77 institutions as their first choice of undergraduate place of study. Hardly any institutions educated more than two senators at the undergraduate level. The top two numerically – Yale with six senators and Princeton with four senators – were atypical also in being leading private institutions. Otherwise the diversity of educational backgrounds reflected America's strong regionalism, sense of state identity, and dispersed elites.[103]

More predictably, the British social elite displays strong cohesion. Of the 25 British non-royal dukes in 1981, the top drawer of the hereditary aristocracy, 15 had been at Oxford or Cambridge, only one had attended another university and that was McGill in Quebec. No fewer than 17 had been at one school, Eton, the clearest possible indication of the way in which an elite whose ancestral estates stretched from Northern Ireland, Perthshire, the Scottish borders, Northumberland, to Derbyshire, Norfolk, Berkshire and Sussex, was drawn together by education. When the *Sunday Times* published a listing of those it believed to be the richest 200 people in Britain, it noted that no fewer than 55 of those 200 had been to one school, Eton, and that 27 of them were landowners; the list included 40 peers *above* the rank of baron, out of 370 men in total holding such titles. Nearly half of all dukes remained among the mega-rich.[104] Much of that wealth goes back two hundred years or more.

American status and wealth were also often inherited. In 1987 241 of the wealthiest 400 Americans listed in *Forbes* magazine had inherited most or all of their fortunes.[105] But this group did not constitute an establishment in a national political, cultural and social scene equivalent to London's. The dispersal of American elites through the various states and cities – and the absence of a capital that was a national commercial, financial, cultural and social as well as political and legal capital – worked against the formation of so clear-cut an aristocracy. The older established elites of Boston, New York City and Philadelphia tended to intermingle more in work and marriage after the Second World War than they had done earlier. But their sense of caste fell off and those whose wealth was based on nineteenth century commerce and industry no longer had the power to rival the new rich of Detroit or Pittsburgh, Delaware or Texas, with their roots essentially in cars, steel, chemicals and oil, respectively, together with the numerous spin-offs from those commodities. The ten leading American philanthropic foundations in 1980–81 (each endowed with assets of at least $460 million) showed the dispersal of wealth: three (Ford, Kellogg and Kresge) emerged from Michigan (in cars, cereals and retailing), three emerged from oil (Pew, Rockefeller and Keck) in Pennsylvania, New York and California; the others varied. Three of these ten biggest foundations were set-up after 1945.[106]

C. Wright Mills' notable study of *The Power Elite* (1956) emphasized that exclusive schools, university societies and clubs were the preserve of the hereditary rich; but he failed to show what proportion of the top decision-makers attended such schools or belonged to such societies at the handful of select universities; the general view is that the old elites wielded no comparable power or indeed influence to that enjoyed by the British establishment. One special case where a close-knit elite exercised considerable power just after the Second World War (at about the time Mills was writing) was in the direction of foreign policy. The financial and political elite certainly merged in the shape of W. Averell Harrison (Groton and Yale), Dean Acheson (Groton and Yale), Charles E. Bohlen (St Paul's and Harvard), and Robert Lovett (The Hill School and Yale), who shared a common social and educational background of the sort Mills described and shaped American responses during the early Cold War.[107] But even those men's families could scarcely challenge the aristocratic or gentry background of those heading the British Foreign Office under Conservative governments. The following Conservative Foreign Secretaries since 1951 were educated at one school, Eton: Sir Anthony Eden 1951–55, the son of a baronet whose title went back to 1672; Harold Macmillan, 1955, whose father-in-law was the 9th Duke of Devonshire; the 14th Earl of Home, 1960–63, 1970–74, whose family titles went back to 1473; the 6th Lord Carrington, 1979–82, whose title goes back to 1796; Francis Pym, 1982–83, one of whose ancestors was a speaker of the House of Commons in the mid-seventeenth century; Douglas Hurd, since 1989, whose grandfather was an M.P. and knighted and whose father was an M.P. and then a life peer. At the beginning of 1990 all five Foreign Office ministers in the government were sons of peers, two of them hereditary peers and one a Sainsbury magnate.[108]

The emergence of new elites in America pushed the old ones into the shadows. New York upper class society folded after the Second World War as an elaborately ritualized order. So, too, 'Divorce, the Depression, flight, and the encroachment of café society withered high society in Chicago and other places', by 1940. In Los Angeles, Hollywood and new tycoons from real estate and finance edged families of older wealth – such as the Huntingtons and Kresses – from such positions of social prestige as may have existed. Given the peculiar relationship to Hollywood and its booming expansion, 'in Los Angeles money and publicity, not birth or tradition, dictated social rank.' It was a city of the present and the future, not the past.[109] Although aggregate data are difficult to secure and rely on, one comparative study using figures from the 1940s and 1950s showed some important differences between Britain and America. Although sons of American fathers classified as being in the elite had a greater chance of staying within the elite than did such sons in Britain, there was also a distinctly higher rate of middle-class entry into the American elite than was the case in Britain. Opportunity for entering the elite was one and a half times greater in America than Britain. This resulted from the facts that the elite virtually doubled in relative size between the two generations (in Britain it fell slightly) and that the middle class also took up a relatively larger share of the total work force in America than in Britain.[110]

The lack of an entrenched elite and the diffusion of business education and values helped secure wide acceptance of the industrial system despite all the criticisms of industrialism's worst effects. In a careful analysis of public attitudes towards big business, as displayed in the specialist press, Louis Galambos has shown that over the period 1880–1940 there was a remarkably low level of outright disapproval, that if disapproval emerged it was generally short-lived and that by 1940 attitudes among professional men, farmers and labourers converged with respect to approval or disapproval of business. Although the last named group naturally offered more unfavourable opinions of big business than did the first two groups, the overall trend of opinion among working class periodicals followed that of the farmers' journals; by the late 1930s favourable or neutral opinions outweighed antagonistic ones. In a survey of opinion carried out in 1950, only 10 per cent of those questioned believed that big business' faults outweighed their benefits. The big businesses attacked most consistently in the period 1890 to 1940 were railway transport companies and, secondarily, transport equipment companies. Other sectors prominently included were oil and food processing giants. For many farmers and small businessmen the middlemen – not the system generally – caused the greatest anxiety and antagonism. Even at the apogee of radical ferment and the student and black protest movements, in July 1968, Gallup conducted a poll asking what set of institutions would be 'the biggest threat to the country in the future?' No fewer than 46 per cent of respondents saw the principal threat as big government; 26 per cent selected big unions; only 12 per cent suggested big business and that tiny minority rose only to 14 per cent among registered Democrats alone.[111]

Any discussion of an enterprise system must take into account the social context in which ideas flourish. The American environment provided such physical space and opportunity and social fluidity that a business culture met few impediments. In education and in society generally business was accepted and promoted. In American high culture, however, the rise of corporations aroused considerable antagonism: in novels from the late nineteenth century onwards; among the old rich; among social critics sceptical about the moral acceptability of organization men. But elsewhere in American culture these disparaging attitudes won relatively little endorsement; universities promoted business education and business links; the middle-brow periodicals addressed to workers, clergymen and professionals only irregularly attacked big business.

Part of the reason for this was that American business was relatively innovative, competitive and open to individual influences and pressures. Sir John Harvey-Jones makes this point in assessing British defects: 'Management is about change, and maintaining a high rate of change.' The British, in his exaggerated but still significant view, remain too wedded to the past. 'It is only in the United Kingdom that we have a particular love of the old and a seeming contempt for the new.' This contrasted sharply with the powerful American sales word 'new'.[112] Building on this enthusiasm for novelty, perhaps Americans' major contribution to modern capitalism was the packaging, advertising and distributing of goods and services. Henry Ford blazed the way with the sale of 15 million model-T Fords between 1908 and 1927. Again, between 1920 and the 1950s a whole range of groceries, food-stuffs and household commodities had become packaged with purchases made at supermarkets, the first of which was opened in 1923 and 30,000 of which existed by 1959. This genius for marketing entered another phase from the 1950s with the explosion of franchising and the accompanying diffusion of small-scale capitalism. By 1965 about 1,200 companies operated through 350,000 franchised dealerships, bottlers and packagers, repairers, restaurants and an array of other services. The system of matching centralized brands, promotion and organization with independent entrepreneurial effort started with car sales at the beginning of the twentieth century. It spread particularly after 1945; one of the most celebrated of franchised organizations was MacDonald's Hamburgers, started only in 1954.[113]

Marketing and selling techniques also evolved through direct selling to become by the late 1980s a phenomenon that has been called 'charismatic capitalism'. By the 1920s brushes, hosiery, and pots and pans were prominent among a variety of articles sold door-to-door in a corporate extension of old-style peddling. From that point companies began to exploit social networks for selling and distribution from the home. In modern times Mary Kay cosmetics and Home Interiors and Gifts offered notable examples of this style of operation; the latter engaged by the late 1980s about 30,000 distributors, typically women operating from home, co-ordinated by only 35 managers. In 1976 some 8 per cent of all American families included an active distributor of one commodity or another and 25 per cent of families reported that they had counted a distributor in their midst at some time in the past. Between 1975 and 1985 distributors involved in direct selling (other than insurance) increased from 1.93 million to 5.12 million. Nor did the development of this form of enterprise simply mean increasing size. Employees are subjected to intensive training accompanied by all the emotion, hope, razzmatazz and presentational slickness that one expects of television evangelism. Individual distributors attend rallies, have their personal self-confidence and assertiveness strengthened, are integrated into regular group contact and support (as well as peer control) with nearby fellow distributors. Emotional identification with the product and with the distributive team is thus built up. It is reinforced by prizes, and prize-giving ceremonies for the most successful sales personnel. Using such intensive techniques the A. L. Williams Company amassed a sales force of 155,000 over ten years and in 1986 sold more term life insurance than did the Prudential, the previous market leader. Direct selling organizations expanded the work-force and, equally important, the culture of participating capitalism.[114]

The expansion of franchising and the allied expansion of the service sector generally, meant that even in the age of mammoth corporations, the number of corporations expanded dramatically from 587,700 in 1947 (up only from 509,400 in 1929) to 1,032,600 in 1961 to 1,905,000 by 1973. The proportion of those corporations which were engaged in manufacturing fell from 19 per cent in 1947 to 11 per cent in 1973, although even that relative decline meant an absolute increase in the number of manufacturing corporations from 112,200 to 209,000. Most of those manufacturing businesses employed under twenty people. Even further evidence for the wide diffusion of enterprise culture comes from the numbers of proprietorships and of the self-employed. Between 1970 and 1985 the number of non-farm proprietorships soared from 5,770,000 to 11,929,000, while the proportion of the non-farm work-force who were self-employed rose from 7 per cent to $7\frac{1}{2}$ per cent at a time when that labour force grew by 30 million. Franchised dealerships, service industries, small manufacturing plants, proprietorships, self-employment and direct selling done with evangelical fervour all indicated the robust embodiment of enterprise values.[115] As one of America's pre-eminent economic historians, Stuart Bruchey, pointed out, 'the overwhelming majority of decisions on what to produce, and how and where and when to produce it, have been made by private persons and businesses, that is to say, by the market.' The country's success depended on its values because the freedom 'to work, save, invest and innovate' resulted from Americans' conviction that such freedom was of vital importance to them.[116]

This behaviour leads free-market economists to an important theoretical point. Building on the Austrian school of economists, Israel M. Kirzner argues against the Keynesian tradition of establishing formal equilibrium models of economic behaviour. The market, he contends, is not a mechanism by which equilibrium may be attained but a process, in which every actor is, in a sense, an entrepreneur. What distinguishes successful entrepreneurship as a particular quality is the use of habitual alertness to price changes, profit opportunities and market differences to initiate transactions. Entrepreneurship is not a specific resource, but part and parcel of the activity of being involved in the market process. Kirzner observes, 'Instead of seeing how the entrepreneur has disturbed the placid status quo, we must see how the status quo is nothing but a seething mass of unexploited maladjustments crying out for correction.' The entrepreneur is not a capital-rich businessman or an innovating genius, as the classic definitions require, but rather a participant in the never-ending transactions that make up a market place of supply and demand differentials and price disparities.[117] This goes straight against American liberals, such as J.K.Galbraith and Lester C.Thurow, who argue that prosperity results from a significantly planned economy directed towards an agreed equilibrium.[118] A comparative judgement here is bound to be subjective; but it seems to many observers that America is a more market-orientated society, in this sense of price alertness and arbitrage, than is the UK.

It would be wrong to suggest that this ideal of a pulsating free-market economy squares entirely with the American reality. Free-market economists point out that from the mid-1950s to the 1970s nearly all federal regulatory agencies (and there were plenty of them) grew rapidly, and more consistently, than did the various industries they regulated. These agencies tended to form bureaucratic relationships with the industries they scrutinized, with the result that government–industry collaborations occur. But it can certainly be stressed, as such leading liberals as Professor Thurow do, that government in the USA at state and federal levels, is far less obtrusive, and absorbs a lower percentage of GNP, than it does in most of America's economic rivals. If anything, according to liberals, the American economy is under-regulated; 'nowhere in the world', writes Thurow, 'is it easier to lay off workers.'[119] Of course, Thurow was writing for the 1980s and not for the 1970s, after the process of deregulation began under President Carter's administration. Republican actions of the 1980s slowed the trend towards increasing regulation and reversed that trend of the 1950s and 1960s in some spheres. On a spectrum between a tightly controlled economy and a free market, America sits rather more to the free-market end; but it would be absurd to overlook the pressures for a shift to the collectivist side.

This discussion has moved between statements of values and empirical manifestations of behaviour. The problem with expressions of belief is that they can be wildly at variance with reality; the corporate president declares his unflinching commitment to free competition while his company does everything in its power to monopolize markets and block the entry to new producers; the best-selling novelist deplores the material world and its values while trimming or even tailoring his or her works to meet the requirements of commercial success. Equally troublesome is the fact that outcomes do not necessarily reflect intentions; regulatory agencies may in effect limit entry of new firms instead of simply policing the behaviour of existing ones. But at least some outcomes relate to underlying beliefs. Millionaires' setting up of philanthropic foundations partly resulted from a determination to avoid heavy federal taxes on estates at death; but their actions reflected also a powerful individualistic impulse to legitimate business success and to celebrate individual businessmen's achievements and values. So, too, the creation of franchising and the continuing surge of business formation since the 1940s indicates the resilience of enterprise values. And the fact that the American spectrum of political debate does not stretch to socialist prescriptions shows the enduring appeal of capitalist or semi-capitalist assumptions and ideas.

This point is well borne out by an empirical study of fundamental values among a sample of respondents made by Jennifer Hochschild; the smallness of the sample was compensated for by the depth of the analysis, and the range of the income distribution of those questioned. Irrespective of wealth or poverty, the respondents followed fairly easily discernible lines of thought. They typically displayed liberal attitudes concerning social and political egalitarianism, endorsing what others have termed an equality of esteem, as well as political democracy; but they typically also upheld economic differentiation among people, assuming that competitive capitalism was the natural economic order. Poor respondents did not press for any redistribution of wealth. Some of them did not want it, or the government intervention necessary to achieve it; others did not believe it could be obtained; others simply regarded the matter with indifference.

The existence of so strong a commitment to the competitive order – albeit counterbalanced by social or political egalitarianism – provided a powerful base for enterprise, one far from being as consistently strong or straightforward in Britain.[120]

The relationship between cultural values and economic performance is unlikely to be precise or well-defined. Yet an examination of the American system of enterprise shows that cultural characteristics – understood in the broadest social and political sense of culture – shape institutional arrangements which themselves may promote entrepreneurial activity. In the emergence of modern managerialism, in the dissemination and celebration of business values, in the spread of half-way forms of self-employment through franchising and direct selling, in the judicial maintenance of competition, and in the resistance to trade unionism and anti-market socialism, the USA has either led the way or, depending how one regards such matters, followed a different path from that trod by Britain. Although America's most distinguished novelists, belles lettrists, and intellectuals may condemn enterprise values in ways similar to those described in Britain, American popular culture, and institutional arrangements, are shaped by the pursuit of business opportunities and profit. 'The business of America is business' may be a comment many Americans regret; but it more truly represents Americans' behaviour and aspirations than would any similar remark about Britain.

NOTES

1. R. C. O. Matthews, 'The Economics of Institutions and the Sources of Growth', *The Economic Journal*, 96 (1986), pp. 903–18; N. F. R. Crafts, 'The Assessment: British Economic Growth Over the Long Run', *Oxford Review of Economic Policy*, 4 (1988), pp. i–xxi.
2. James Raven, 'British History and the Enterprise Culture', *Past and Present*, 123 (1989), pp. 178–204.
3. Bruce R. Scott and George C. Lodge (eds.), *U.S. Competitiveness in the World Economy* (Boston, Mass.: Harvard Business School Press, 1985), pp. 14, 131, 143; again 'Our focus is not on a short-term crisis but on a longer-term decline like that which has characterized the United Kingdom for the last century' (p. 3). See also explicit comparisons with Britain in W. W. Rostow, *The Barbaric Counter-Revolution: Cause and Cure* (London: Macmillan, 1984), pp. xii–xxvii. Bernard Elbaum and William Lazonick (eds.), *The Decline of the British Economy* (Oxford: Clarendon Press, 1986), p. v, argue that 'the United States

may have even more to learn from the decline of Britain' than from Japanese success. Also, Kevin Phillips, 'Toward a Bipartisan Competitiveness Strategy' in David R. Obey and Paul Sarbanes (eds.), *The Changing American Economy* (Oxford: Basil Blackwell, 1986), pp. 213–14.

4. Milton Friedman and Rose Friedman, *Free to Choose: A Personal Statement* (Harmondsworth, Middx.: Penguin, 1980), pp. 19–26, 330–59.

5. Robert Z. Lawrence, *Can America Compete?* (Washington, DC: Brookings Institution, 1984), pp. 137–45. I categorize this as centrist with some caution, since the argument scarcely regards further government intervention favourably. Barry Eichengreen, 'International Competition in the Products of US Basic Industries', in Martin Feldstein (ed.), *The United States in the World Economy* (Chicago: University of Chicago Press, 1988), pp. 279–353, esp. pp. 341–2.

6. Lester C. Thurow, *The Zero-Sum Society: Distribution and the Possibilities for Economic Change* (Harmondsworth, Middx.: Penguin, 1981), pp. 191–4, 203–14; Rostow, *The Barbaric Counter-Revolution*, pp. 70–6, 95, 115–23; George C. Lodge and William C. Crum, 'The Pursuit of Remedies,' in Scott and Lodge, *U.S. Competitiveness*, pp. 479–502, esp. pp. 490–502.

7. Harry Magdoff and Paul M Sweezy, *The End of Prosperity: The American Economy in the 1970s* (New York: Monthly Review Press, 1979), pp. 21, 30–2, 125, 136 argued that Keynesianism had failed to prevent economic fluctuations and to provide full employment and predicted that capitalism would fail (overthrown by the working class) because its only options had become major depression or inflation.

8. Friedmans, *Free to Choose*, pp. 118–25, 176–8; Milton and Rose Friedman, *The Tyranny of the Status Quo* (Harmondsworth, Middx.: Penguin, 1985), pp. 11–12. For other critiques of the effects of big government, see William E. Simon, *A Time for Truth* (New York: Berkeley Books, 1979), pp. 11–13, 93, 216–27; Robert Higgs, *Crisis and Leviathan: Critical Episodes in the Growth of American Government* (New York: Oxford University Press, 1987), pp. 189–95, 256–62; James M. Buchanan, Charles K. Rowley, and Robert D. Tollison (eds.), *Deficits* (Oxford: Basil Blackwell, 1987), pp. 3–8. Businessmen initially supported the New Deal measures of 1933, but disillusion set in from 1934. Arthur A. Ekirch, Jr, *Ideologies and Utopias: The Impact of the New Deal on American Thought* (Chicago: Quadrangle, 1971), pp. 190–3.

9. Lawrence, *Can America Compete?*, pp. 92, 145; Rostow, *Barbaric Counter-Revolution*, pp. xii–xxvii, 1–3; Edward F. Denison, *Accounting for Slower Economic Growth: The United States in the 1970s* (Washington, DC: Brookings Institution, 1979), pp. 125–6, 145–6, and *Accounting for United States Economic Growth 1929–1969* (Washington, DC: Brookings Institution, 1974), pp. 83, 222; Bruce R. Scott, 'US Competitiveness' in Scott and Lodge (eds.), *U.S. Competitiveness*, pp. 13–70, esp. pp. 68–70.

10. Rostow, *Barbaric Counter-Revolution*, pp. 77–86, 125–6.

11. Scott and Lodge, *U.S. Competitiveness*, pp. 10–12, 500–2. A vigorous argument for national industrial strategic planning and investment (which recognizes the political obstacles in the way of such a departure) is presented in Ira C. Magaziner and Robert B. Reich, *Minding America's Business: The Decline and Rise of the American Economy* (New York: Vintage, 1983), pp. 350–1, 370–80.

12. Kevin Phillips, 'Toward a Bipartisan Competitiveness Strategy', in Obey and Sarbanes, *The Changing American Economy*, pp. 210–18.

13. S. J. Prais, 'Comment on the Paper by Professor Giersch and Dr. Walter', *The Economic Journal*, 93 (1983), pp. 84–8.

14. Herman Van der Wee, *Prosperity and Upheaval: The World Economy, 1945–1980*, trans. by Robin Hogg and Max R. Hall (Harmondsworth, Middx.: Penguin, 1987), p. 51.

15. Lawrence, *Can America Compete?*, pp. 18, 33.

16. Edward F. Denison, 'The Interruption of Productivity Growth in the United States', *The Economic Journal*, 93 (1983), 56–77, esp. pp. 76–7.

17. Charles Feinstein, 'Economic Growth since 1870: Britain's Performance in International Perspective', *Oxford Review of Economic Policy*, 4 (1988), 1–13.

18. Van der Wee, *Prosperity and Upheaval*, pp. 141, 165, 170–2, 180–1, 189, 208, 231.

19. Scott, 'U.S. Competitiveness' in Scott and Lodge, *U.S. Competitiveness*, p. 55.

20. Eichengreen, 'International Competition' in Feldstein, *United States in the World Economy*, p. 292.

21. Rostow, *Barbaric Counter-Revolution*, pp. 4–20.

22. Eichengreen, 'International Competition' in Feldstein, *United States in the World Economy*, pp. 293, 332, 337–42; Scott, 'U.S. Competitiveness' in Scott and Lodge, *U.S. Competitiveness in the World Economy*, p. 58.

23. OECD, Department of Economics and Statistics, *Main Economic Indicators*, March 1989 (Paris: OECD 1989), pp. 15, 172.

24. This is the thrust of a useful introduction to the subject: Alan Sked, *Britain's Decline: Problems and Perspectives* (Oxford: Basil Blackwell, 1987). The Friedmans argue the opposite: that a dependency culture, in which the state involves itself pervasively in family and social welfare undermines morality and a sense of personal responsibility. Friedmans, *Free to Choose*, pp. 135, 149, 157–8.

25. Rostow, *Barbaric Counter-Revolution*, p. 5.

26. Van der Wee, *Prosperity and Upheaval*, p. 51; Caves and Krause, 'Introduction and Summary', and Caves (with comments by S. J. Prais), 'Productivity Differences Among Industries' in Richard E. Caves and Lawrence B. Krause (eds.) *Britain's Economic Performance* (Washington, DC: Brookings Institution, 1980), pp. 2–3, 136–7, 155, 193–5. This low British productivity occurred despite capital investment in machinery. The same relative fall against the US is documented in Stephen Davies and Richard E Caves, *Britain's Productivity Gap* (Cambridge: Cambridge University Press, 1987), pp. 1–4.

27. Central Statistical Office, *Social Trends*, 10 (London, HMSO, 1979), p. 219; *Social Trends*, 18 (London, HMSO, 1988), p. 149.
28. Feinstein, 'Economic Growth since 1870', pp. 6–7.
29. Eichengreen, 'International Competition' in Feldstein, *The United States in the World Economy*, pp. 284, 299–300, 318.
30. The view that American engineering training is lamentably deficient compared with Japanese and German training and retention of engineers is put in Sheldon Weinig, 'Managing Better' in Obey and Sarbanes, *The Changing American Economy*, pp. 205–6.
31. Paul Kennedy, *The Rise and Fall of the Great Powers. Economic Change and Military Conflict from 1500 to 2000* (New York: Random House, 1987), pp. 519, 521, 527–30; Friedmans, *The Tyranny of the Status Quo*, pp. 71–81 argue that wasteful defence spending results from bureaucrats' and politicians' actions yet stress that the rise in non-defence spending greatly exceeds increasing defence costs.
32. Lawrence, *Can America Compete?*, p. 134; Steven Muller, 'The View of the Big Performers', *Annals of the American Academy of Political and Social Science*, vol. 502 (March, 1989), 120–9; Les Young, 'Electronics and Computing' in *idem*, pp. 82–93. One economic historian notes that massive US government spending on research in defence, atomic energy and space exploration 'broadened and deepened the scientific base of industry and had a positive qualitative and quantitative impact on the technological lead of the United States over the rest of the world'. Van der Wee, *Prosperity and Upheaval*, p. 203. A leading economic historian of an earlier generation claimed, 'In their definition of military objectives, defence departments in all Western countries, and above all in the USA, were very liberal, and financed a great deal of research only remotely related to defence and much of it serving the interests of pure science. For these and other reasons general technology and science stood to benefit from high and rising expenditures on defence-inspired research'. M. M. Postan, *An Economic History of Western Europe 1945–1964* (London: Methuen, 1967), p. 146.
33. David P. Calleo, *The Imperious Economy* (Cambridge, Mass.: Harvard University Press, 1982), p. 213.
34. Bruce R. Scott, 'National Strategies' in Scott and Lodge, *U.S. Competitiveness in the World Economy*, pp. 96–7, 111–24; quotation on p. 137; Friedmans, *Free to Choose*, pp. 310–16, 350–3, 355, 358; Friedmans, *The Tyranny of the Status Quo*, pp. 112–14. But falling American productivity in the 1970s was not related at all to any shifts in savings rates. Denison, 'The Interruption of Productivity Growth', p. 72.
35. Charles L. Schultze, 'Saving, Investment, and Profitability in Europe', in Robert Z. Lawrence and Charles L. Schultze (eds.), *Barriers to European Growth: A Transatlantic View* (Washington, DC: Brookings Institution, 1987), p. 510.
36. Robert Bacon and Walter Eltis, *Britain's Economic Problem: Too Few Producers* (London: Macmillan, 1978 edn.), pp. 153–6, 163.
37. Lodge and Crum, 'The Pursuit of Remedies', in Scott and Lodge, *U.S. Competitiveness in the World Economy*, pp. 486–7. For vigorous

denunciations of protectionism see the remarks of former President Richard Nixon and former Secretary of State George Schultz in Annelise Anderson and Dennis L. Bark (eds.), *Thinking About America: The United States in the 1990s* (Stanford: Hoover Institution Press, 1988), pp. 10, 526 (also p. 231). For a liberal economist's rejection of protectionism, see Thurow, *The Zero-Sum Society*, p. 6.

38. Lawrence, *Can America Compete?*, pp. 126–7 argues that low tariffs are in American interests and that more sophisticated countermeasures than protectionism can be taken against unfair competition; Robert A. Pollard, *Economic Security and the Origins of the Cold War, 1945–1950* (New York: Columbia University Press, 1985), pp. 5–9, 11–17, 60–6.

39. Martin Feldstein, 'Introduction' in Feldstein, *The United States in the World Economy*, pp. 1–7; Scott, 'U.S. Competitiveness' in Scott and Lodge, *U.S. Competitiveness in the World Economy*, pp. 41–6, 64–70, Scott points out that America's slide in international manufacturing competitiveness occurred when the dollar was falling in the 1970s as well as when it was overvalued during the 1980s. He adds: 'as a safe haven for capital and as the world's leading reserve currency, the United States may face the prospect of a dollar that has a more or less permanent tendency to be overvalued. Like Switzerland, we may have to learn to compete under such conditions rather than simply blame our failure on them' (p. 65). Lawrence, *Can America Compete?*, pp. 7–8 lays little stress on exchange rates.

40. George C. Lodge, *The New American Ideology* (New York: Alfred A. Knopf, 1975), pp. 223–6.

41. Jack Baranson, *The Japanese Challenge to U.S. Industry* (Lexington, Mass.: Lexington Books, 1981), offers a wide-ranging discussion of factors, including infant industry protectionism, intense competition within the Japanese internal market, non-tariff barriers to imports, and such cultural influences as the readiness to go easy on short-term dividends (pp. 24–5, 147–61).

42. Lawrence, *Can America Compete?*, pp. 31, 36; Robert E. Lipsey, 'Changing Patterns of International Investment in and by the United States' in Feldstein, *The United States in the World Economy*, pp. 494–7.

43. Calleo, *The Imperious Economy*, pp. 185–6; Kennedy, *The Rise and Fall of the Great Powers*, pp. 529–30.

44. Rachel McCulloch, 'International Competition in Services' in Feldstein (ed.), *The United States in the World Economy*, p. 383.

45. John Harvey-Jones, *Making It Happen: Reflections on Leadership* (Glasgow: Fontana, 1988), p. 122. There is an excellent example of this phenomenon in the case of F. G. Dalgety, who was born in Canada in 1817, became a merchant in Australia and then in the 1850s and 1860s headed the leading colonial wool importing house in London. In 1864 72% of his investments were in his firm and 5% in his London house and furniture. By 1893, just before his death, investments in his firm had increased substantially in value but constituted only 35%

of his total holdings. Property in England accounted for 38%, mostly in the shape of a country estate and the house he built on it in the early 1870s. Dalgety wrote in 1873, 'I value reputation and social position beyond any amount of profit and will not sacrifice either for gain.' Eton figured largely in the education of his sons, three of whom were at the time of his death officers in the army or navy, one of whom was farming in New Zealand and the last of whom was at Cambridge; of his daughters who had married when he died, one married the heir to an earldom (though an impoverished one) and the other married an army officer whose father had been a Lord Justice of Appeal. Although his own father had been a very junior army officer, Dalgety displayed a distinct long-term aversion to the commerce which enabled him to gentrify his family, M. J. Daunton, 'Firm and Family in the City of London in the Nineteenth Century: the Case of F. G. Dalgety', *Historical Research*, 62 (1989), 154–77.

46. Jim Potter, '"You Too Can Have Statistics Like Mine": Some Economic Comparisons' in Richard Rose (ed.), *Lessons From America: An Exploration* (London: Macmillan, 1974), pp. 97–8.

47. Naomi R. Lamoreaux, *The Great Merger Movement in American Business, 1895–1904* (Cambridge: Cambridge University Press, 1985), pp. 2–4, 188–92.

48. Alfred D. Chandler, Jr, *The Visible Hand: Managerial Revolution in American Business* (Cambridge, Mass.: Belknap, 1977); Van Der Wee, *Prosperity and Upheaval*, pp. 207, 220.

49. Martin J. Sklar, *The Corporate Reconstruction of American Capitalism 1890–1916* (Cambridge: Cambridge University Press, 1988), pp. 106, 147–52, 182, 187.

50. *Ibid.*, pp. 105, 421–5.

51. *Ibid.*, p. 438.

52. *Ibid.*, pp. 223–5, 254; Christopher L. Tomlins, *The State and the Unions: Labor Relations, Law, and the Organized Labor Movement in America, 1880–1960* (Cambridge: Cambridge University Press, 1985), pp. 83–4; Henry Pelling, *A History of British Trade Unionism* (Harmondsworth, Middx.: Penguin, 1976 edn.), p. 132. There is a good discussion of the different intellectual traditions in Melvyn Stokes, 'American Progressives and the European Left', *Journal of American Studies*, 17 (1983), 5–28.

53. Bureau of the Census, US Department of Commerce, *Historical Statistics of the United States, Colonial Times to 1957* (Washington, DC: US Government Printing Office, 1960), p. 97; Pelling, *A History of British Trade Unionism*, pp. 294–5.

54. Werner Sombart, *Why is there no Socialism in the United States?*, trans. by Patricia M. Hocking and C. T. Husbands and ed. by C. T. Husbands (London: Macmillan, 1976), pp. 27–8; Henry F. Bedford, *Socialism and the Workers in Massachusetts, 1886–1912* (Amherst, Mass.: University of Massachusetts Press, 1966), pp. 1, 181–2, 195–8, 206–12, 220, 244, 252, 288. An important set of further reflections is provided in John H. M. Laslett and Seymour M. Lipset (eds.), *Failure*

of a Dream? Essays in the History of American Socialism (Berkeley: University of California Press, 1984 edn). One factor noted is the importance of a high rate of social mobility other than for black and native American minorities (pp. 436–42).

55. James Weinstein, *The Decline of Socialism in America, 1912–1925* (New York: Monthly Review Press, 1967), pp. 1, 23–4, 108–15, 327–39.

56. Sombart, *Why is there no Socialism in the United States?*, pp. 95, 106, 119; James Joll, *Gramsci* (Glasgow: Fontana, 1977), pp. 105–7.

57. Steve Jeffreys, *Management and Managed: Fifty years of crisis at Chrysler* (Cambridge: Cambridge University Press, 1986), pp. 217–24. There is a school of academic thought which argues for a powerful, only half suppressed radicalism among American workers: e.g. David Montgomery, *Workers' control in America: Studies in the history of work, technology, and labor struggles* (Cambridge: Cambridge University Press, 1979), p. 175 asserts that workers do support 'an articulate socialist leadership' and 'broadly-based grass roots struggles' and thereby 'cut away at the very roots of their employers' power over them.' This is a distinctly minority view.

58. Sombart, *Why is there no Socialism in the United States?*, pp. 18, 55–7, 109, 117–18; Edward F. Denison, 'Economic Growth' in Richard E. Caves and associates, *Britain's Economic Prospects* (Washington, DC: Brookings Institution, 1968), p. 276. Denison's explanation for relative British sluggishness was multi-faceted, including stress on the greater supply of new labour for industrialization in the 1950s in other countries, from immigration, or from the shaking out of agricultural or traditional small-business over-employment: pp. 263–6.

59. David M. Potter, *People of Plenty: Economic Abundance and the American Character* (Chicago: University of Chicago Press, 1954); Seymour M. Lipset, *The First New Nation: The United States in Historical and Comparative Perspective* (London: Heinemann, 1964), pp. 170–9, 197–8.

60. The effects of poor labour relations on British industry are not simply to be measured in days lost through strikes. Because of the uncertainty of industrial relations in the 1970s, British firms held larger stocks of raw materials and goods being processed, suffered from considerable variations in production rates, avoided building larger plants where poor industrial relations tended to be exacerbated, and found that a far higher proportion of their plant managers' time was devoted to industrial relations than was the case in Germany. Davies and Caves, *Britain's Productivity Gap*, pp. 7–8.

61. Simon, *A Time for Truth*, pp. 46–7. A more restrained statement of the arrival of capitalism in the first immigrant ships is in Carl Degler, *Out of Our Past: The Forces That Shaped Modern America* (New York: Harper and Row, 1959), Ch. 1.

62. Drew R. McCoy, *The Last of the Fathers: James Madison and the Republican Legacy* (Cambridge: Cambridge University Press, 1989), p. 162.

63. Richard Hofstadter, *The Age of Reform from Bryan to F.D.R.* (London: Jonathan Cape, 1962), pp. 23–4, 47.

64. R. Richard Wohl, 'The "Rags to Riches Story": An Episode of Secular Idealism', in Reinhard Bendix and Seymour M. Lipset (eds.), *Class, Status, and Power: Social Stratification in Comparative Perspective* (London:RKP, 1967 edn), pp. 501–6.

65. Emily S. Watts, *The Businessman in American Literature* (Athens: University of Georgia Press, 1982), pp. 5, 150–9.

66. *Ibid.*, pp. 3–4; Walter F. Taylor, *The Economic Novel in America* (Chapel Hill: University of North Carolina Press, 1942), pp. 308, 313–14, 325–7.

67. Richard Hofstadter, *Anti-Intellectualism in American Life* (London: Jonathan Cape, 1964), p. 234; Taylor, *The Economic Novel*, p. 324. It has been noted that American writers of quality in the literary critics' eyes nearly all deplored the economic system at the end of the nineteenth century. It is also significant that of the 73 best-selling books in the years 1898–1914, merely three are judged to possess any literary merit. Andrew Hook, *American Literature in Context, III 1865–1900* (London: Methuen, 1983), p. 6.

68. Irvin G. Wyllie, *The Self-Made Man in America: The Myth of Rags to Riches* (New York: Free Press, 1954), pp. 152–65, 173–4.

69. Hofstadter, *Anti-Intellectualism in American Life*, e.g. pp. 253–71.

70. Daniel J. Boorstin, *The Americans: The Democratic Experience* (London: Cardinal, 1988, original edn. 1973), pp. 492–3; Edward C. Kirkland, *Dream and Thought in the Business Community, 1860–1900* (Ithaca, NY: Cornell University Press, 1956), pp. 83, 93–7, 104, 109.

71. Boorstin, *The Americans: The Democratic Experience*, pp. 482–4, 486–7.

72. Jean-Jacques Servan-Schreiber, trans. by Ronald Steel, *The American Challenge* (London: Hamish Hamilton, 1968), p. xi; Boorstin, *The Americans: The Democratic Experience*, pp. 497–9.

73. James O. Robertson, *America's Business* (New York: Hill and Wang, 1985), pp. 166–7; Robert F. Dalzell, Jr. *Enterprising Elite: The Boston Associates and the World They Made* (Cambridge, Mass.: Harvard University Press, 1987), pp. 228–9.

74. Walter Isaacson and Evan Thomas, *The Wise Men: Six Friends and the World They Made* (New York: Simon and Schuster, 1986), p. 60.

75. Allan Nevins, *Study in Power: John D. Rockefeller, Industrialist and Philanthropist*, 2 vols. (New York: Charles Scribner, 1953) II, 157; Lewis B. Mayhew, *Graduate and Professional Education 1980: A Survey of Institutional Plans* (New York: McGraw-Hill, 1970), p. 11; US Department of Commerce, Bureau of the Census, *Statistical Abstract of the United States, 1988*, 108th edn. (Washington, DC: US Department of Commerce, 1987), p. 150.

76. Richard Perlman, 'Education and Training: An American Perspective', *Oxford Review of Economic Policy*, 4 (1988), 82–93; this argues

that many college graduates may be slightly over-educated for the jobs they hold, but do not feel dissatisfied with that fact; there is a good individual rate of return on college education (especially protection from unemployment).

77. Logan Wilson, *American Academics: Then and Now* (New York: Oxford University Press, 1979), p. 269; Richard N. Smith, *The Harvard Century: The Making of a University to a Nation* (New York: Simon and Schuster, 1986), p. 326.

78. P. Sargent Florence. *The Logic of British and American Industry* (London:RKP, 1953), p. 357, which points out that Birmingham's Faculty of Commerce (1901) was early in the field, even by US standards, but made little headway in advancing the cause of management education in universities; Michael Shanks, *The Innovators: The Economics of Technology* (Harmondsworth, Middx.: Penguin, 1967), pp. 69, 210–11; David Granick, *Managerial Comparisons of Four Developed Countries: France, Britain, United States, and Russia* (Cambridge, Mass.: M.I.T. Press, 1972), pp. 175, 178, 358, 364, 374–6. Richard Caves argued that 'Britain's economic malaise stems largely from its productivity problem, whose origins lie deep in the social system'. Poor management, poor investment in training workers, strained industrial relations, and strikes in large plants provided probable reasons. Caves and Krause, *Britain's Economic Performance*, pp. 19, 153, 196–8. This point is strongly repeated in Davies and Caves, *Britain's Productivity Gap*, pp. 94–7.

79. Michael Sanderson, 'Technical Education and Economic Decline: 1890–1980s', *Oxford Review of Economic Policy*, 4 (1988), 38–50; Margaret Ackrill, 'Britain's Managers and the British Economy, 1870s to the 1980s', *idem.*, pp. 59–73.

80. Granick, *Managerial Comparisons of Four Developed Countries*, p. 170; Reinhard Bendix, *Work and Authority in Industry: Ideologies of Management in the Course of Industrialization* (New York: John Wiley, 1956), pp. 229–30.

81. Alistair Cooke, *Talk About America, 1951–1968* (Harmondsworth, Middx.: Penguin, 1981), pp. 196–8.

82. Smith, *The Harvard Century*, pp. 325–6.

83. Hofstadter, *The Age of Reform*, p. 241; Bendix, *Work and Authority in Industry*, pp. 274–82, 298–9, 308, 313–28; Douglas McGregor, *The Human Side of Enterprise* (New York: McGraw-Hill, 1960), pp. 45–9, 55–7, 65, 110–19. It has been argued that American personnel practices emerged partly from the specific conditions of the 1920s, 1930s and 1940s – the desire to reduce foremen's erratic power in the early years and a New Deal and war-time desire for a contented, stable work-force later on – and partly from the natural tendency of an emergent profession to self-aggrandizement, in this case the desire of personnel managers to establish themselves as intermediaries between workers and general management. Sanford W. Jacoby, *Employing Bureaucracy: Managers, Unions, and the Transformation of Work in American Industry, 1900–1945* (New York: Columbia University Press, 1985).

84. G. Pellicelli, 'Management 1920–1970' in Carlo M. Cipolla (ed.), *The Fontana Economic History of Europe: The Twentieth Century*, Part I (Glasgow: Collins, 1976), pp. 184–216.

85. T. J. Peters and N. K. Austin, *A Passion for Excellence: the Leadership Difference* (Glasgow: Fontana, 1986). For an example of bustling advocacy of a new management style being used as a positive defence against Marxism, see the essay written in 1953, Abram T. Collier, 'Business Leadership and a Creative Society' reprinted in Eliza G. C. Collins, *Executive Success: Making It In Management* (New York: *Harvard Business Review*, Executive Books Series 1983), p. 183.

86. David E. Noble, *Forces of Production: A Social History of Industrial Automation* (New York: Oxford University Press, 1986), pp. 191–2, 200–3, 235, 243–4, 332, 334–9.

87. Alfred D. Chandler, 'The United States: Seedbed of Managerial Capitalism', in Alfred D. Chandler, Jr and Herman Daems (eds.), *Managerial Hierarchies: Comparative Perspectives on the Rise of the Modern Industrial Enterprise* (Cambridge, Mass.: Harvard University Press, 1980), pp. 9–40.

88. Robertson, *America's Business*, p. 167; Leonard S. Reich, *The Making of American Industrial Research: Science and Business at G.E. And Bell, 1876–1926* (Cambridge: Cambridge University Press, 1985), pp. 249–56.

89. Van der Wee, *Prosperity and Upheaval*, pp. 201–3; Magaziner and Reich, *Minding America's Business*, p. 59; Merton J. Peck, 'Science and Technology' in Caves, *Britain's Economic Prospects*, p. 451; Julia Wrigley, 'Technical Education and Industry in the Nineteenth Century' in Elbaum and Lazonick, *The Decline of the British Economy*, pp. 210–11 shows the considerably higher American industrial research effort of the 1950s compared with Britain's.

90. Servan-Schreiber, *The American Challenge*, p. 46; Shanks, *The Innovators*, pp. 43–4, 79; Noble, *Forces of Production*, p. 249.

91. Harold G. Vatter, 'Technological Innovation and Social Change in the United States, 1870–1980' in John Colton and Stuart Bruchey (eds.), *Technology, the Economy, and Society: The American Experience* (New York: Columbia University Press, 1987), p. 27; Shanks, *The Innovators*, p.46.

92. Servan-Schreiber, *The American Challenge*, pp. 23–5; Volker R. Berghahn, *The Americanisation of West German Industry 1945–1973* (Leamington Spa: Berg, 1986), pp. 89–90, 100–3, 225–37, 247–58, 295, 310–12, 320–35.

93. Daniel T. Rodgers, *The Work Ethic in Industrial America, 1850–1920* (Chicago: Chicago University Press, 1978), pp. 5, 9–14, 17–18.

94. *Ibid.*, pp. 22–9, 102–3, 110–11.

95. *Ibid.*, p. 230; Joseph F. Wall, *Andrew Carnegie* (New York: Oxford University Press, 1970), pp. 882–4; Peter Collier and David Horowitz, *The Rockefellers: An American Dynasty* (New York: Holt, Rhinehart and Winston, 1976), pp. 48–9.

96. Wall, *Andrew Carnegie*, pp. 816–17, 828, 834, 838–9, 864.

97. Thomas C. Cochrane, *Challenges to American Values: Society, Business and Religion* (New York: Oxford University Press, 1985), pp. 86, 90; Boorstin, *The Americans: The Democratic Experience*, p. 468; Harold M. Keele and Joseph C. Kiger (eds.), *Foundations* (Westport, Conn.: Greenwood Press, 1984), pp. xxvii, 457; *Directory of Grant-Making Trusts 1987*, 10th Compilation (Tonbridge, Kent: Charities Aid Foundation, 1987), pp. 665, 930 (the figure for Wolfson is presumably £200 million, not £200,000 as printed); Lewis H. Lapham, *Money and Class in America: Notes and Observations on Our Civil Religion* (New York: Weidenfeld and Nicolson, 1988), pp. 15, 22, 27–8. Lapham claims that there is no 'establishment' in America (p. 12 note 7) and that wealth is the only sure guide to status: 'The restlessness of the American experience lends to money a greater power than it enjoys in less mobile societies' (p. 78).
98. Ralph E. Pumphrey, 'The Introduction of Industrialists into the British Peerage: A Study in Adaptation of a Social Institution', *American Historical Review*, LXV (1959), 1–16, argues that by 1911 the aristocracy was becoming an increasingly middle-class institution. But that contention is sustained solely by examining the professional and social backgrounds of newly-created peers. No attempt is made to examine life-styles or country-house ownership, or to trace what happened to these newly created peers' offspring. The evidence cannot by itself disprove the gentrification thesis.
99. Frederick C. Jaher, 'The Boston Brahmins in the Age of Industrial Capitalism', in Frederick C Jaher (ed.), *The Age of Industrialism in America: Essays in Social Structure and Cultural Values* (New York: The Free Press, 1968), pp. 193–6, 198–9, 202, 211, 228–35.
100. *Ibid.*, pp. 214–16.
101. C. Wright Mills, *The Power Elite* (New York: Oxford University Press 1956), p. 55.
102. Anthony Sampson, *The Changing Anatomy of Britain* (London: Hodder and Stoughton, 1982), pp. 52, 158–9, 178–9. I suspect there is generally more to the shared 'culture' of an educational background than is admitted in W. D. Rubinstein, 'Education and the Social Origins of British Elites, 1880–1970', *Past and Present*, 112 (1986), 163–207.
103. Educational information on US senators is gleaned from the biographical entries for each senator by state in Michael Barone and Grant Ujifusa, *The Almanac of American Politics, 1982* (Washington DC: Barone and Co., 1981). I have taken the first college or university attended where senators attended more than one as undergraduates. Graduate school attendance is more by way of professional, usually legal, training.
104. Sampson, *The Changing Anatomy of Britain*, pp. 26–7; *Sunday Times*, 2 April 1989. There were 374 peers of the rank of viscount, earl, marquees and duke listed in *Whitaker's Almanack 1989* (London: J. Whitaker, 1988), pp. 157–66.
105. Lapham, *Money and Class in America*, p. 22.

106. Frederic D. Jaher, *The Urban Establishment: Upper Strata in Boston, New York, Charleston, Chicago, and Los Angeles* (Urbana: University of Illinois Press, 1982), pp. 280–1,; Keele and Kiger (eds.), *Foundations*, p. 457.

107. Mills, *The Power Elite*, pp. 62–70; on the foreign policy elite, see Isaacson and Thomas, *The Wise Men*, chs. 1–3, 6.

108. The Foreign Office ministers in 1989 were listed in *The Times*, 9 August 1989; their backgrounds were checked in *Who's Who*.

109. Jaher, *The Urban Establishment*, pp. 280–1, 552, 682–3.

110. Thomas Fox and S. M. Miller, 'Intra-Country Variations: Occupational Stratification and Mobility', in Bendix and Lipset, *Class, Status, and Power*, pp. 574–81.

111. Louis Galambos, *The Public Image of Big Business in America, 1880–1940: A Quantitative Study in Social Change* (Baltimore, Md.: Johns Hopkins University Press, 1975), pp. 256, 265–6; George H. Gallup, *The Gallup Poll: Public Opinion 1935–1971*, 3 vols. (New York: Random House, 1972), III, p. 2154.

112. Harvey-Jones, *Making It Happen*, pp. 122–3. One historian of British business concluded, 'Perhaps the outstanding impression of British managers over the past century is their general slowness to embrace change'. Three of the most notable top managers responsible for combatting trade unions' restrictive practices in the 1980s were Michael Edwardes (a South African), Ian McGregor (whose long career had been mostly in the USA), and Rupert Murdoch (an Australian). Ackrill, 'Britain's Managers and the British Economy', pp. 68, 72.

113. Boorstin, *The Americans: The Democratic Experience*, pp. 429–34, 440–7, 551–5.

114. Nicole W. Biggart, *Charismatic Capitalism: Direct Selling Organizations in America* (Chicago: University of Chicago Press, 1989), pp. 1–12, 20–1, 26, 47, 51, 135–54.

115. Harold G. Vatter, 'The Position of Small Business in the Structure of American Manufacturing, 1870–1970' in Stuart W. Bruchey (ed.), *Small Business in American Life* (New York: Columbia University Press, 1980), pp. 146, 155; *Statistical Abstract of the United States 1988*, pp. 368, 497.

116. Stuart Bruchey, *The Wealth of the Nation* (New York: Harper and Row, 1988), p. 232.

117. Israel M. Kirzner, *Perception, Opportunity, and Profit: Studies in the Theory of Entrepreneurship* (Chicago: University of Chicago Press, 1979), pp. 119, 158, 180–1.

118. J. K. Galbraith, *Economics and the Public Purpose* (Harmondsworth, Middx.: Penguin, 1975), pp. 312–35; Thurow. *The Zero-Sum Society*, pp. 19–20, 163, 191–2, 204, 211, 214.

119. George J. Stigler, *The Citizen and the Stage: Essays on Regulation* (Chicago: University of Chicago Press, 1975), pp. 152, 162–6, 187–8; Thurow, *The Zero-Sum Society*, p. 7.

120. Jennifer L. Hochschild, *What's Fair? American Beliefs about Distributive Justice* (Cambridge, Mass.: Harvard University Press, 1981), pp. 22, 228–37, 258, 278, 283; J. R. Pole, *The Pursuit of Equality in American History* (Berkeley: University of California Press, 1978), ch. 11 offers wide-ranging reflections on the dilemmas raised by American political and social egalitarianism.

Index